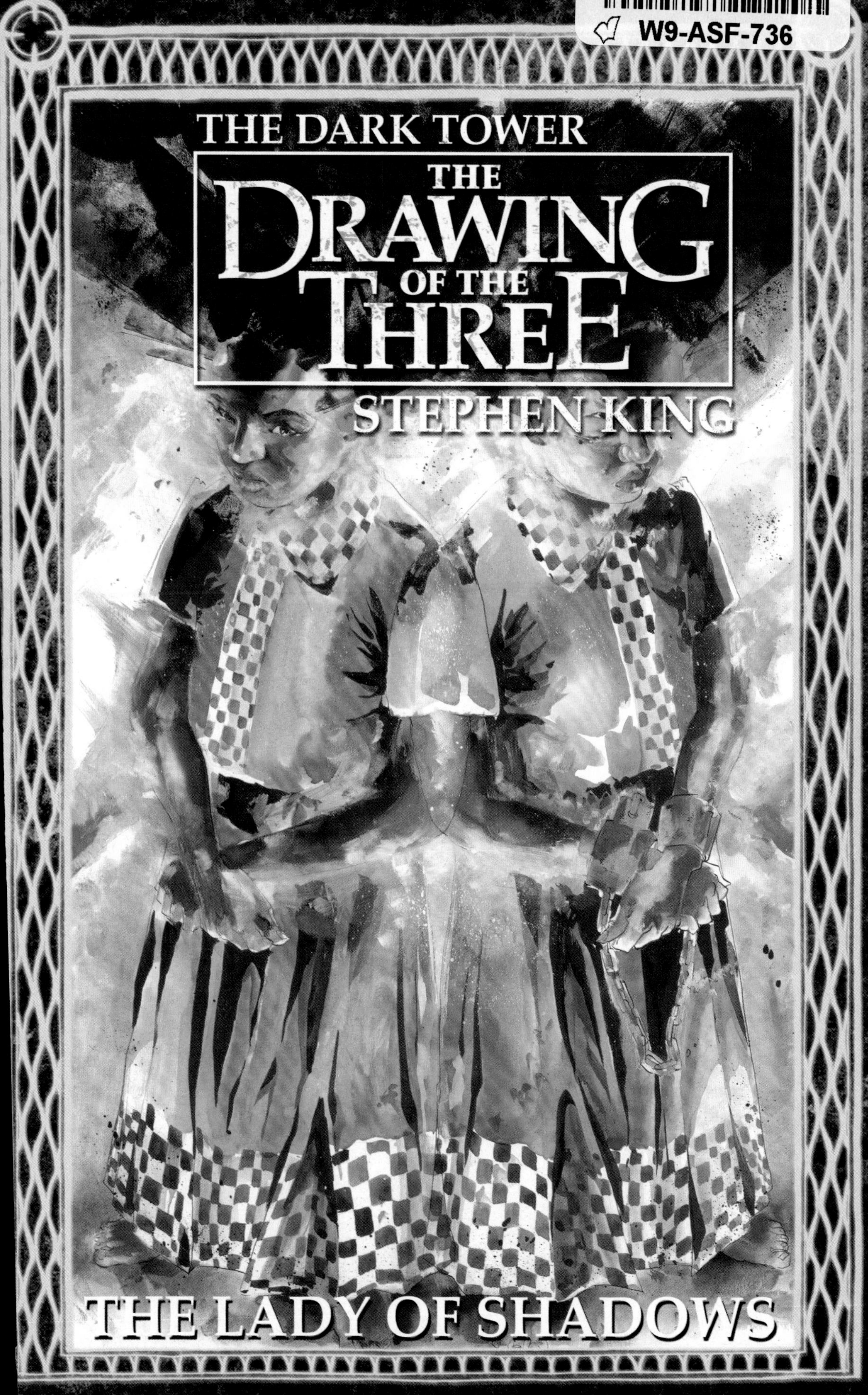
THE DARK TOWER
THE DRAWING OF THE THREE
STEPHEN KING
THE LADY OF SHADOWS

THE DARK TOWER

THE DRAWING OF THE THREE

STEPHEN KING

CREATIVE DIRECTOR AND EXECUTIVE DIRECTOR
STEPHEN KING

PLOT AND CONSULTATION
ROBIN FURTH

SCRIPT
PETER DAVID

ARTIST
JONATHAN MARKS

COLORISTS
LEE LOUGHRIDGE WITH
JONATHAN MARKS

LETTERING
VC'S JOE SABINO

COVER ARTIST
NIMIT MALAVIA

EDITOR
EMILY SHAW

CONSULTING EDITOR
RALPH MACCHIO

THE LADY OF SHADOWS

COLLECTION EDITOR
MARK D. BEAZLEY

ASSOCIATE EDITOR
SARAH BRUNSTAD

ASSOCIATE MANAGING EDITOR
ALEX STARBUCK

EDITOR, SPECIAL PROJECTS
JENNIFER GRÜNWALD

VP, PRODUCTION & SPECIAL PROJECTS
JEFF YOUNGQUIST

SVP PRINT, SALES & MARKETING
DAVID GABRIEL

EDITOR IN CHIEF
AXEL ALONSO

CHIEF CREATIVE OFFICER
JOE QUESADA

PUBLISHER
DAN BUCKLEY

SPECIAL THANKS TO CHUCK VERRILL, MARSHA DEFILIPPO & BRIAN STARK

DARK TOWER: THE DRAWING OF THE THREE — LADY OF SHADOWS. Contains material originally published in magazine form as DARK TOWER: THE DRAWING OF THE THREE — LADY OF SHADOWS #1-5. First printing 2016. ISBN# 978-0-7851-9282-4. Published by MARVEL WORLDWIDE, INC., a subsidiary of MARVEL ENTERTAINMENT, LLC. OFFICE OF PUBLICATION: 135 West 50th Street, New York, NY 10020. **Printed in Canada.** ALAN FINE, President, Marvel Entertainment; DAN BUCKLEY, President, TV, Publishing and Brand Management; JOE QUESADA, Chief Creative Officer; TOM BREVOORT, SVP of Publishing; DAVID BOGART, SVP of Operations & Procurement, Publishing; C.B. CEBULSKI, VP of International Development & Brand Management; DAVID GABRIEL, SVP Print, Sales & Marketing; JIM O'KEEFE, VP of Operations & Logistics; DAN CARR, Executive Director of Publishing Technology; SUSAN CRESPI, Editorial Operations Manager; ALEX MORALES, Publishing Operations Manager; STAN LEE, Chairman Emeritus. For information regarding advertising in Marvel Comics or on Marvel.com, please contact Jonathan Rheingold, VP of Custom Solutions & Ad Sales, at jrheingold@marvel.com. For Marvel subscription inquiries, please call 800-217-9158. **Manufactured between 1/22/2016 and 2/29/2016 by SOLISCO PRINTERS, SCOTT, QC, CANADA.**

10 9 8 7 6 5 4 3 2 1

THE DARK TOWER
THE DRAWING OF THE THREE
STEPHEN KING

THE LADY OF SHADOWS
CHAPTER ONE

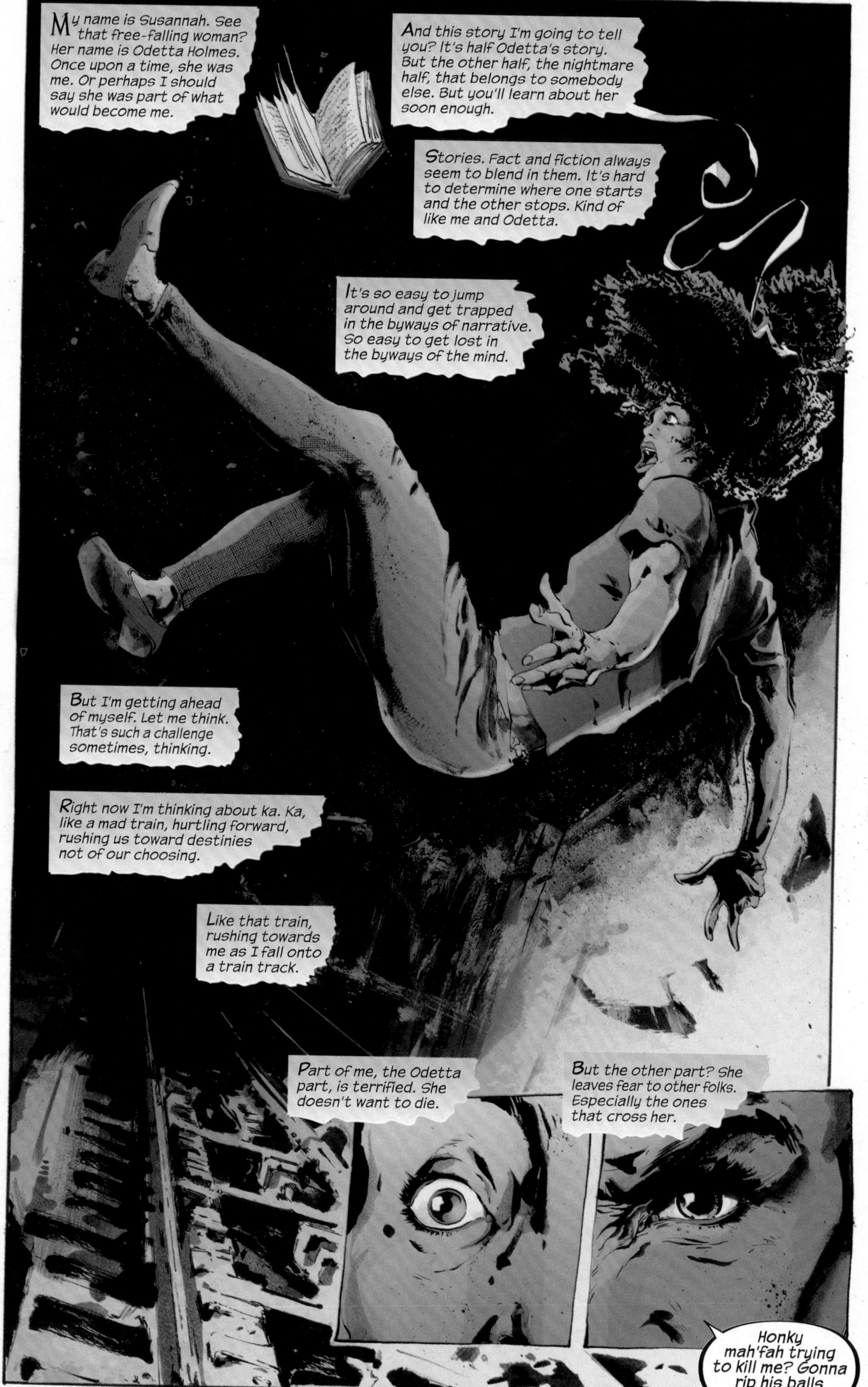
My name is Susannah. See that free-falling woman? Her name is Odetta Holmes. Once upon a time, she was me. Or perhaps I should say she was part of what would become me.
And this story I'm going to tell you? It's half Odetta's story. But the other half, the nightmare half, that belongs to somebody else. But you'll learn about her soon enough.
Stories. Fact and fiction always seem to blend in them. It's hard to determine where one starts and the other stops. Kind of like me and Odetta.
It's so easy to jump around and get trapped in the byways of narrative. So easy to get lost in the byways of the mind.
But I'm getting ahead of myself. Let me think. That's such a challenge sometimes, thinking.
Right now I'm thinking about ka. Ka, like a mad train, hurtling forward, rushing us toward destinies not of our choosing.
Like that train, rushing towards me as I fall onto a train track.
Part of me, the Odetta part, is terrified. She doesn't want to die.
But the other part? She leaves fear to other folks. Especially the ones that cross her.
Honky mah'fah trying to kill me? Gonna rip his balls off!

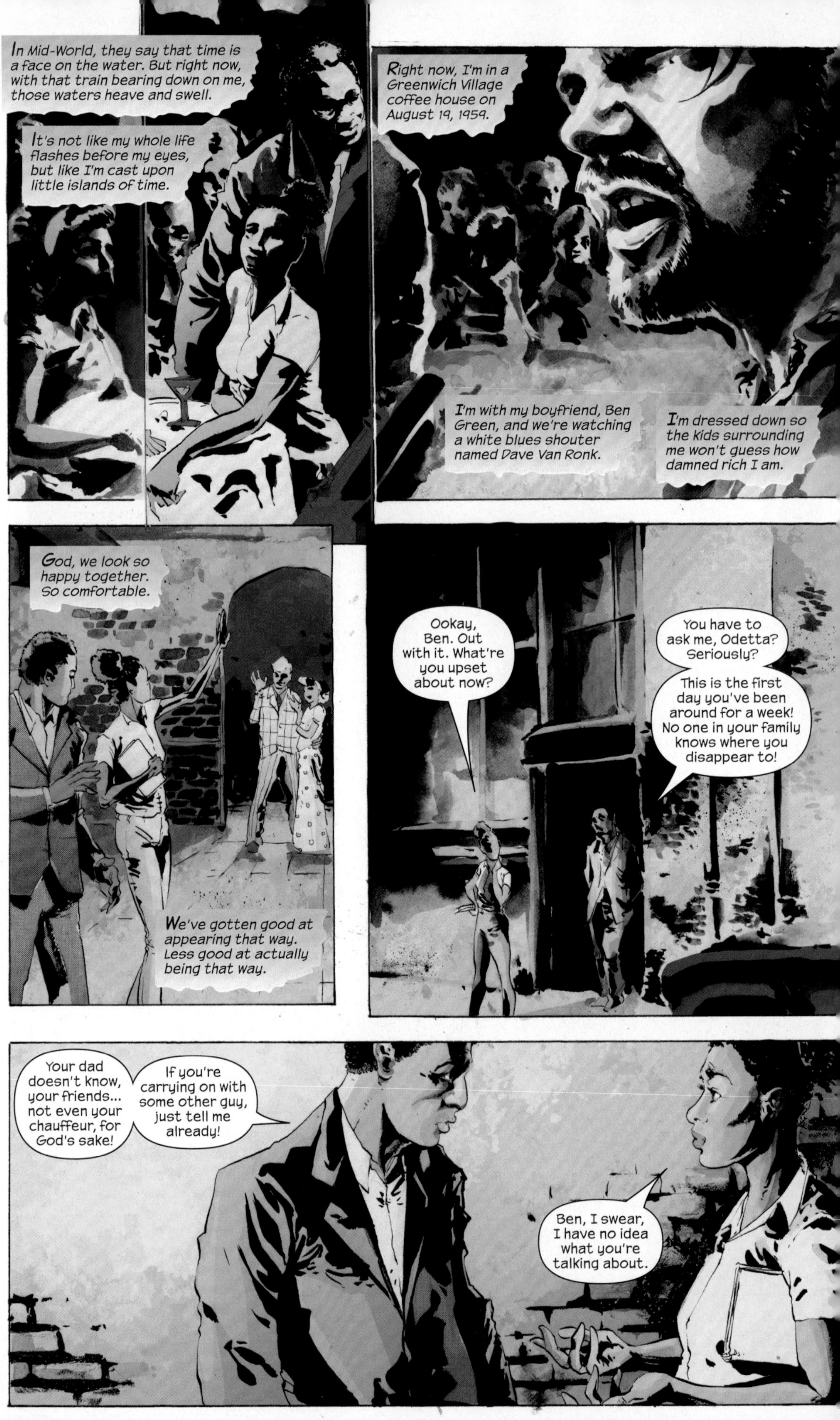
In Mid-World, they say that time is a face on the water. But right now, with that train bearing down on me, those waters heave and swell.
It's not like my whole life flashes before my eyes, but like I'm cast upon little islands of time.
Right now, I'm in a Greenwich Village coffee house on August 19, 1959.
I'm with my boyfriend, Ben Green, and we're watching a white blues shouter named Dave Van Ronk.
I'm dressed down so the kids surrounding me won't guess how damned rich I am.
God, we look so happy together. So comfortable.
We've gotten good at appearing that way. Less good at actually being that way.
Ookay, Ben. Out with it. What're you upset about now?
You have to ask me, Odetta? Seriously?
This is the first day you've been around for a week! No one in your family knows where you disappear to!
Your dad doesn't know, your friends... not even your chauffeur, for God's sake!
If you're carrying on with some other guy, just tell me already!
Ben, I swear, I have no idea what you're talking about.

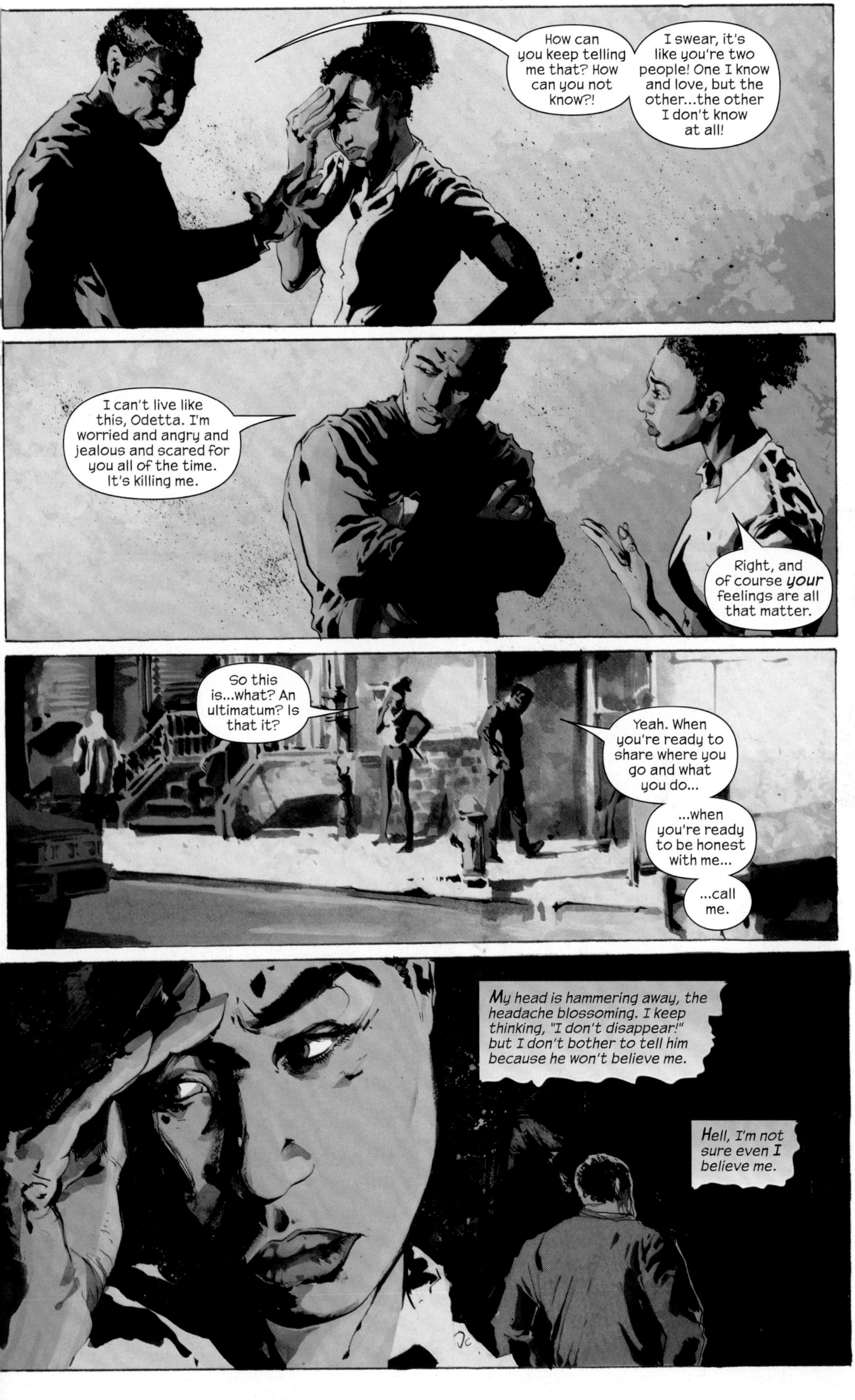

How can you keep telling me that? How can you not know?!
I swear, it's like you're two people! One I know and love, but the other...the other I don't know at all!
I can't live like this, Odetta. I'm worried and angry and jealous and scared for you all of the time. It's killing me.
Right, and of course *your* feelings are all that matter.
So this is...what? An ultimatum? Is that it?
Yeah. When you're ready to share where you go and what you do...
...when you're ready to be honest with me...
...call me.
My head is hammering away, the headache blossoming. I keep thinking, "I don't disappear!" but I don't bother to tell him because he won't believe me.
Hell, I'm not sure even I believe me.

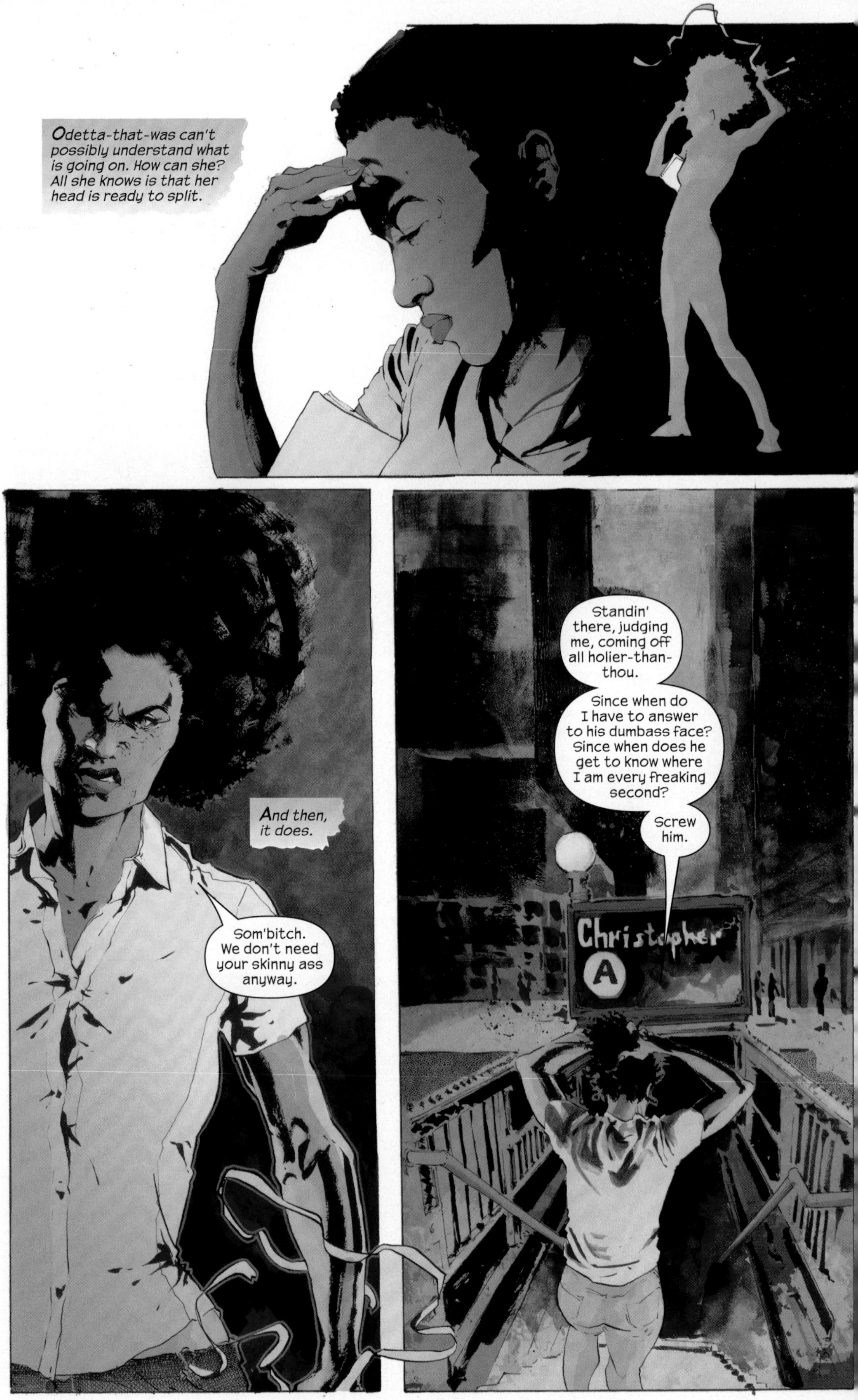
Odetta-that-was can't possibly understand what is going on. How can she? All she knows is that her head is ready to split.
And then, it does.
Som'bitch. We don't need your skinny ass anyway.
Standin' there, judging me, coming off all holier-than-thou.
Since when do I have to answer to his dumbass face? Since when does he get to know where I am every freaking second?
Screw him.
Christopher
A

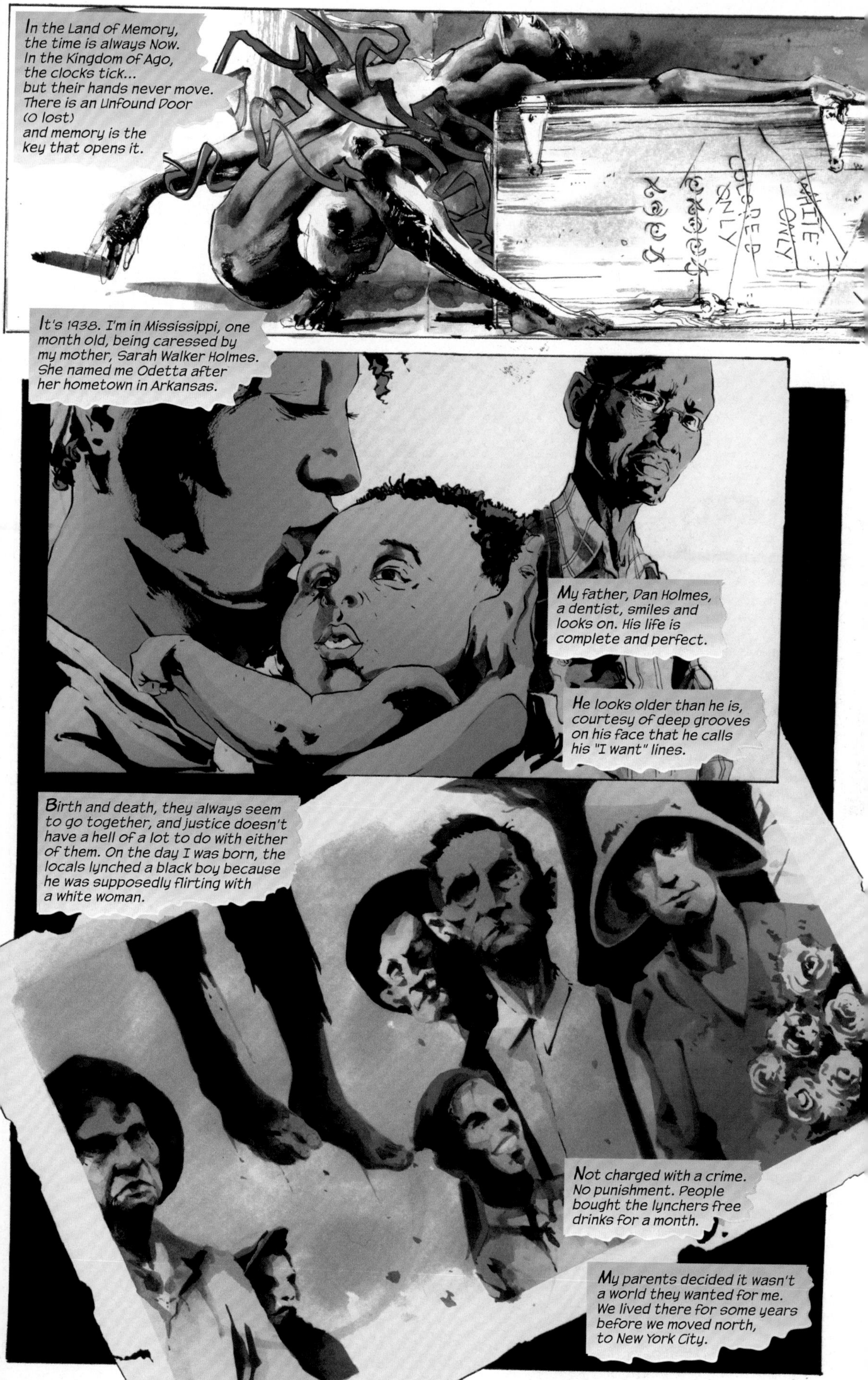
In the Land of Memory, the time is always Now. In the Kingdom of Ago, the clocks tick... but their hands never move. There is an Unfound Door (O lost) and memory is the key that opens it.
It's 1938. I'm in Mississippi, one month old, being caressed by my mother, Sarah Walker Holmes. She named me Odetta after her hometown in Arkansas.
My father, Dan Holmes, a dentist, smiles and looks on. His life is complete and perfect.
He looks older than he is, courtesy of deep grooves on his face that he calls his "I want" lines.
Birth and death, they always seem to go together, and justice doesn't have a hell of a lot to do with either of them. On the day I was born, the locals lynched a black boy because he was supposedly flirting with a white woman.
Not charged with a crime. No punishment. People bought the lynchers free drinks for a month.
My parents decided it wasn't a world they wanted for me. We lived there for some years before we moved north, to New York City.

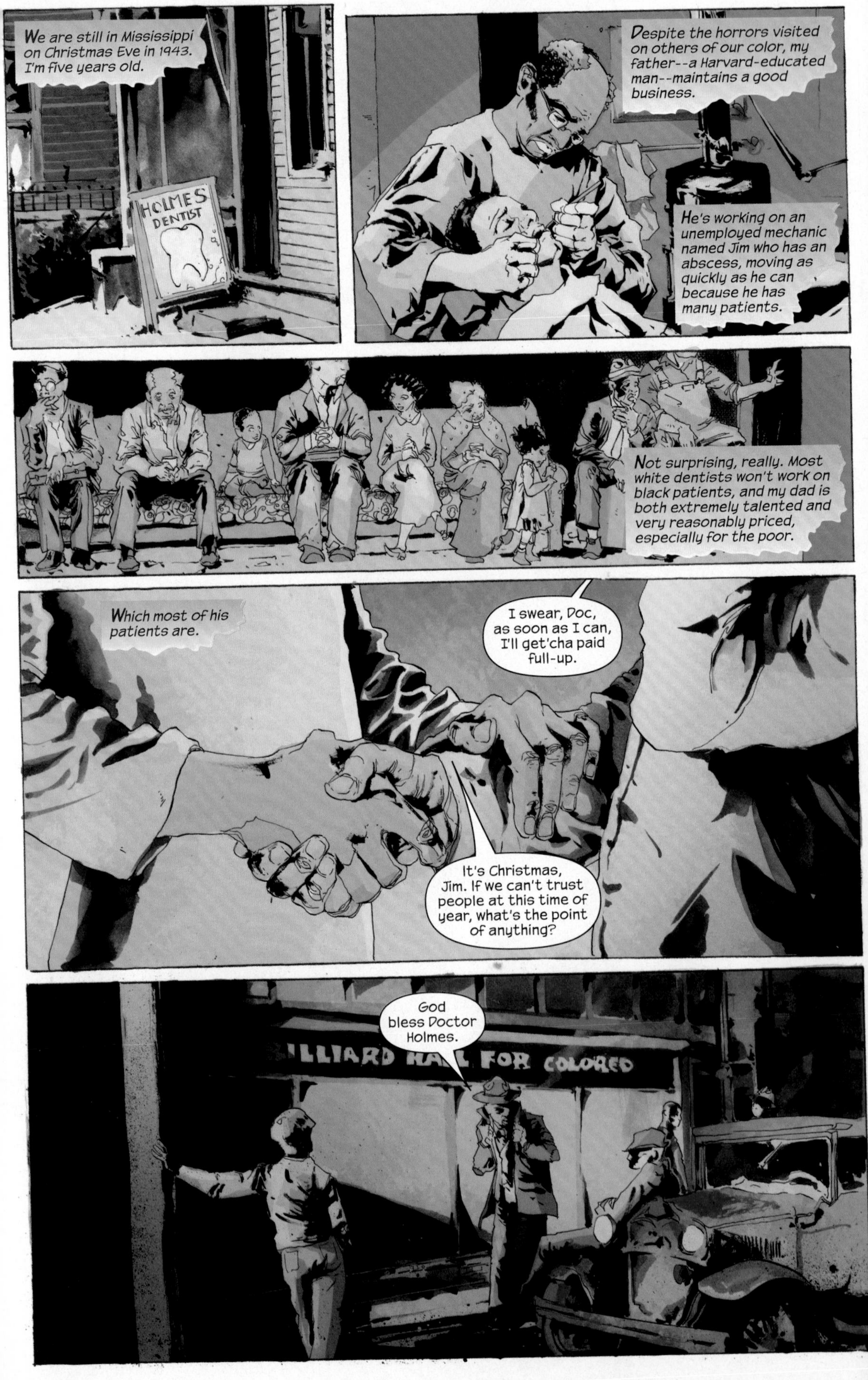
We are still in Mississippi on Christmas Eve in 1943. I'm five years old.
HOLMES DENTIST
Despite the horrors visited on others of our color, my father--a Harvard-educated man--maintains a good business.
He's working on an unemployed mechanic named Jim who has an abscess, moving as quickly as he can because he has many patients.
Not surprising, really. Most white dentists won't work on black patients, and my dad is both extremely talented and very reasonably priced, especially for the poor.
Which most of his patients are.
I swear, Doc, as soon as I can, I'll get'cha paid full-up.
It's Christmas, Jim. If we can't trust people at this time of year, what's the point of anything?
God bless Doctor Holmes.
ILLIARD HALL FOR COLORED

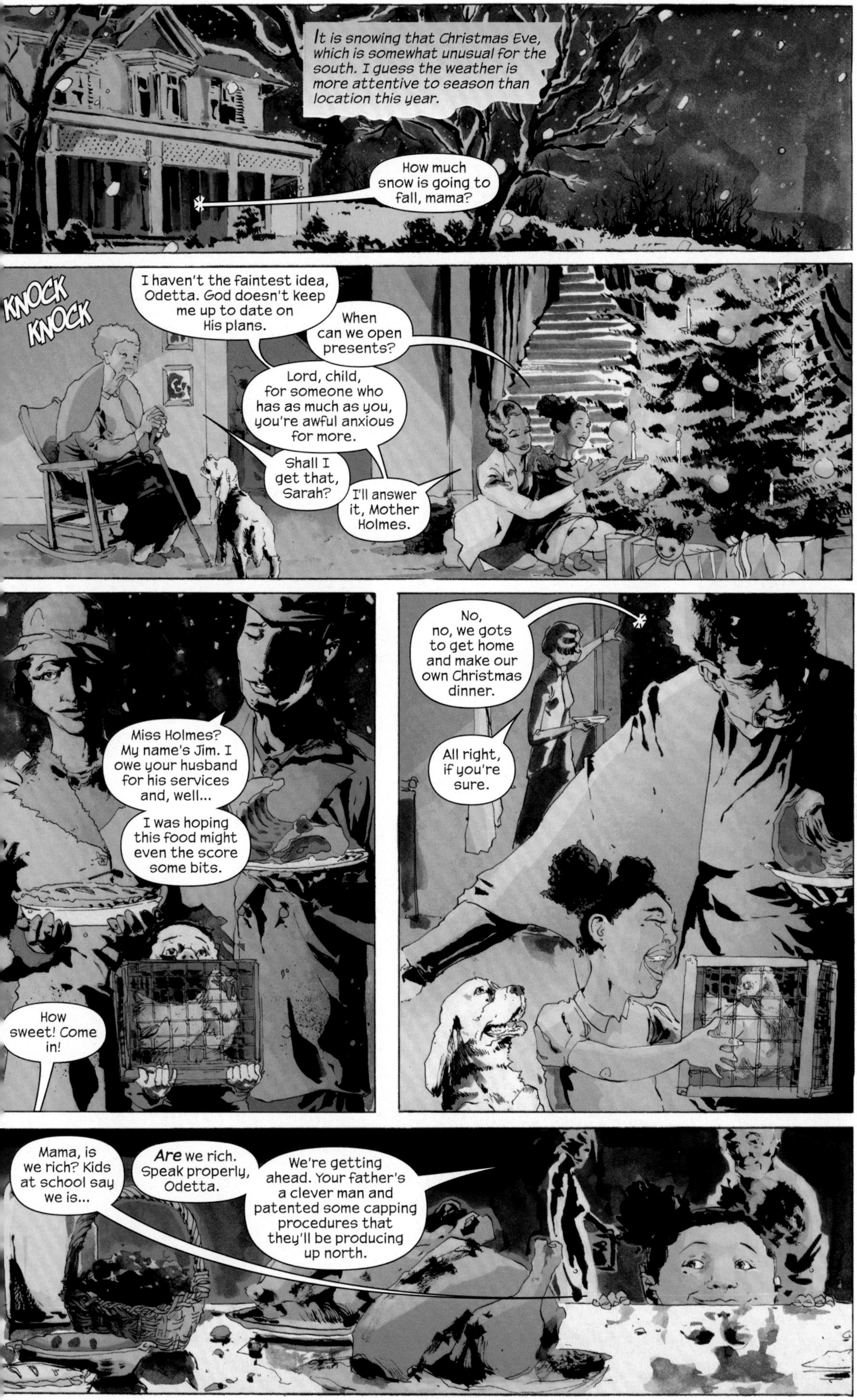
It is snowing that Christmas Eve, which is somewhat unusual for the south. I guess the weather is more attentive to season than location this year.
How much snow is going to fall, mama?
KNOCK KNOCK
I haven't the faintest idea, Odetta. God doesn't keep me up to date on His plans.
When can we open presents?
Lord, child, for someone who has as much as you, you're awful anxious for more.
Shall I get that, Sarah?
I'll answer it, Mother Holmes.
Miss Holmes? My name's Jim. I owe your husband for his services and, well...
I was hoping this food might even the score some bits.
How sweet! Come in!
No, no, we gots to get home and make our own Christmas dinner.
All right, if you're sure.
Mama, is we rich? Kids at school say we is...
Are we rich. Speak properly, Odetta.
We're getting ahead. Your father's a clever man and patented some capping procedures that they'll be producing up north.

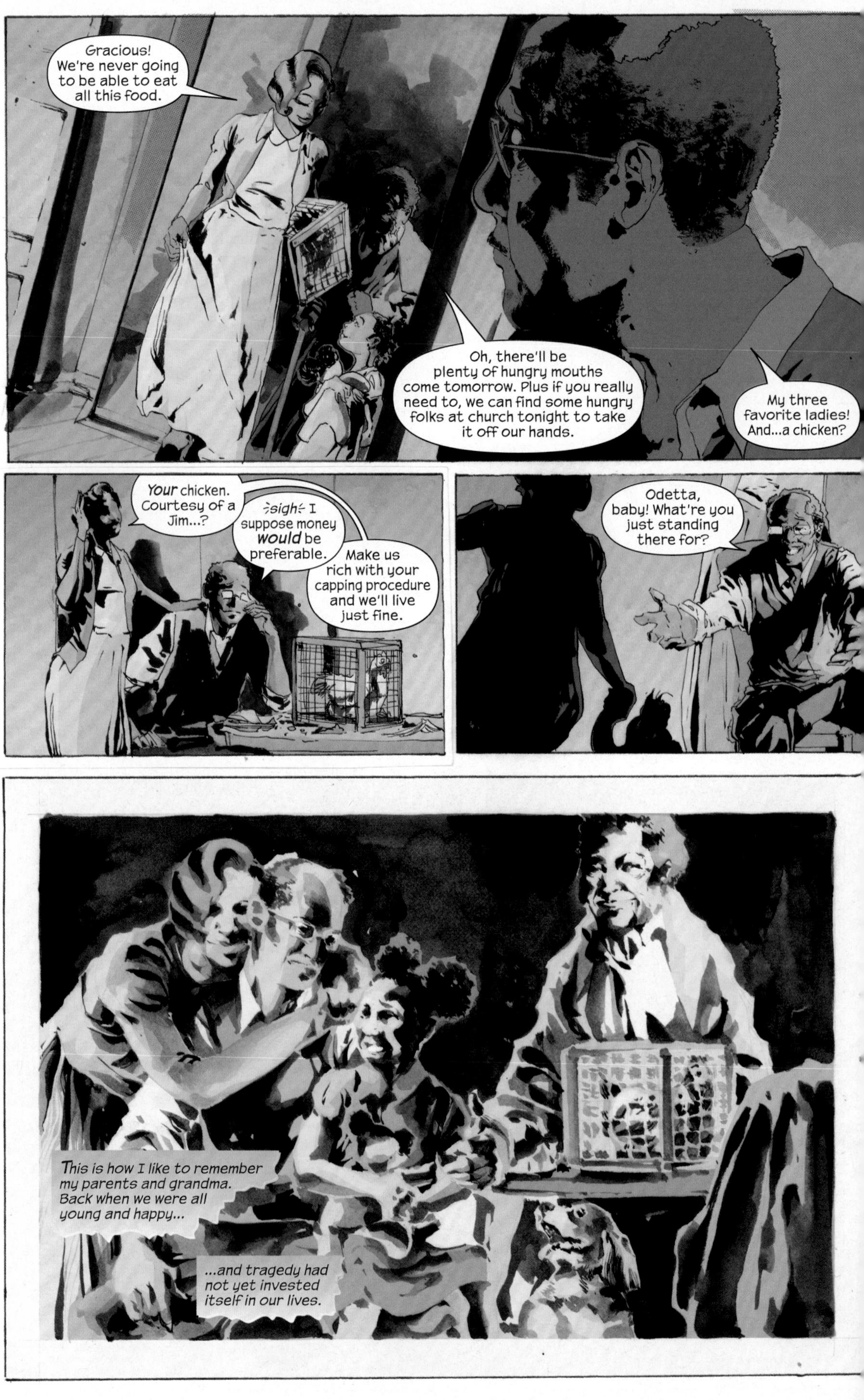

Gracious! We're never going to be able to eat all this food.
Oh, there'll be plenty of hungry mouths come tomorrow. Plus if you really need to, we can find some hungry folks at church tonight to take it off our hands.
My three favorite ladies! And...a chicken?
Your chicken. Courtesy of a Jim...?
sigh I suppose money would be preferable.
Make us rich with your capping procedure and we'll live just fine.
Odetta, baby! What're you just standing there for?
This is how I like to remember my parents and grandma. Back when we were all young and happy...
...and tragedy had not yet invested itself in our lives.

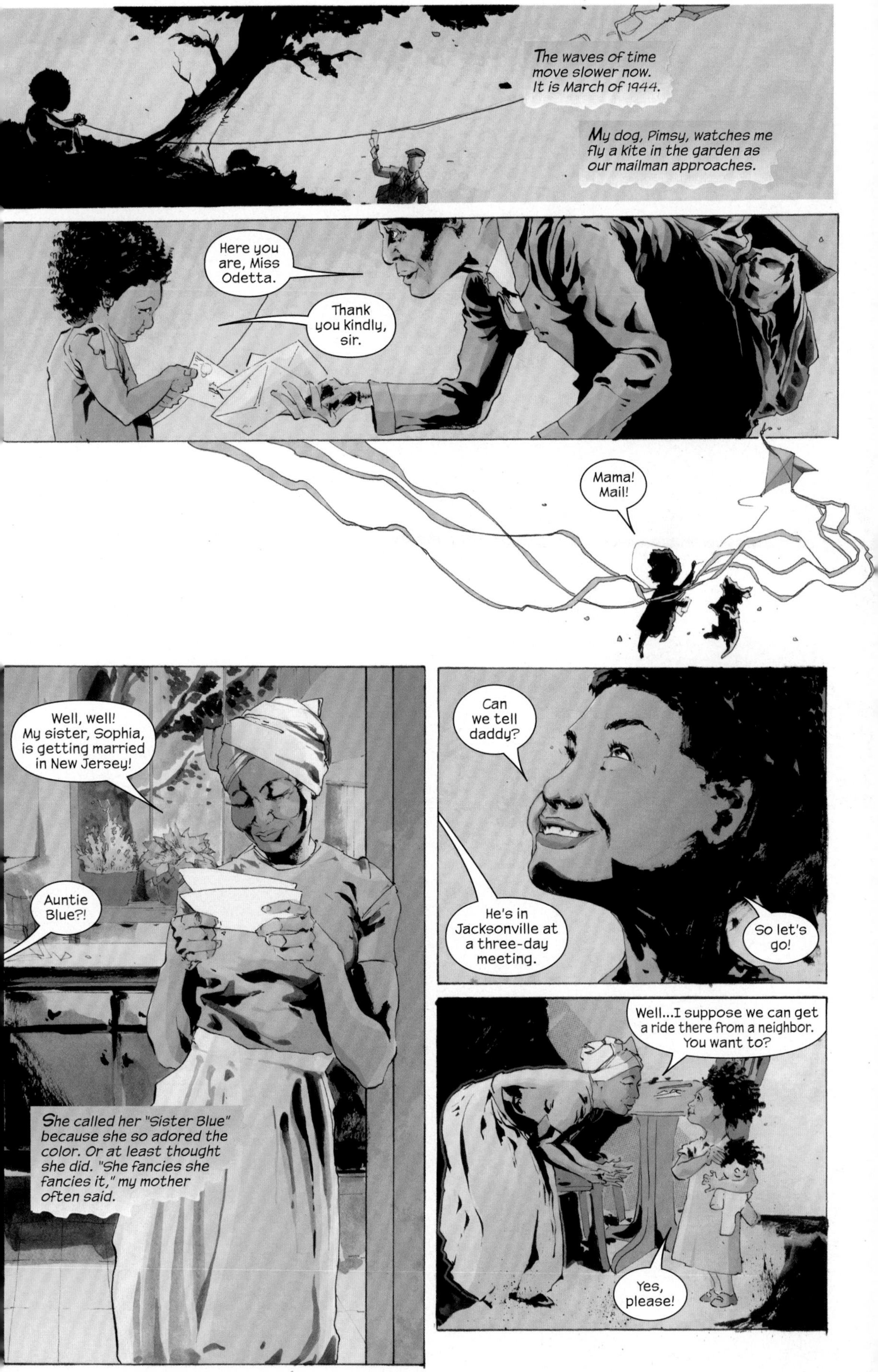
The waves of time move slower now. It is March of 1944.
My dog, Pimsy, watches me fly a kite in the garden as our mailman approaches.
Here you are, Miss Odetta.
Thank you kindly, sir.
Mama! Mail!
Well, well! My sister, Sophia, is getting married in New Jersey!
Auntie Blue?!
She called her "Sister Blue" because she so adored the color. Or at least thought she did. "She fancies she fancies it," my mother often said.
Can we tell daddy?
He's in Jacksonville at a three-day meeting.
So let's go!
Well...I suppose we can get a ride there from a neighbor. You want to?
Yes, please!

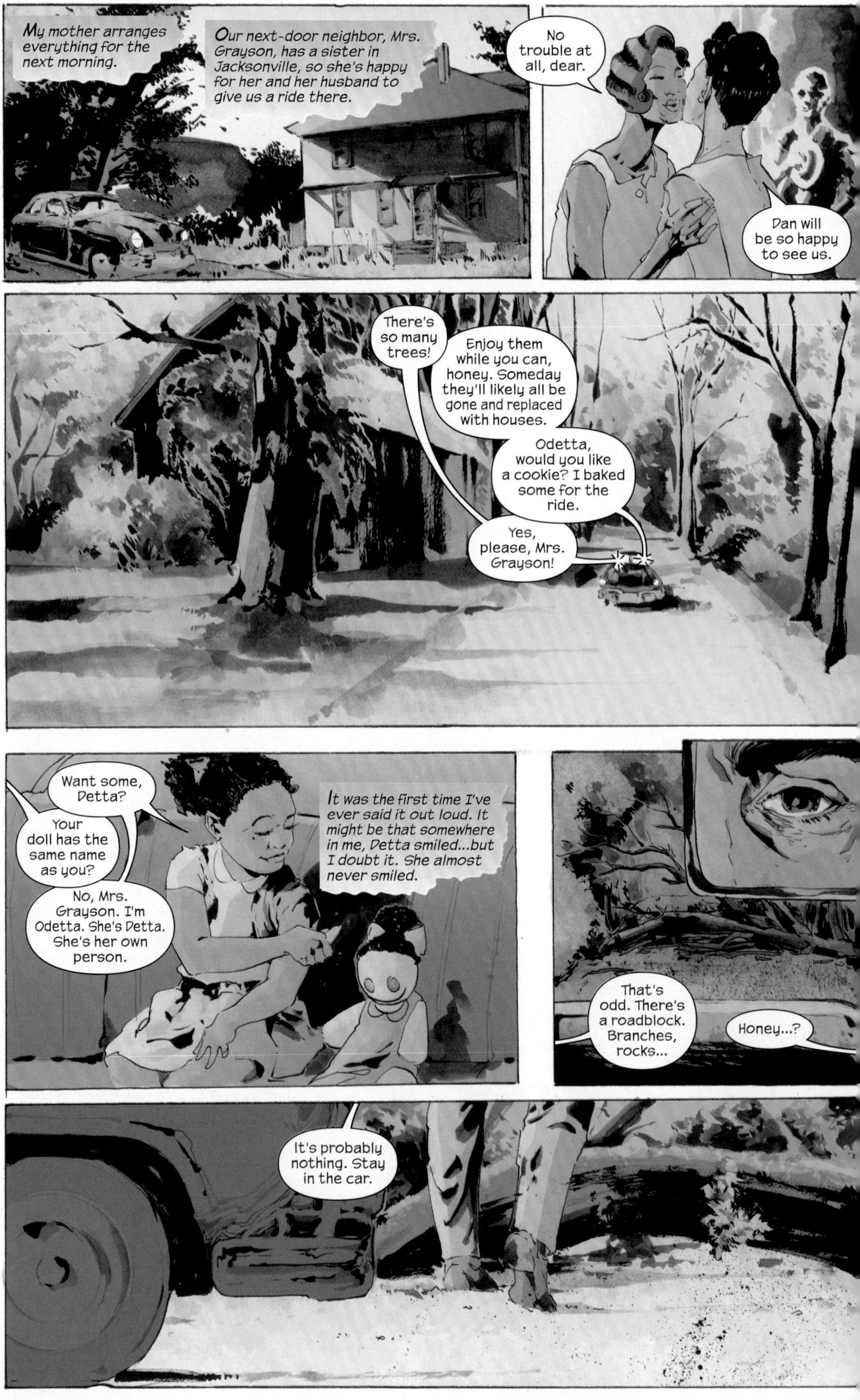
My mother arranges everything for the next morning.
Our next-door neighbor, Mrs. Grayson, has a sister in Jacksonville, so she's happy for her and her husband to give us a ride there.
No trouble at all, dear.
Dan will be so happy to see us.
There's so many trees!
Enjoy them while you can, honey. Someday they'll likely all be gone and replaced with houses.
Odetta, would you like a cookie? I baked some for the ride.
Yes, please, Mrs. Grayson!
Want some, Detta?
Your doll has the same name as you?
No, Mrs. Grayson. I'm Odetta. She's Detta. She's her own person.
It was the first time I've ever said it out loud. It might be that somewhere in me, Detta smiled...but I doubt it. She almost never smiled.
That's odd. There's a roadblock. Branches, rocks...
Honey...?
It's probably nothing. Stay in the car.

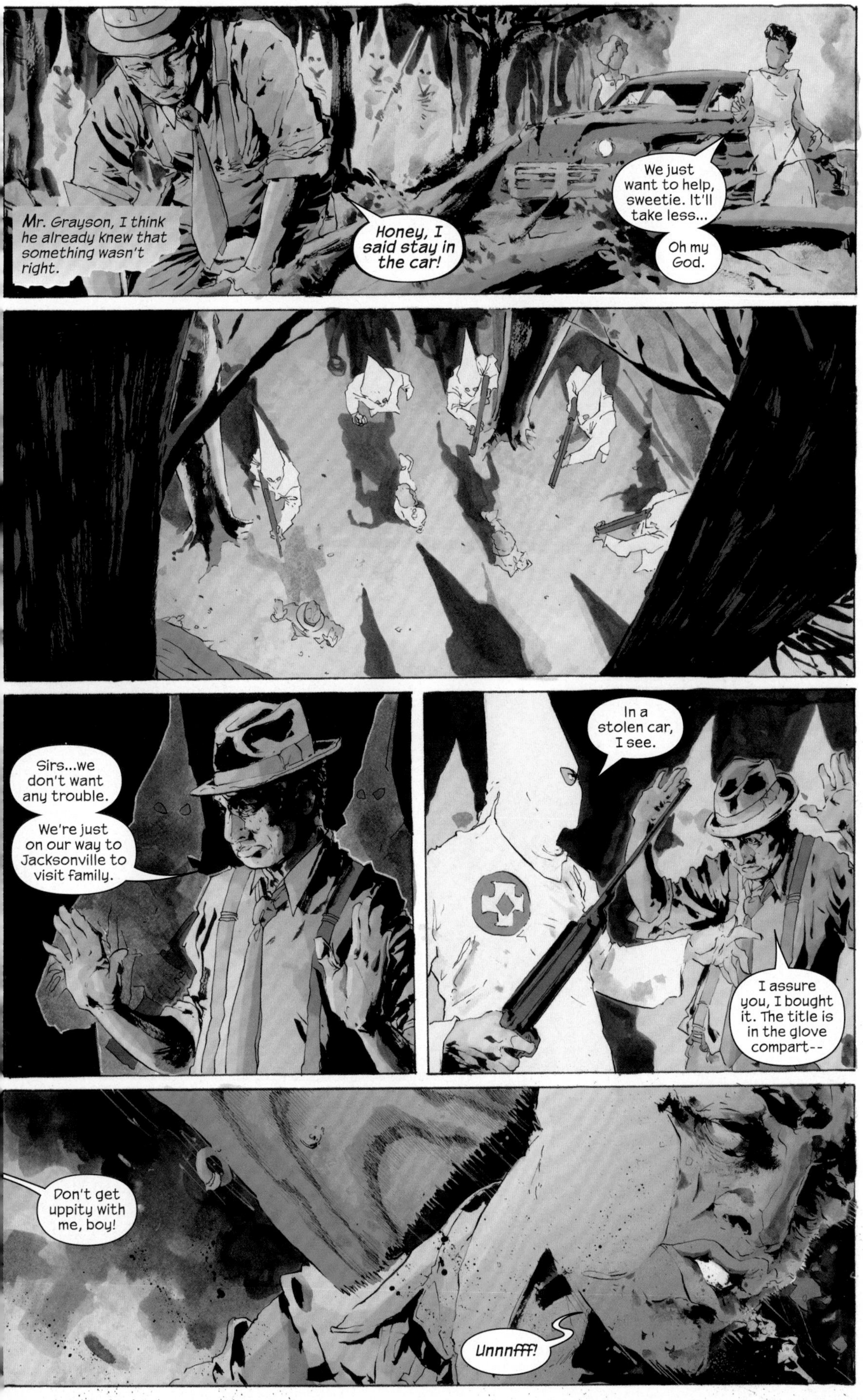
Mr. Grayson, I think he already knew that something wasn't right.
Honey, I said stay in the car!
We just want to help, sweetie. It'll take less...
Oh my God.
Sirs...we don't want any trouble.
We're just on our way to Jacksonville to visit family.
In a stolen car, I see.
I assure you, I bought it. The title is in the glove compart--
Don't get uppity with me, boy!
Unnnfff!

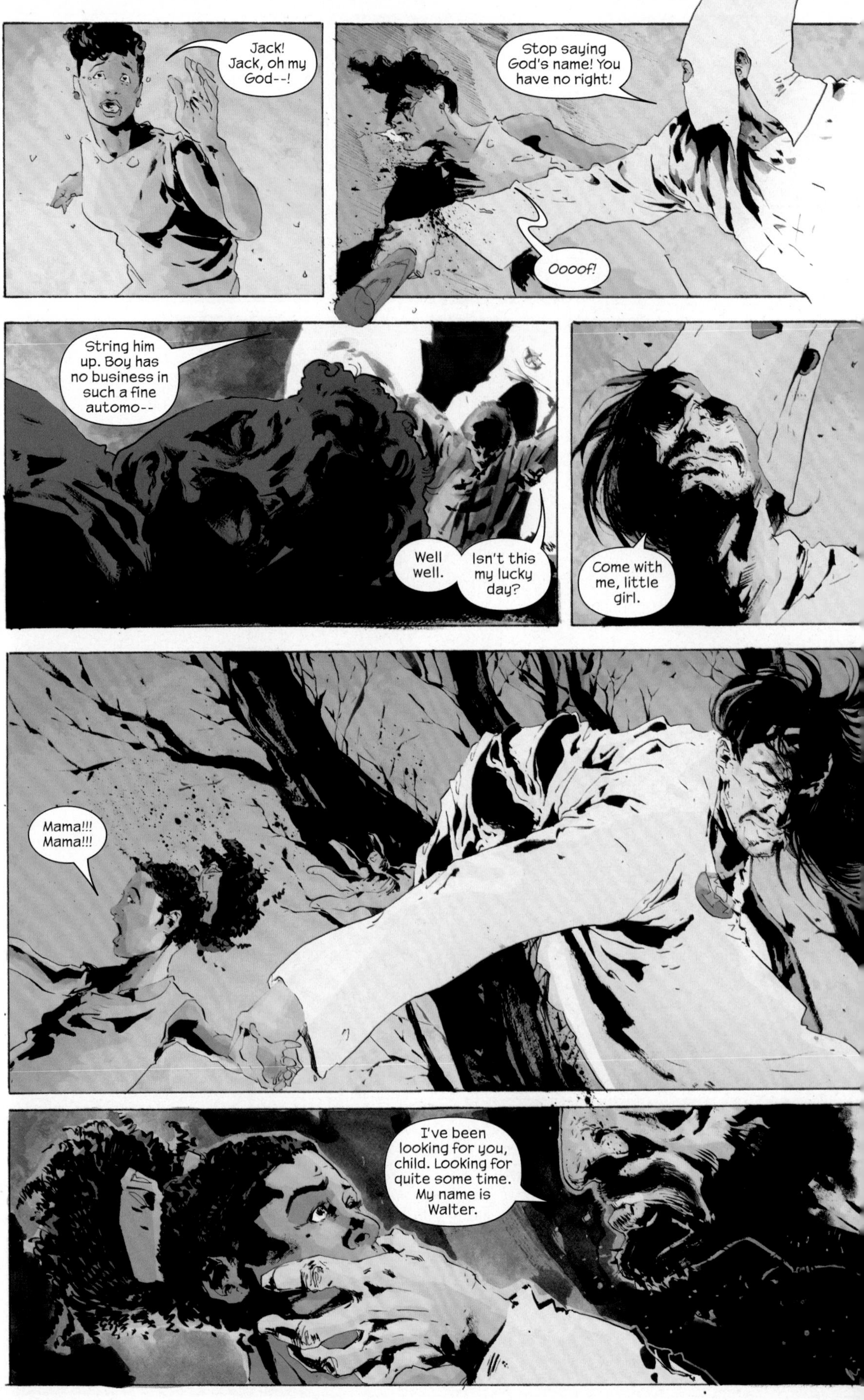
Jack! Jack, oh my God--!
Stop saying God's name! You have no right!
Oooof!
String him up. Boy has no business in such a fine automo--
Well well.
Isn't this my lucky day?
Come with me, little girl.
Mama!!! Mama!!!
I've been looking for you, child. Looking for quite some time. My name is Walter.

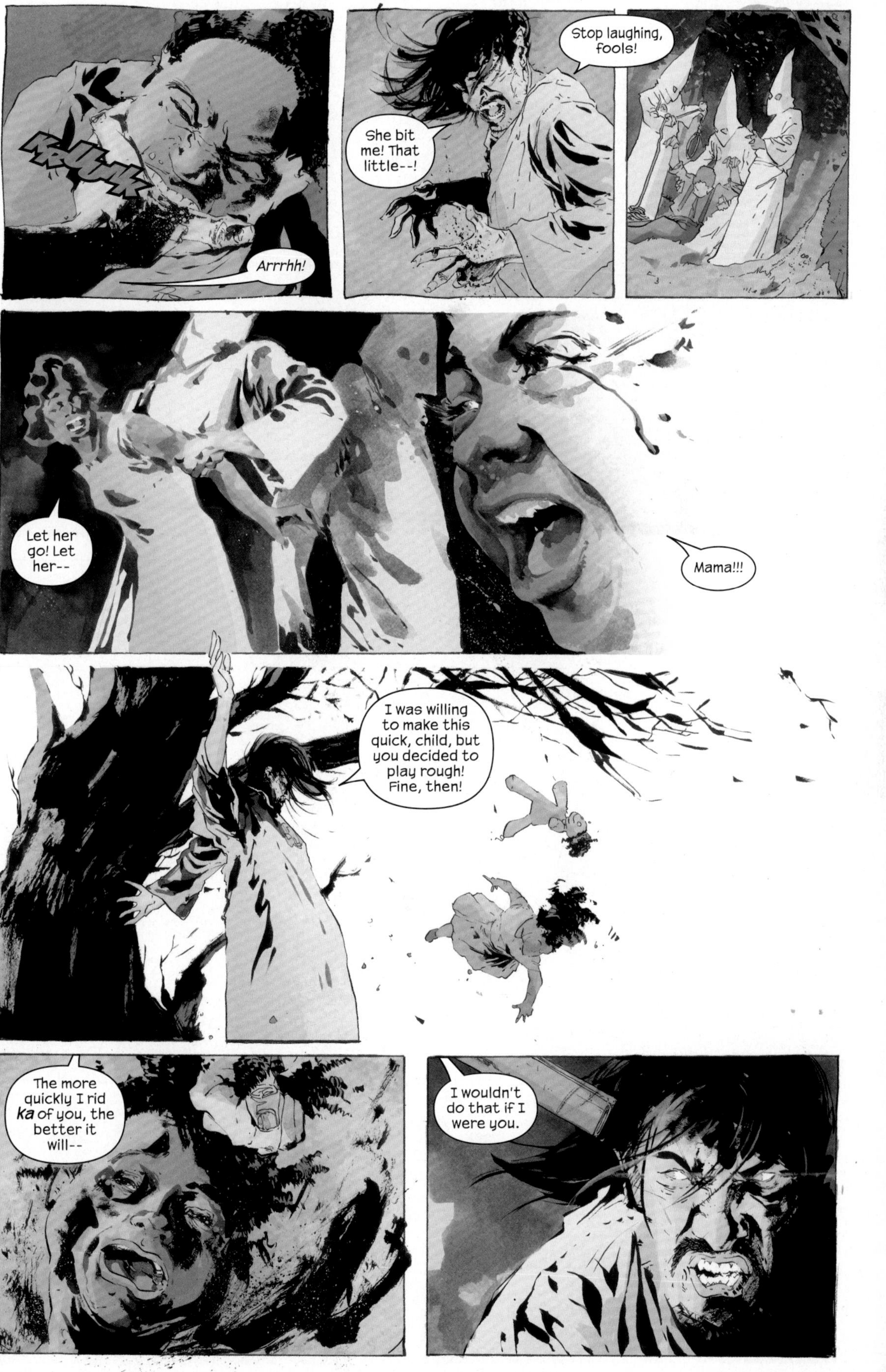
KRUNK
Arrrhh!
Stop laughing, fools!
She bit me! That little--!
Let her go! Let her--
Mama!!!
I was willing to make this quick, child, but you decided to play rough! Fine, then!
The more quickly I rid *ka* of you, the better it will--
I wouldn't do that if I were you.

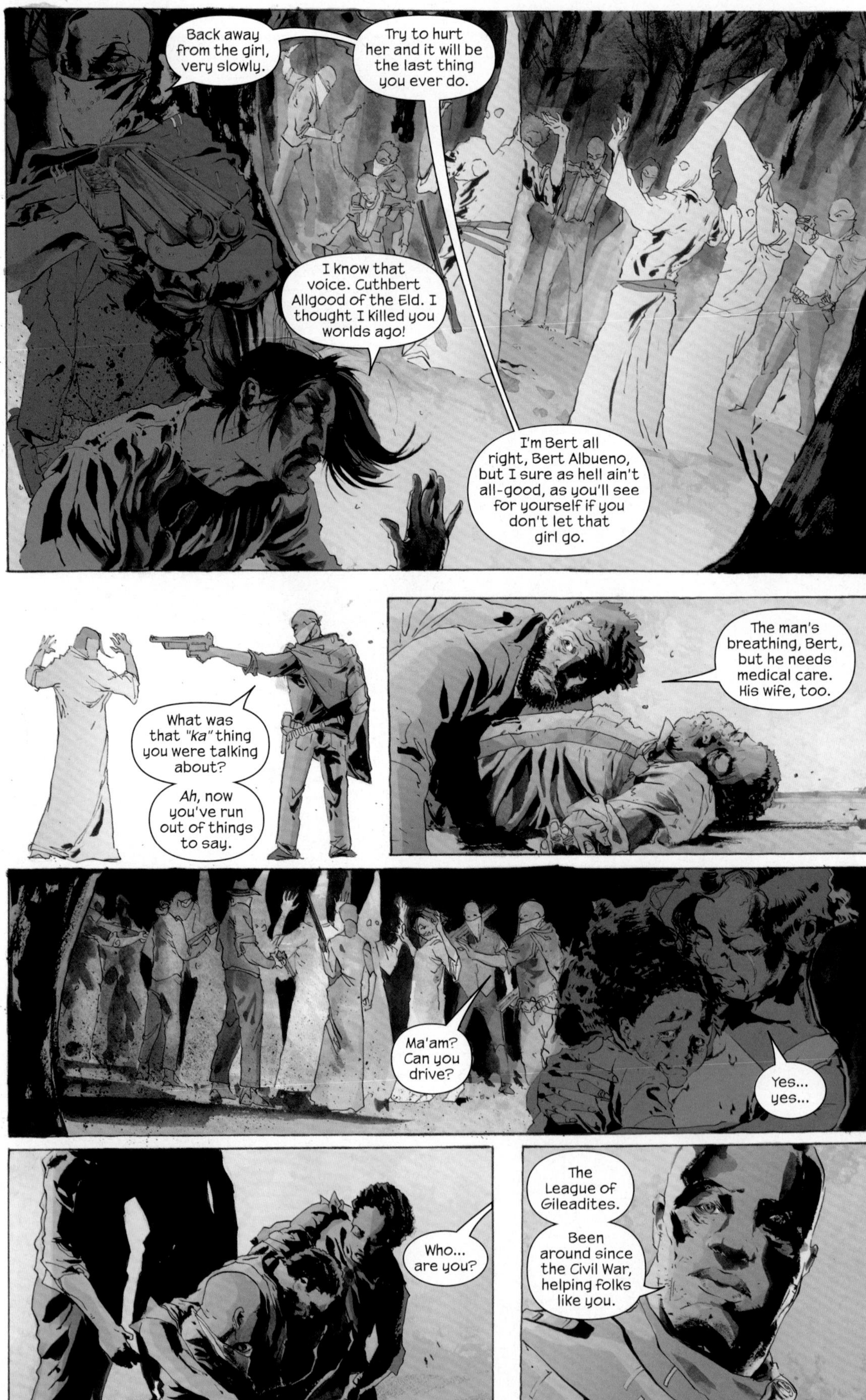

Back away from the girl, very slowly.
Try to hurt her and it will be the last thing you ever do.
I know that voice. Cuthbert Allgood of the Eld. I thought I killed you worlds ago!
I'm Bert all right, Bert Albueno, but I sure as hell ain't all-good, as you'll see for yourself if you don't let that girl go.
What was that "*ka*" thing you were talking about?
Ah, now you've run out of things to say.
The man's breathing, Bert, but he needs medical care. His wife, too.
Ma'am? Can you drive?
Yes... yes...
Who... are you?
The League of Gileadites.
Been around since the Civil War, helping folks like you.

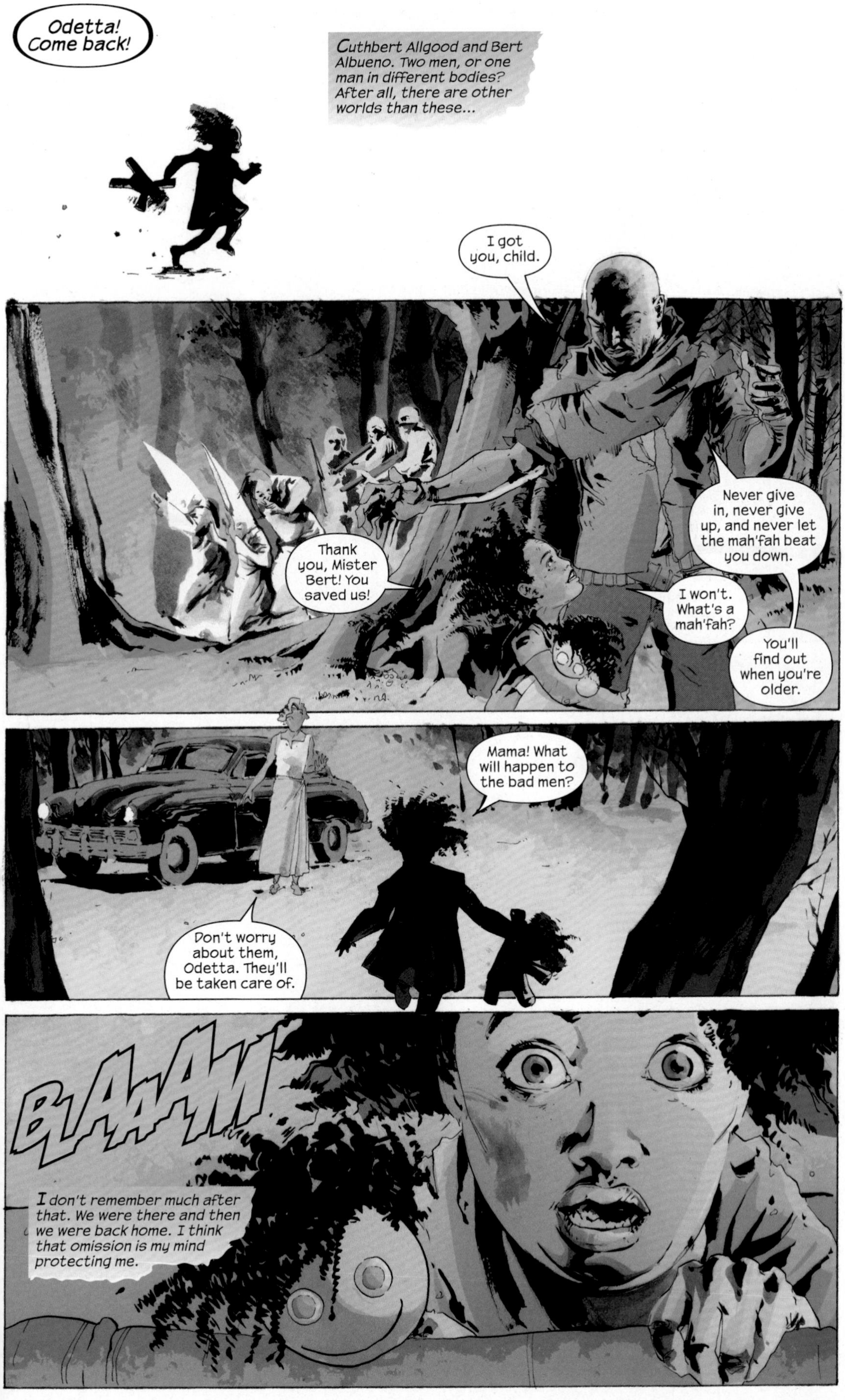

Odetta! Come back!
Cuthbert Allgood and Bert Albueno. Two men, or one man in different bodies? After all, there are other worlds than these...
I got you, child.
Thank you, Mister Bert! You saved us!
Never give in, never give up, and never let the mah'fah beat you down.
I won't. What's a mah'fah?
You'll find out when you're older.
Mama! What will happen to the bad men?
Don't worry about them, Odetta. They'll be taken care of.
BLAAAM
I don't remember much after that. We were there and then we were back home. I think that omission is my mind protecting me.

I just heard from the hospital, sweetheart. Both the Graysons are out of danger. They'll be fine.

But what about Odetta? What she saw! So much blood!

Don't fret, honeychild. She thinks the whole thing was a bad dream.

Well, thank *God* for that.

Better to thank the "*League of Gileadites.*"

I read about them. They were formed by John Brown a hundred years ago.

Can't believe they're still around, but good thing.

Still want to go to Blue's wedding?

Of course! She's my only sister.

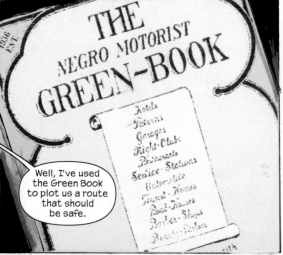

THE NEGRO MOTORIST GREEN-BOOK

Hotels
Taverns
Garages
Night Clubs
Restaurants
Service Stations
Automotive
Tourist Homes
Road Houses
Barber Shops
Beauty Salons

Well, I've used the Green Book to plot us a route that should be safe.

Safe? I don't know what that word means anymore. I'm terrified just to get into the car.

Our car is just like the Grayson's. Maybe we'll be targeted next!

My God, what kind of world are we leaving to our daughter?

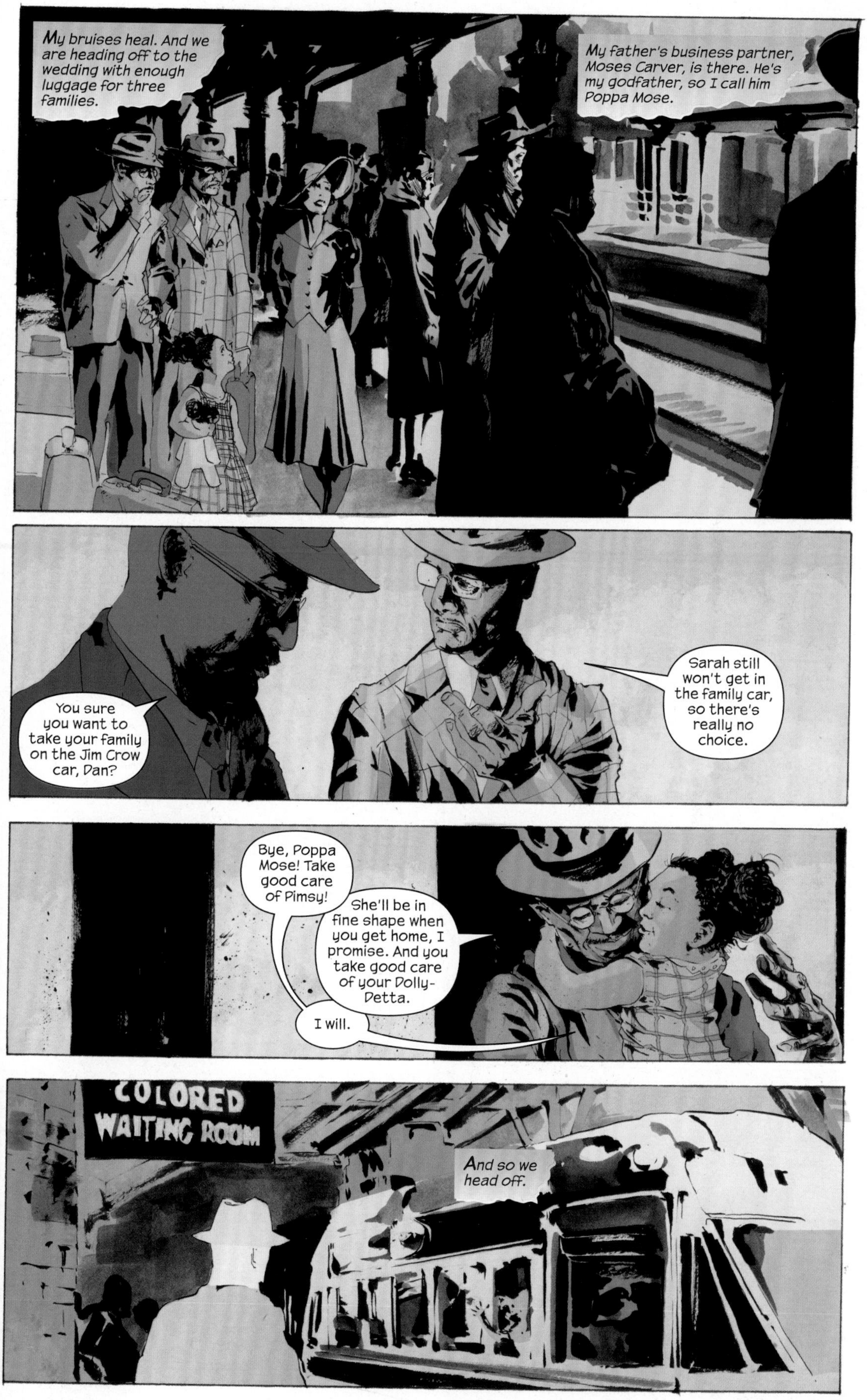

My bruises heal. And we are heading off to the wedding with enough luggage for three families.
My father's business partner, Moses Carver, is there. He's my godfather, so I call him Poppa Mose.
You sure you want to take your family on the Jim Crow car, Dan?
Sarah still won't get in the family car, so there's really no choice.
Bye, Poppa Mose! Take good care of Pimsy!
She'll be in fine shape when you get home, I promise. And you take good care of your Dolly-Detta.
I will.
COLORED WAITING ROOM
And so we head off.

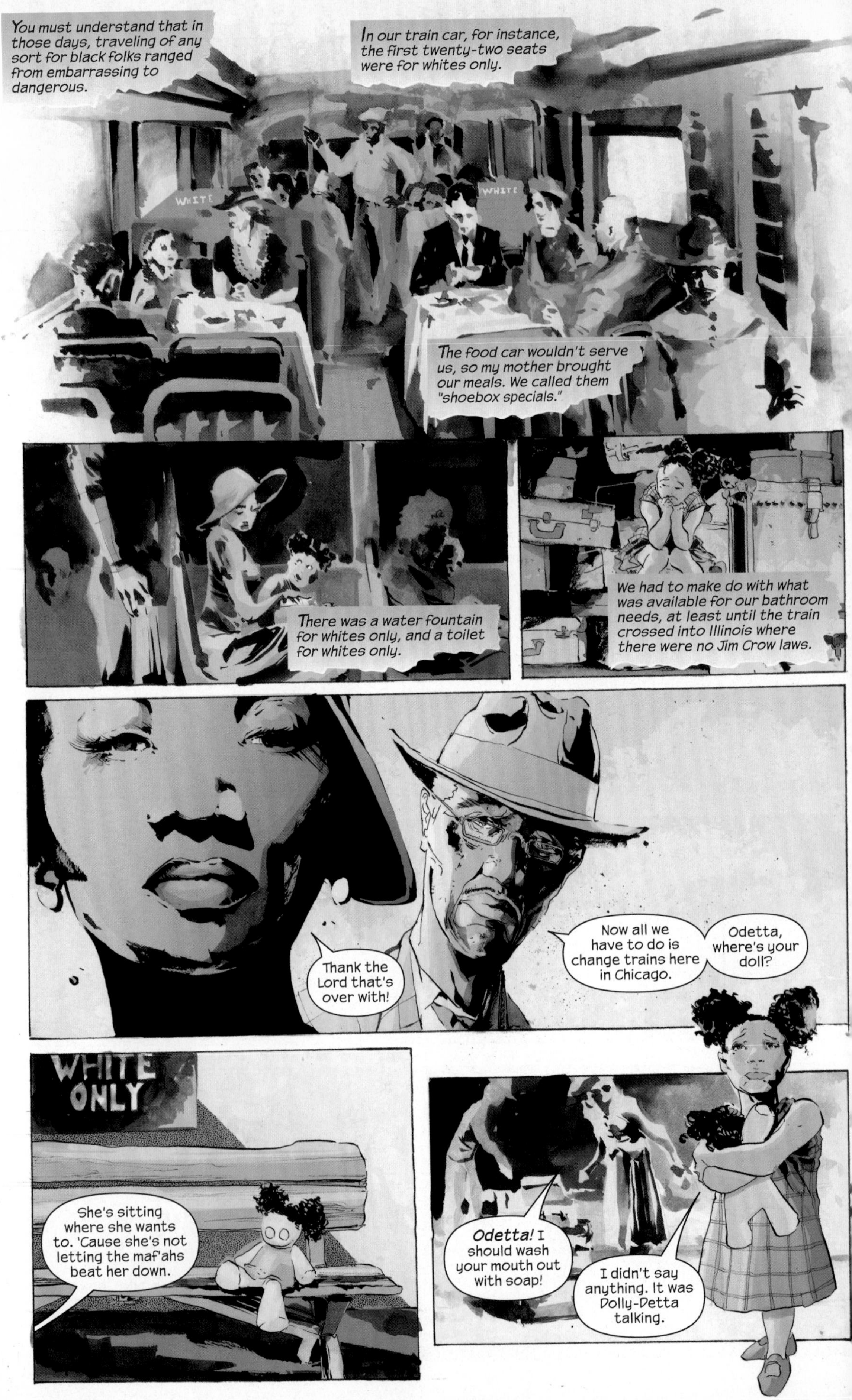
You must understand that in those days, traveling of any sort for black folks ranged from embarrassing to dangerous.
In our train car, for instance, the first twenty-two seats were for whites only.
WHITE
WHITE
The food car wouldn't serve us, so my mother brought our meals. We called them "shoebox specials."
There was a water fountain for whites only, and a toilet for whites only.
We had to make do with what was available for our bathroom needs, at least until the train crossed into Illinois where there were no Jim Crow laws.
Thank the Lord that's over with!
Now all we have to do is change trains here in Chicago.
Odetta, where's your doll?
WHITE ONLY
She's sitting where she wants to. 'Cause she's not letting the maf'ahs beat her down.
Odetta! I should wash your mouth out with soap!
I didn't say anything. It was Dolly-Detta talking.

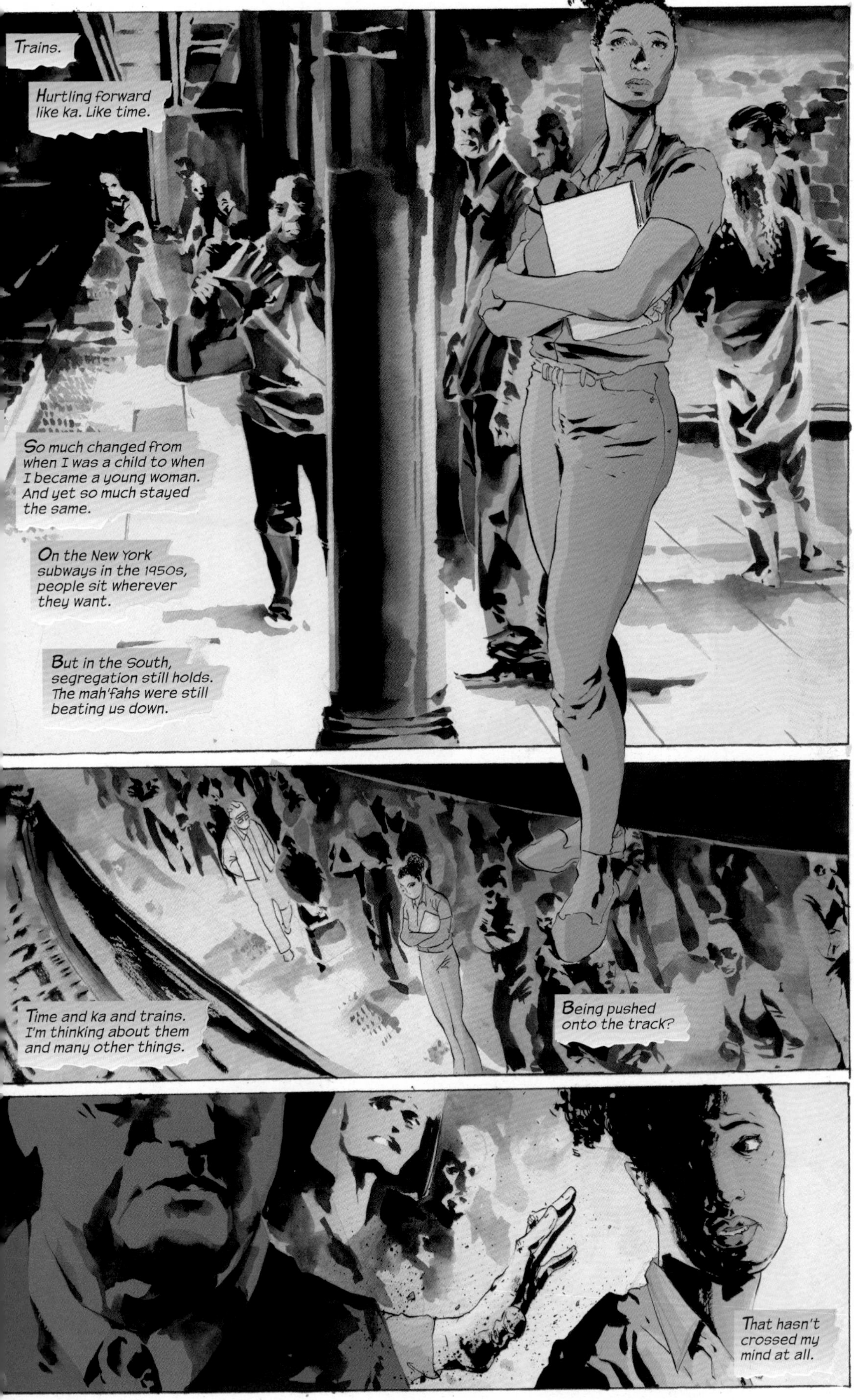
Trains.
Hurtling forward like ka. Like time.
So much changed from when I was a child to when I became a young woman. And yet so much stayed the same.
On the New York subways in the 1950s, people sit wherever they want.
But in the South, segregation still holds. The mah'fahs were still beating us down.
Time and ka and trains. I'm thinking about them and many other things.
Being pushed onto the track?
That hasn't crossed my mind at all.

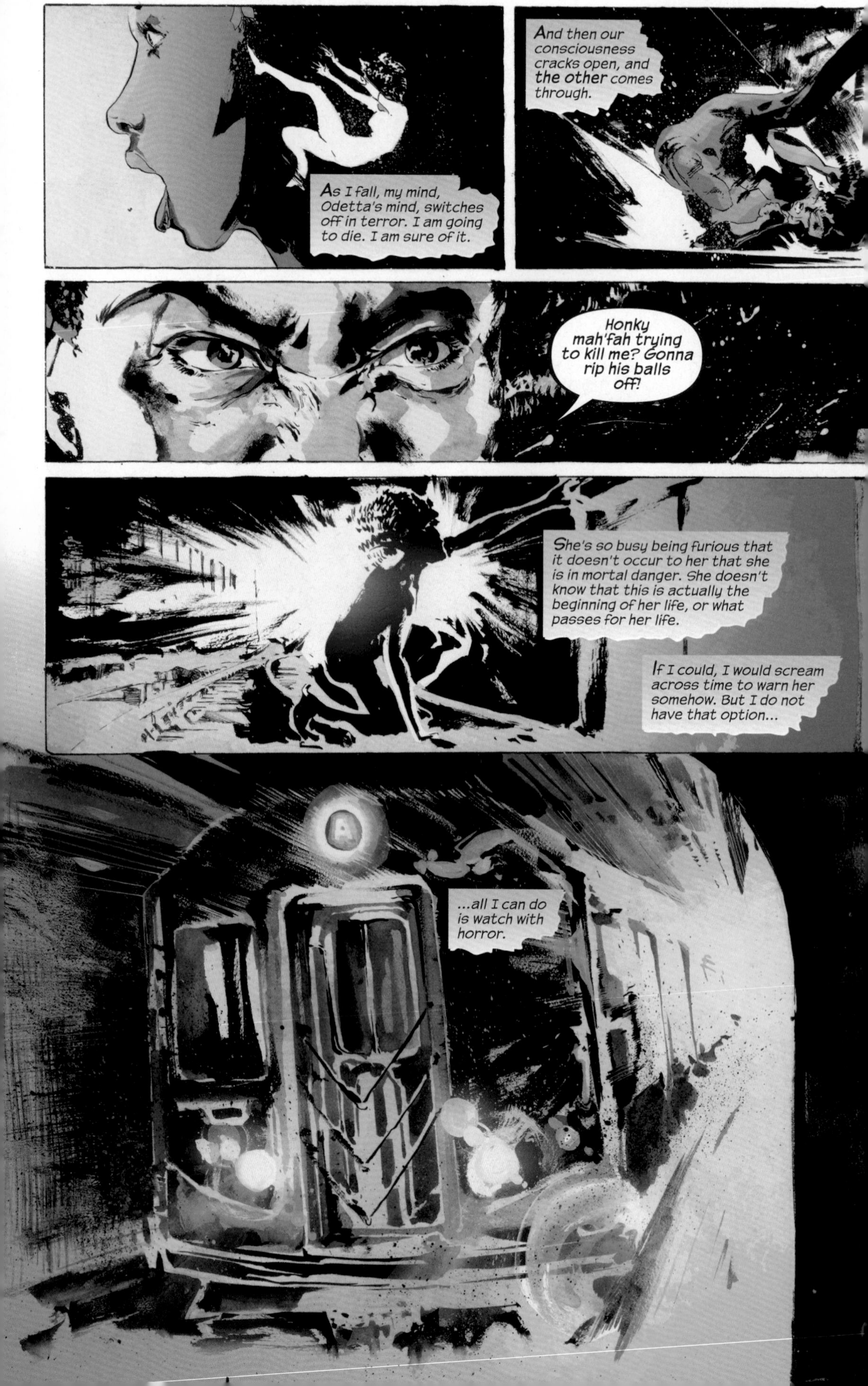
As I fall, my mind, Odetta's mind, switches off in terror. I am going to die. I am sure of it.
And then our consciousness cracks open, and the other comes through.
Honky mah'fah trying to kill me? Gonna rip his balls off!
She's so busy being furious that it doesn't occur to her that she is in mortal danger. She doesn't know that this is actually the beginning of her life, or what passes for her life.
If I could, I would scream across time to warn her somehow. But I do not have that option...
A
...all I can do is watch with horror.

THE DARK TOWER
THE DRAWING OF THE THREE
STEPHEN KING

THE LADY OF SHADOWS
CHAPTER TWO

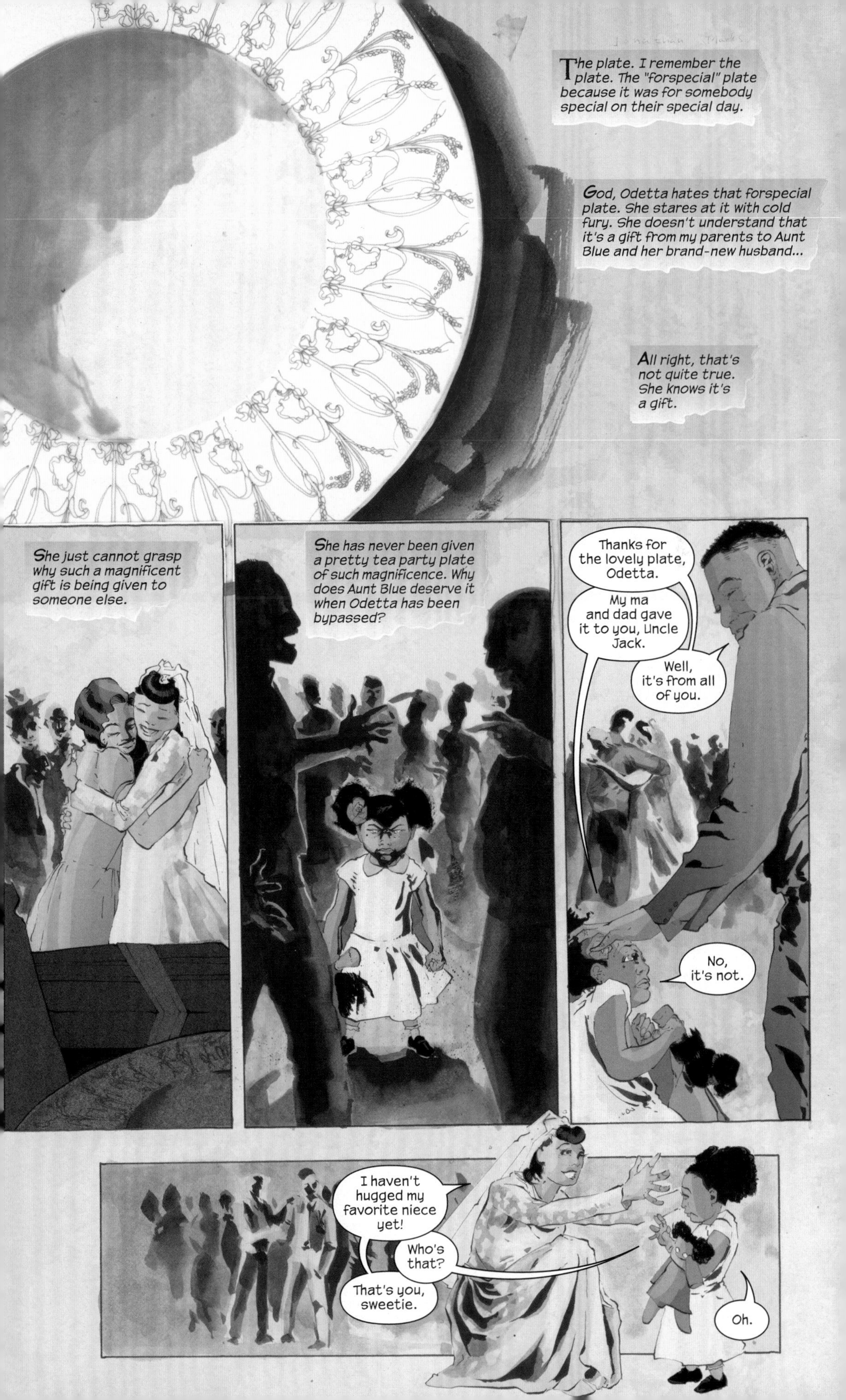
The plate. I remember the plate. The "forspecial" plate because it was for somebody special on their special day.
God, Odetta hates that forspecial plate. She stares at it with cold fury. She doesn't understand that it's a gift from my parents to Aunt Blue and her brand-new husband...
All right, that's not quite true. She knows it's a gift.
She just cannot grasp why such a magnificent gift is being given to someone else.
She has never been given a pretty tea party plate of such magnificence. Why does Aunt Blue deserve it when Odetta has been bypassed?
Thanks for the lovely plate, Odetta.
My ma and dad gave it to you, Uncle Jack.
Well, it's from all of you.
No, it's not.
I haven't hugged my favorite niece yet!
Who's that?
That's you, sweetie.
Oh.

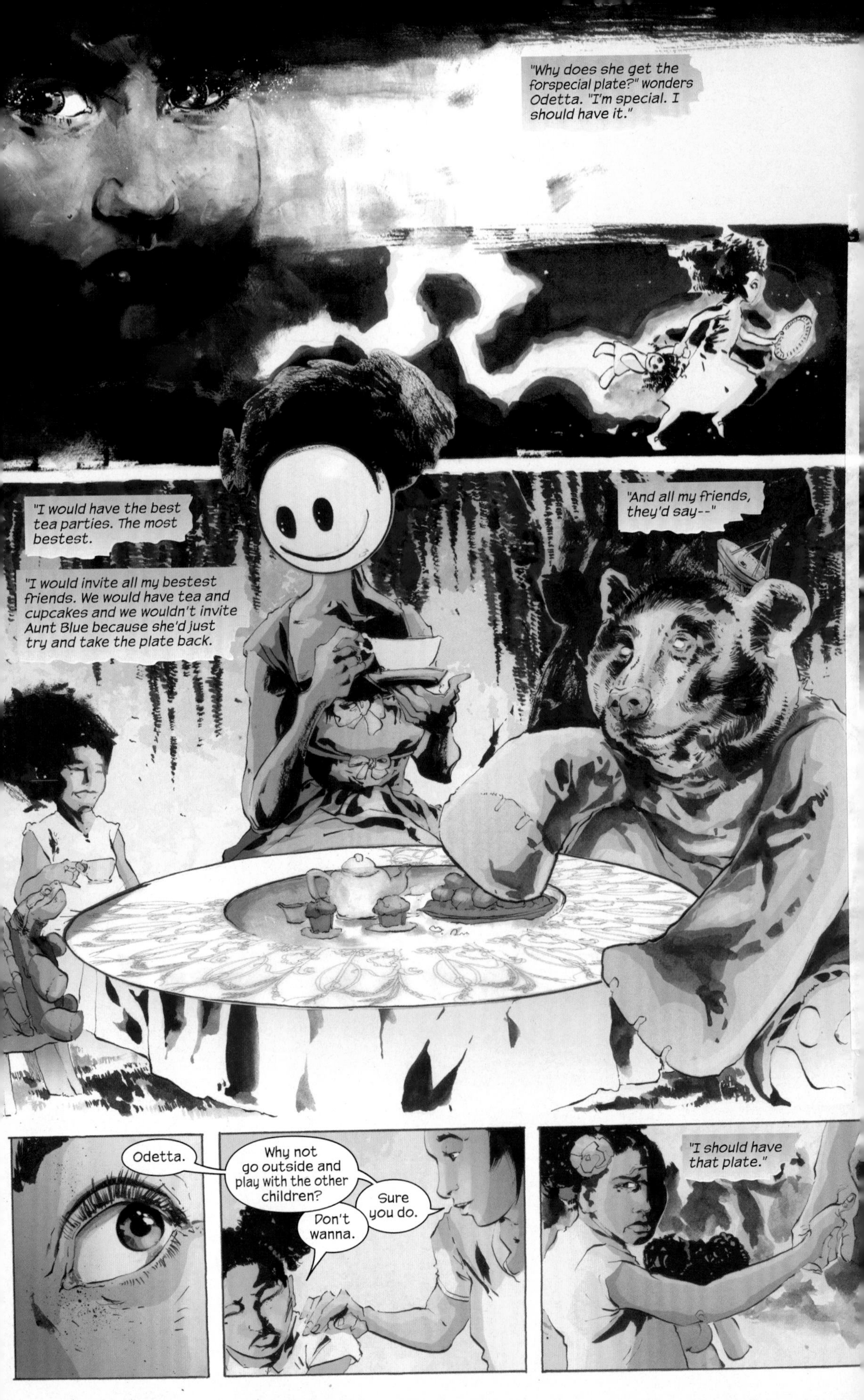
"Why does she get the forspecial plate?" wonders Odetta. "I'm special. I should have it."
"I would have the best tea parties. The most bestest.
"I would invite all my bestest friends. We would have tea and cupcakes and we wouldn't invite Aunt Blue because she'd just try and take the plate back.
"And all my friends, they'd say--"
Odetta.
Why not go outside and play with the other children?
Don't wanna.
Sure you do.
"I should have that plate."

It is the next day as we prepare to take a train to New York City. My mind remains with the plate.

Sure we can't give you a lift?

With all that luggage of ours you're carrying? You're lucky if you fit, Mr. Howard! Besides, we already called a cab.

Okay, then! Meet you at the station!

My father tells me about how my face will glow when I see the animals dance on the Central Park clock. I ask if that will hurt and he laughs.

Moments later we're all laughing as the cabbie pulls up...

And then sees that his fare is colored. And he drives off like his head is on fire and his ass is catching.

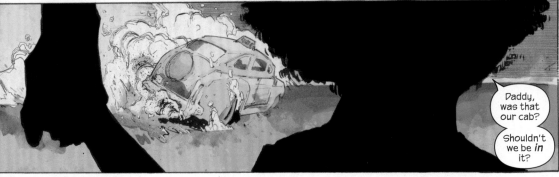

Daddy, was that our cab?

Shouldn't we be *in* it?

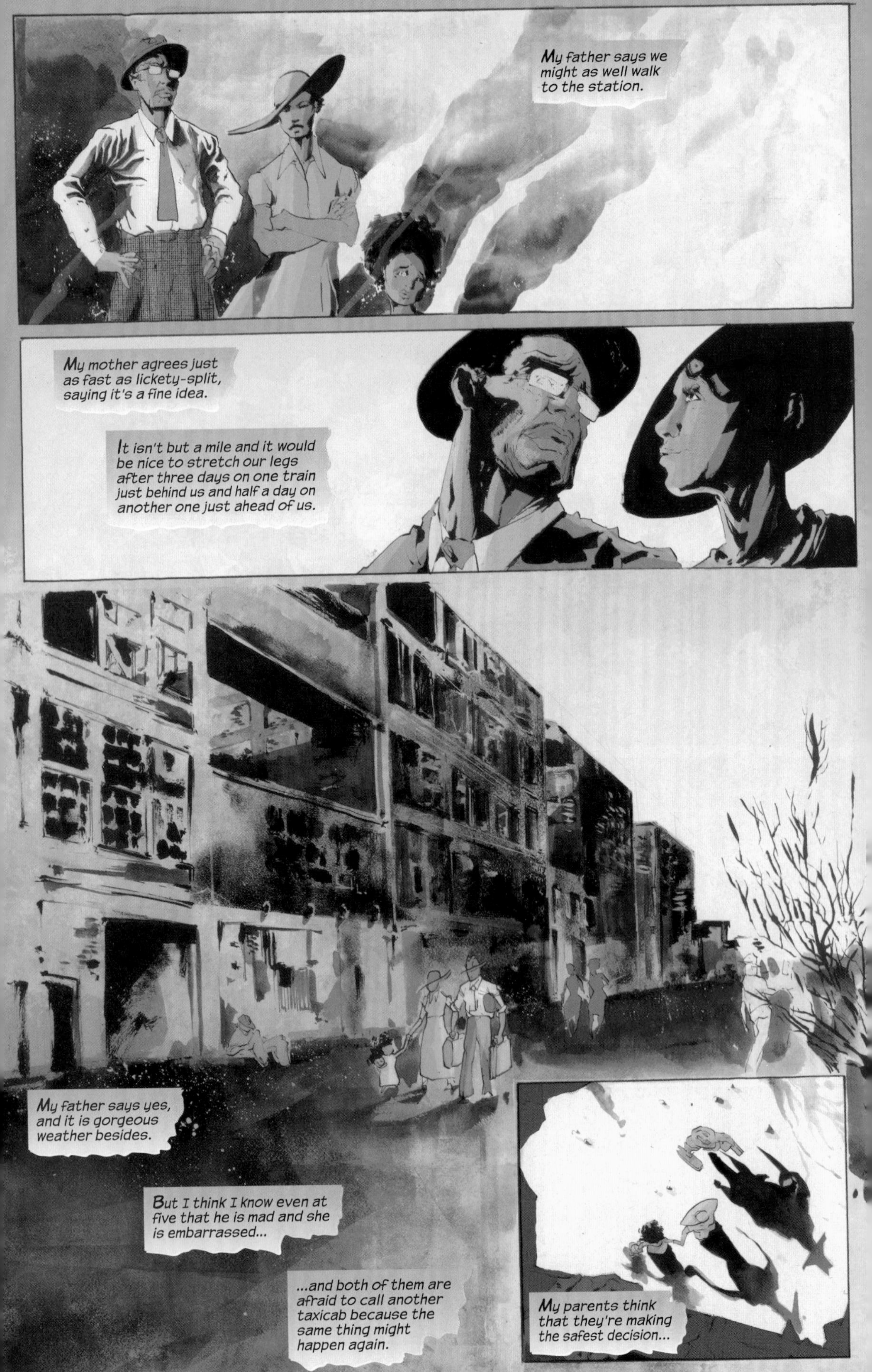
My father says we might as well walk to the station.
My mother agrees just as fast as lickety-split, saying it's a fine idea.
It isn't but a mile and it would be nice to stretch our legs after three days on one train just behind us and half a day on another one just ahead of us.
My father says yes, and it is gorgeous weather besides.
But I think I know even at five that he is mad and she is embarrassed...
...and both of them are afraid to call another taxicab because the same thing might happen again.
My parents think that they're making the safest decision...

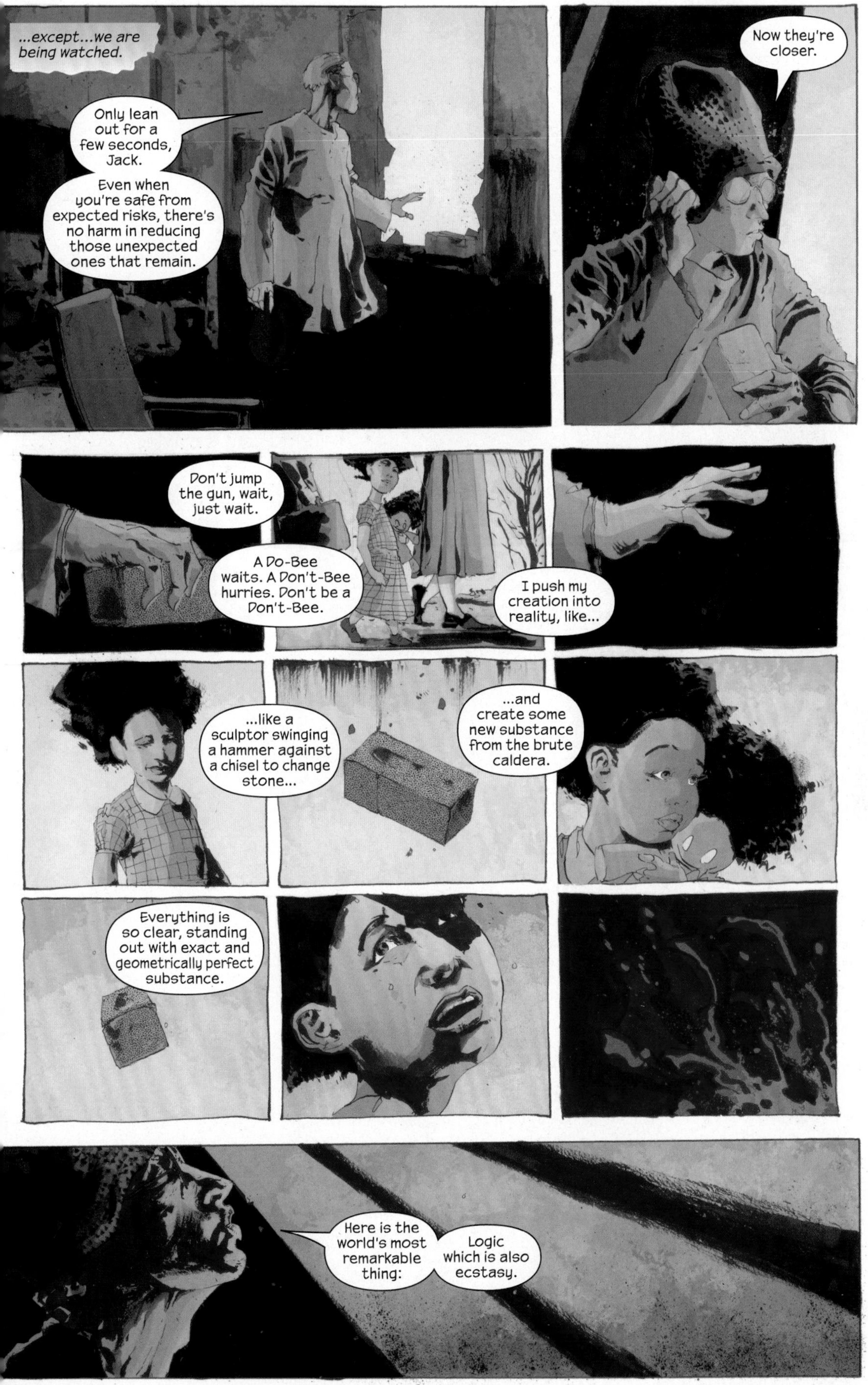
...except...we are being watched.
Only lean out for a few seconds, Jack.
Even when you're safe from expected risks, there's no harm in reducing those unexpected ones that remain.
Now they're closer.
Don't jump the gun, wait, just wait.
A Do-Bee waits. A Don't-Bee hurries. Don't be a Don't-Bee.
I push my creation into reality, like...
...like a sculptor swinging a hammer against a chisel to change stone...
...and create some new substance from the brute caldera.
Everything is so clear, standing out with exact and geometrically perfect substance.
Here is the world's most remarkable thing:
Logic which is also ecstasy.

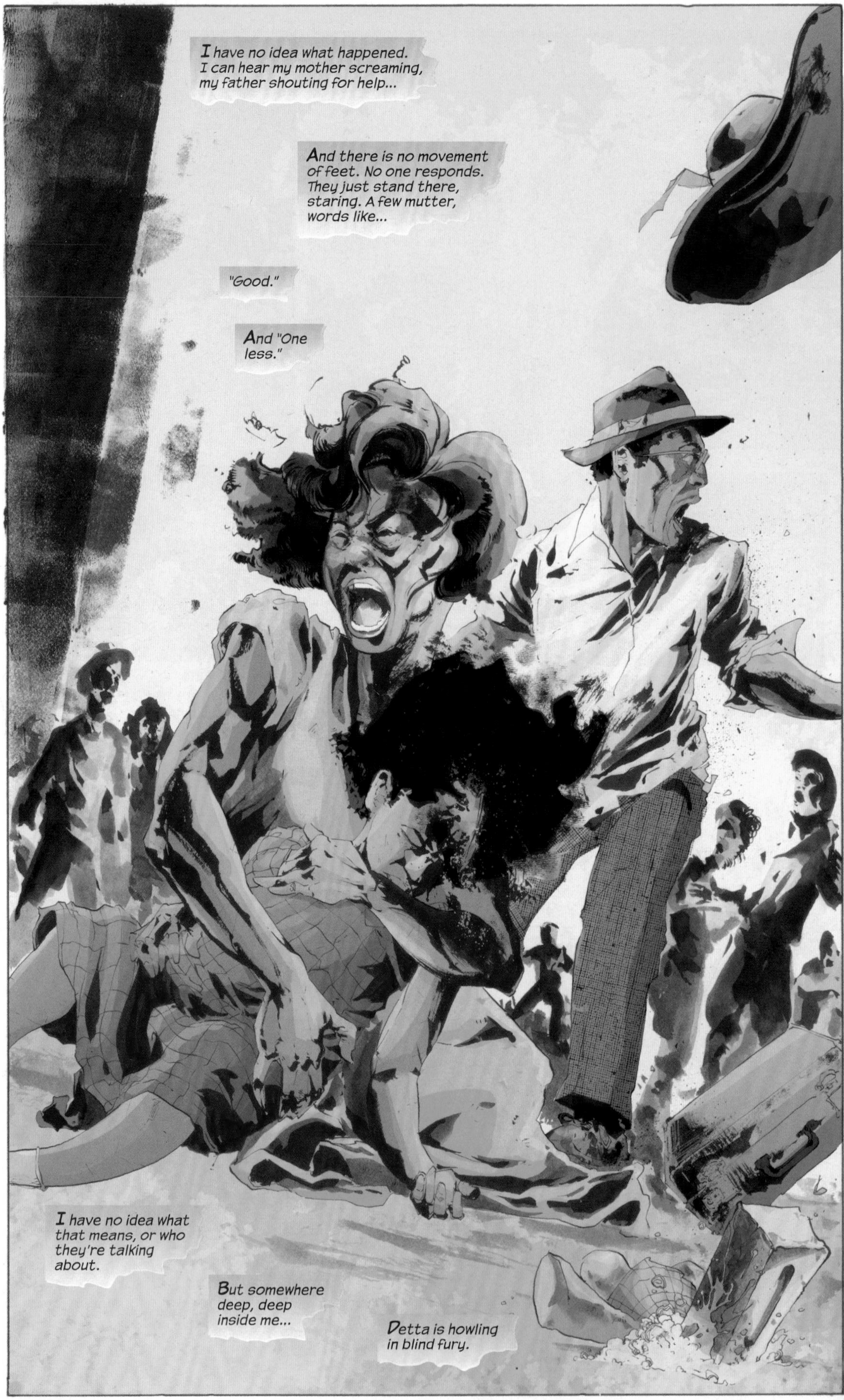
I have no idea what happened. I can hear my mother screaming, my father shouting for help...
And there is no movement of feet. No one responds. They just stand there, staring. A few mutter, words like...
"Good."
And "One less."
I have no idea what that means, or who they're talking about.
But somewhere deep, deep inside me...
Detta is howling in blind fury.

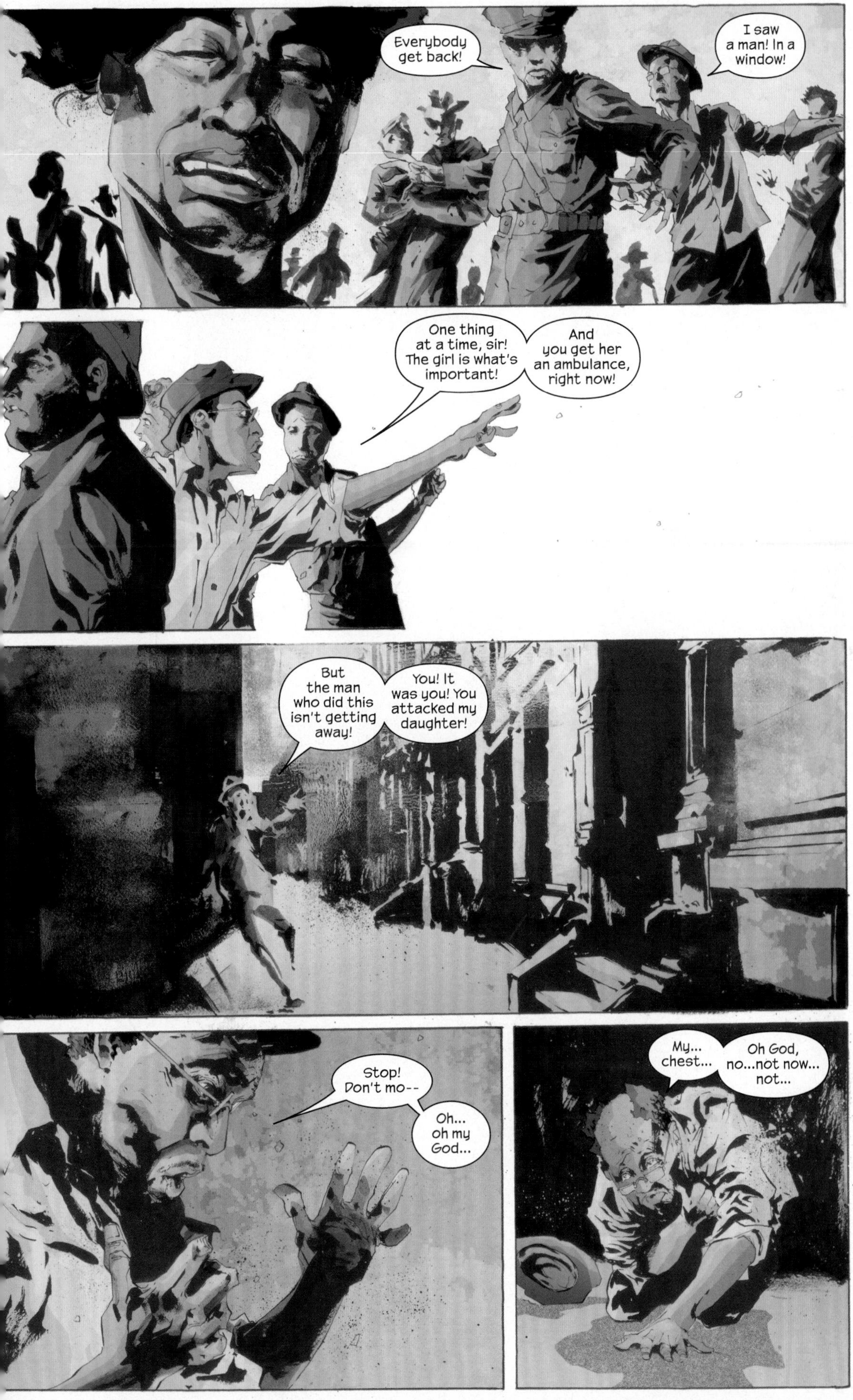
Everybody get back!
I saw a man! In a window!
One thing at a time, sir! The girl is what's important!
And you get her an ambulance, right now!
But the man who did this isn't getting away!
You! It was you! You attacked my daughter!
Stop! Don't mo--
Oh... oh my God...
My... chest...
Oh God, no...not now... not...

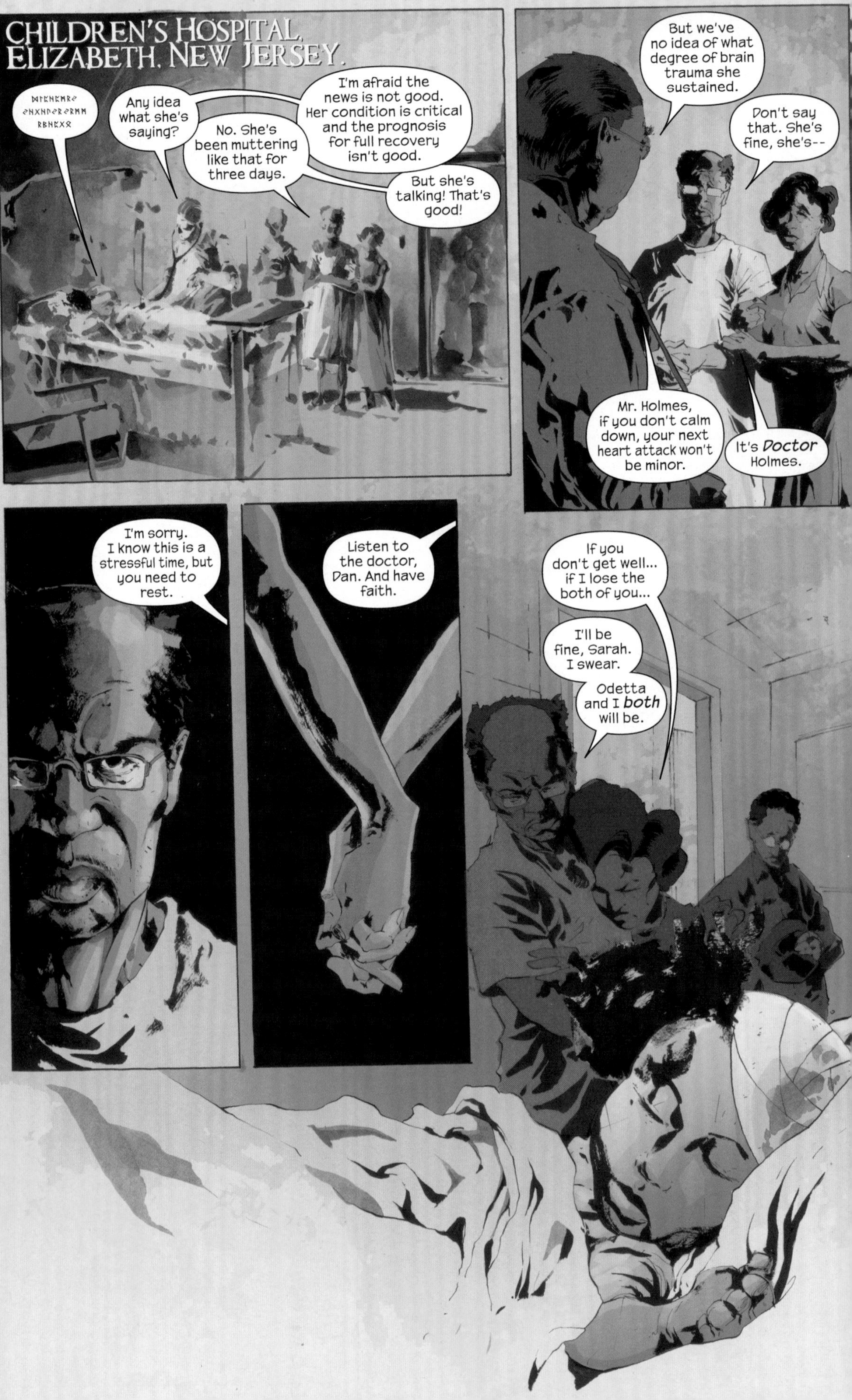
CHILDREN'S HOSPITAL, ELIZABETH, NEW JERSEY.
Any idea what she's saying?
No. She's been muttering like that for three days.
I'm afraid the news is not good. Her condition is critical and the prognosis for full recovery isn't good.
But she's talking! That's good!
But we've no idea of what degree of brain trauma she sustained.
Don't say that. She's fine, she's--
Mr. Holmes, if you don't calm down, your next heart attack won't be minor.
It's *Doctor* Holmes.
I'm sorry. I know this is a stressful time, but you need to rest.
Listen to the doctor, Dan. And have faith.
If you don't get well... if I lose the both of you...
I'll be fine, Sarah. I swear.
Odetta and I *both* will be.

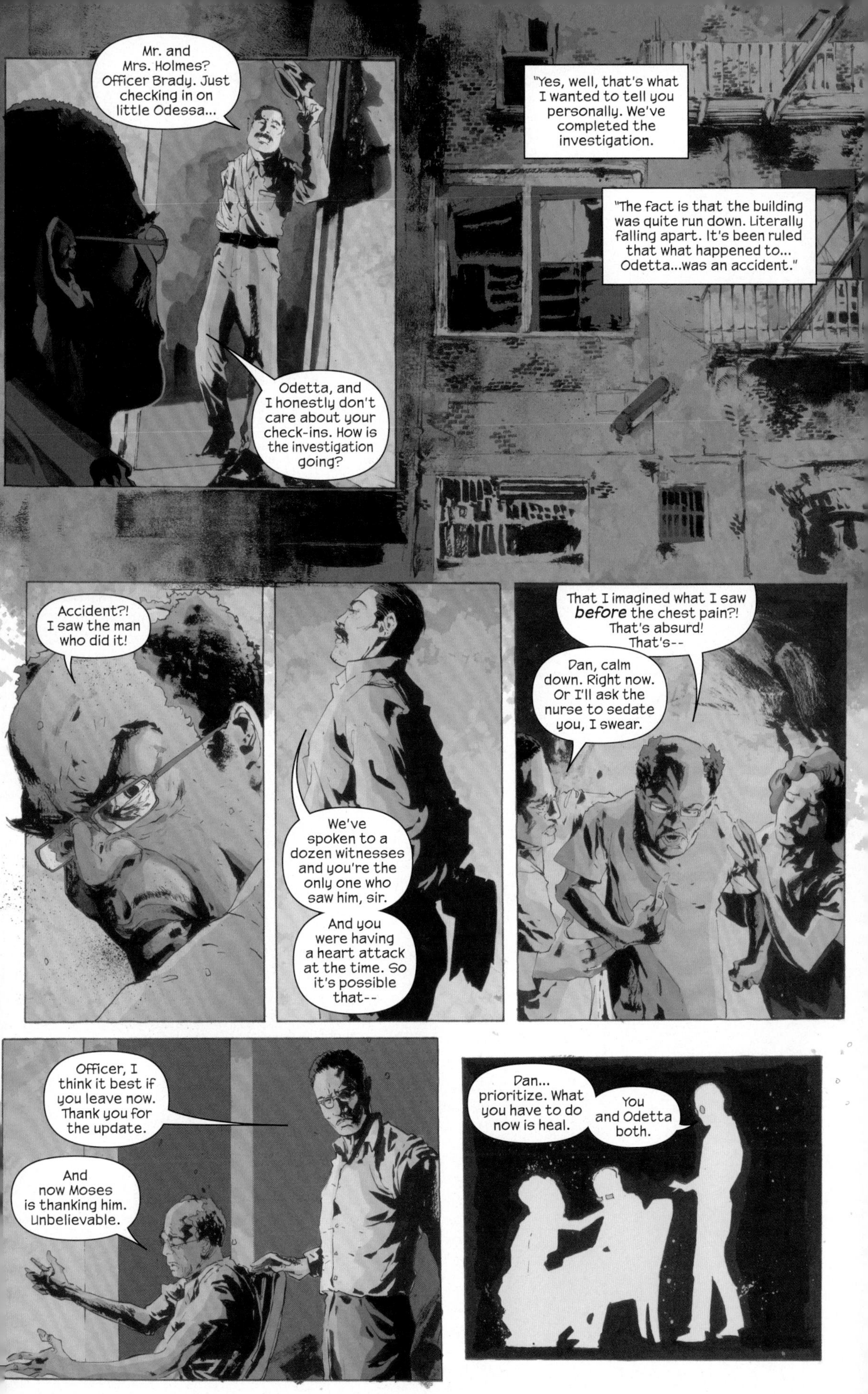
Mr. and Mrs. Holmes? Officer Brady. Just checking in on little Odessa...
Odetta, and I honestly don't care about your check-ins. How is the investigation going?
"Yes, well, that's what I wanted to tell you personally. We've completed the investigation.
"The fact is that the building was quite run down. Literally falling apart. It's been ruled that what happened to... Odetta...was an accident."
Accident?! I saw the man who did it!
We've spoken to a dozen witnesses and you're the only one who saw him, sir.
And you were having a heart attack at the time. So it's possible that--
That I imagined what I saw *before* the chest pain?! That's absurd! That's--
Dan, calm down. Right now. Or I'll ask the nurse to sedate you, I swear.
Officer, I think it best if you leave now. Thank you for the update.
And now Moses is thanking him. Unbelievable.
Dan... prioritize. What you have to do now is heal.
You and Odetta both.

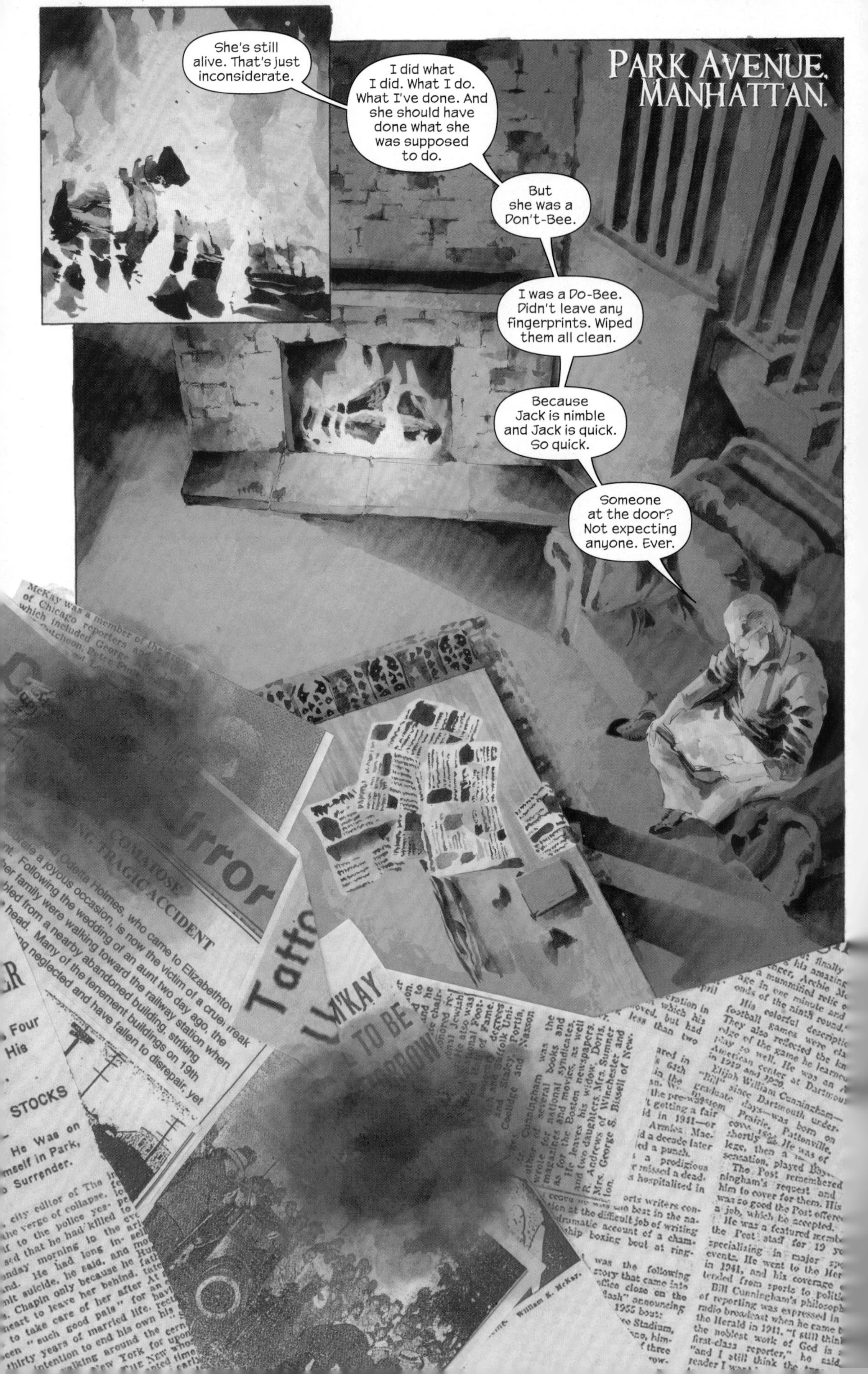
PARK AVENUE, MANHATTAN.
She's still alive. That's just inconsiderate.
I did what I did. What I do. What I've done. And she should have done what she was supposed to do.
But she was a Don't-Bee.
I was a Do-Bee. Didn't leave any fingerprints. Wiped them all clean.
Because Jack is nimble and Jack is quick. So quick.
Someone at the door? Not expecting anyone. Ever.

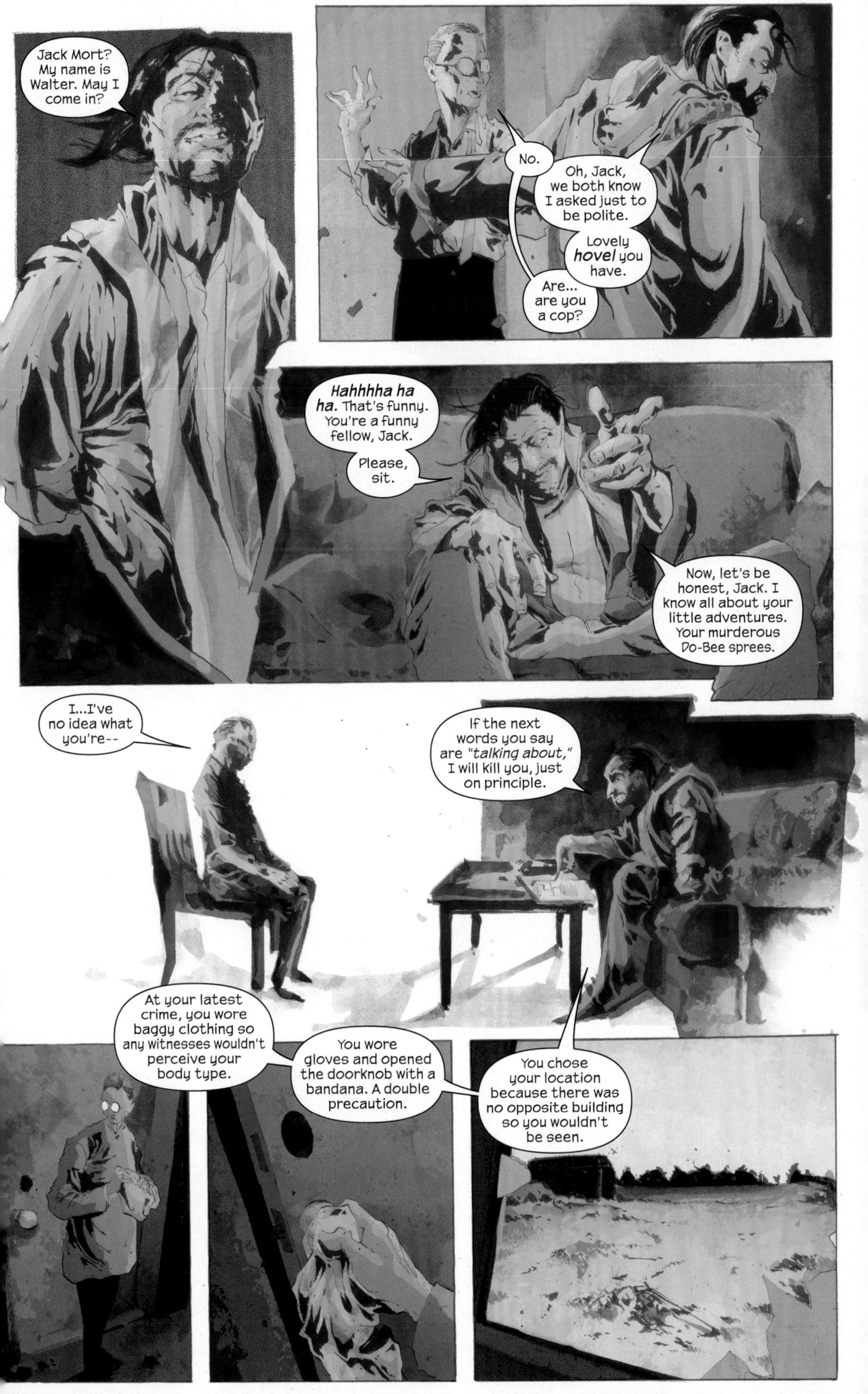

Jack Mort? My name is Walter. May I come in?
No.
Oh, Jack, we both know I asked just to be polite.
Lovely *hovel* you have.
Are... are you a cop?
Hahhhha ha ha. That's funny. You're a funny fellow, Jack.
Please, sit.
Now, let's be honest, Jack. I know all about your little adventures. Your murderous Do-Bee sprees.
I...I've no idea what you're--
If the next words you say are "*talking about,*" I will kill you, just on principle.
At your latest crime, you wore baggy clothing so any witnesses wouldn't perceive your body type.
You wore gloves and opened the doorknob with a bandana. A double precaution.
You chose your location because there was no opposite building so you wouldn't be seen.

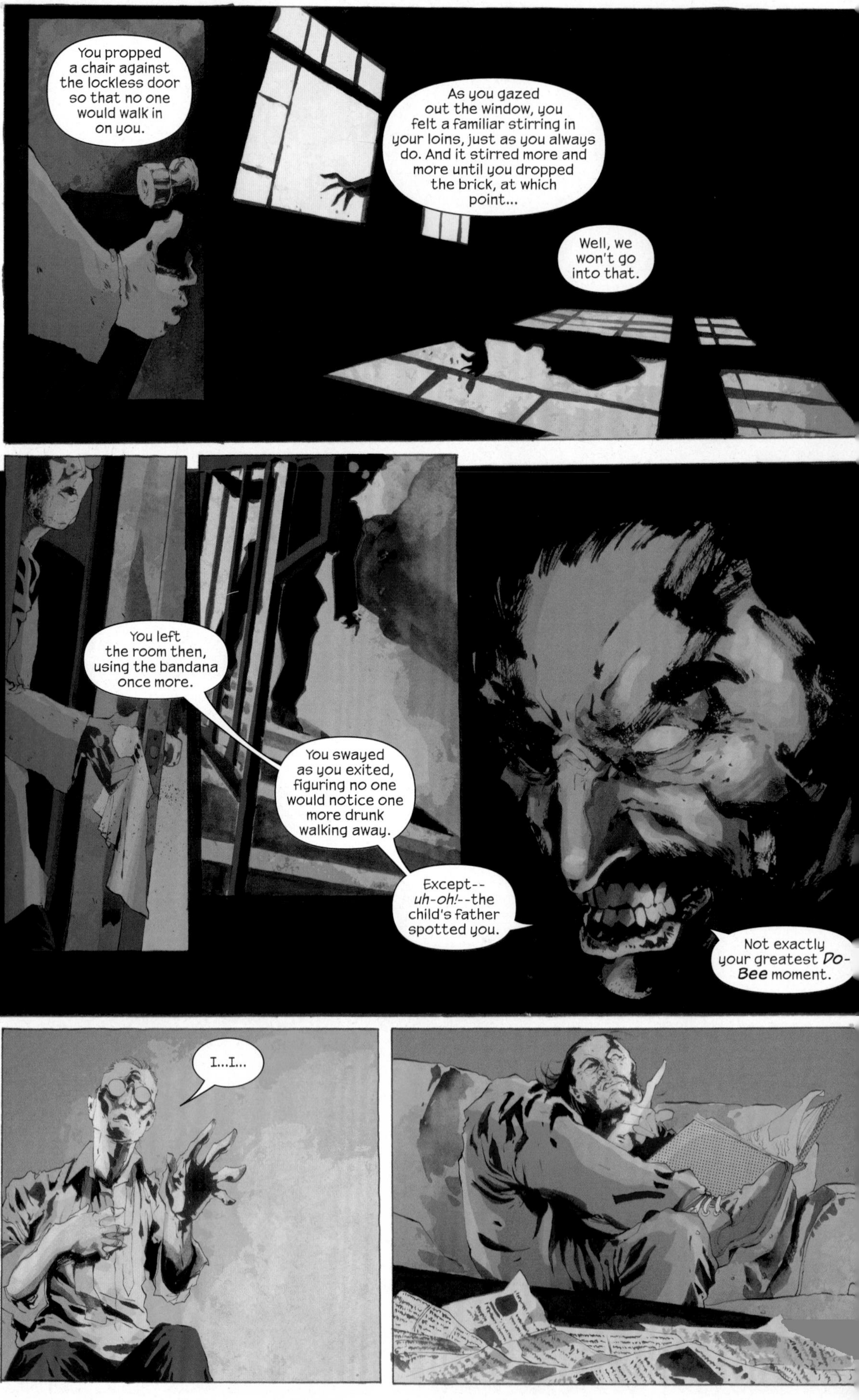
You propped a chair against the lockless door so that no one would walk in on you.
As you gazed out the window, you felt a familiar stirring in your loins, just as you always do. And it stirred more and more until you dropped the brick, at which point...
Well, we won't go into that.
You left the room then, using the bandana once more.
You swayed as you exited, figuring no one would notice one more drunk walking away.
Except-- *uh-oh!*--the child's father spotted you.
Not exactly your greatest *Do-Bee* moment.
I...I...

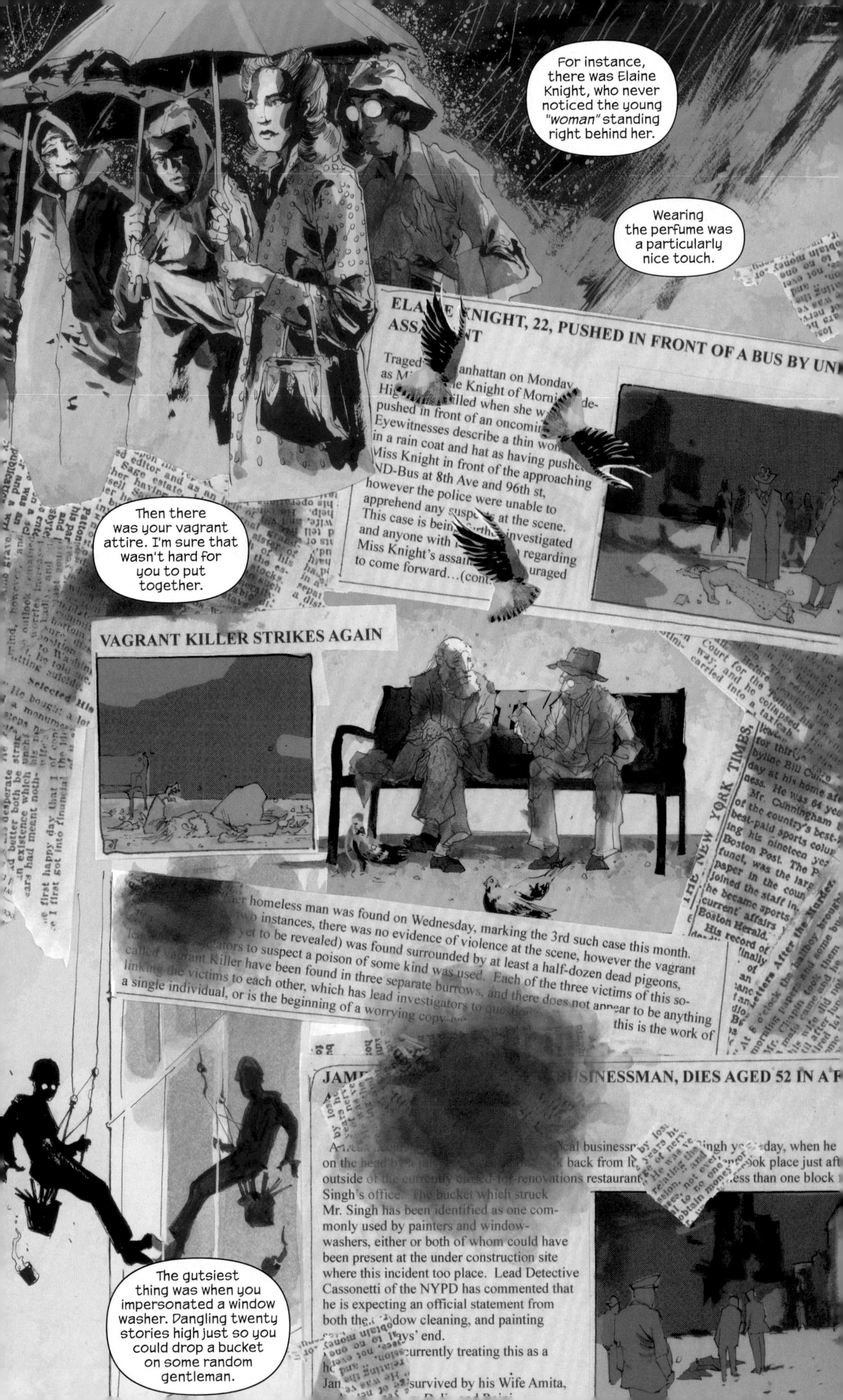

For instance, there was Elaine Knight, who never noticed the young *"woman"* standing right behind her.
Wearing the perfume was a particularly nice touch.
PUSHED IN FRONT OF A BUS BY UN
pushed in front of an oncomi
Eyewitnesses describe a thin wo
in a rain coat and hat as having pushe
Miss Knight in front of the approaching
however the police were unable to
This case is bein
and anyone with
Miss Knight's assa
to come forward...(cont
Then there was your vagrant attire. I'm sure that wasn't hard for you to put together.
VAGRANT KILLER STRIKES AGAIN
homeless man was found on Wednesday, marking the 3rd such case this month.
instances, there was no evidence of violence at the scene, however the vagrant
yet to be revealed) was found surrounded by at least a half-dozen dead pigeons,
to suspect a poison of some kind was used. Each of the three victims of this so-
Vagrant Killer have been found in three separate burrows, and there does not appear to be anything
linking the victims to each other, which has lead investigators to
a single individual, or is the beginning of a worrying copy-
this is the work of
THE NEW YORK TIMES
BUSINESSMAN, DIES AGED 52 IN A F
Singh's office.
Mr. Singh has been identified as one commonly used by painters and window-washers, either or both of whom could have been present at the under construction site where this incident too place. Lead Detective Cassonetti of the NYPD has commented that he is expecting an official statement from both the window cleaning, and painting
currently treating this as a
survived by his Wife Amita,
The gutsiest thing was when you impersonated a window washer. Dangling twenty stories high just so you could drop a bucket on some random gentleman.

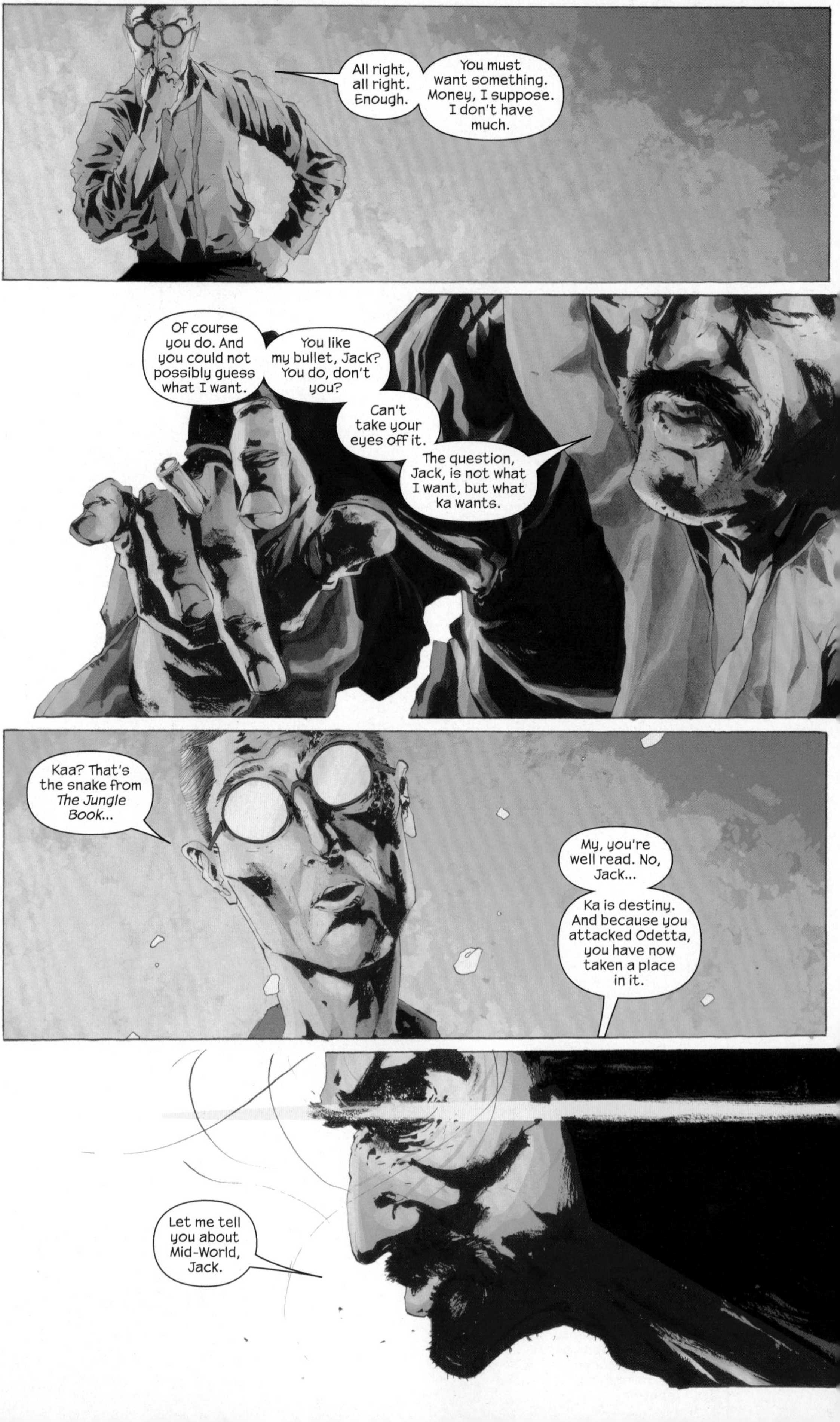
All right, all right. Enough.
You must want something. Money, I suppose. I don't have much.
Of course you do. And you could not possibly guess what I want.
You like my bullet, Jack? You do, don't you?
Can't take your eyes off it.
The question, Jack, is not what I want, but what ka wants.
Kaa? That's the snake from *The Jungle Book*...
My, you're well read. No, Jack...
Ka is destiny. And because you attacked Odetta, you have now taken a place in it.
Let me tell you about Mid-World, Jack.

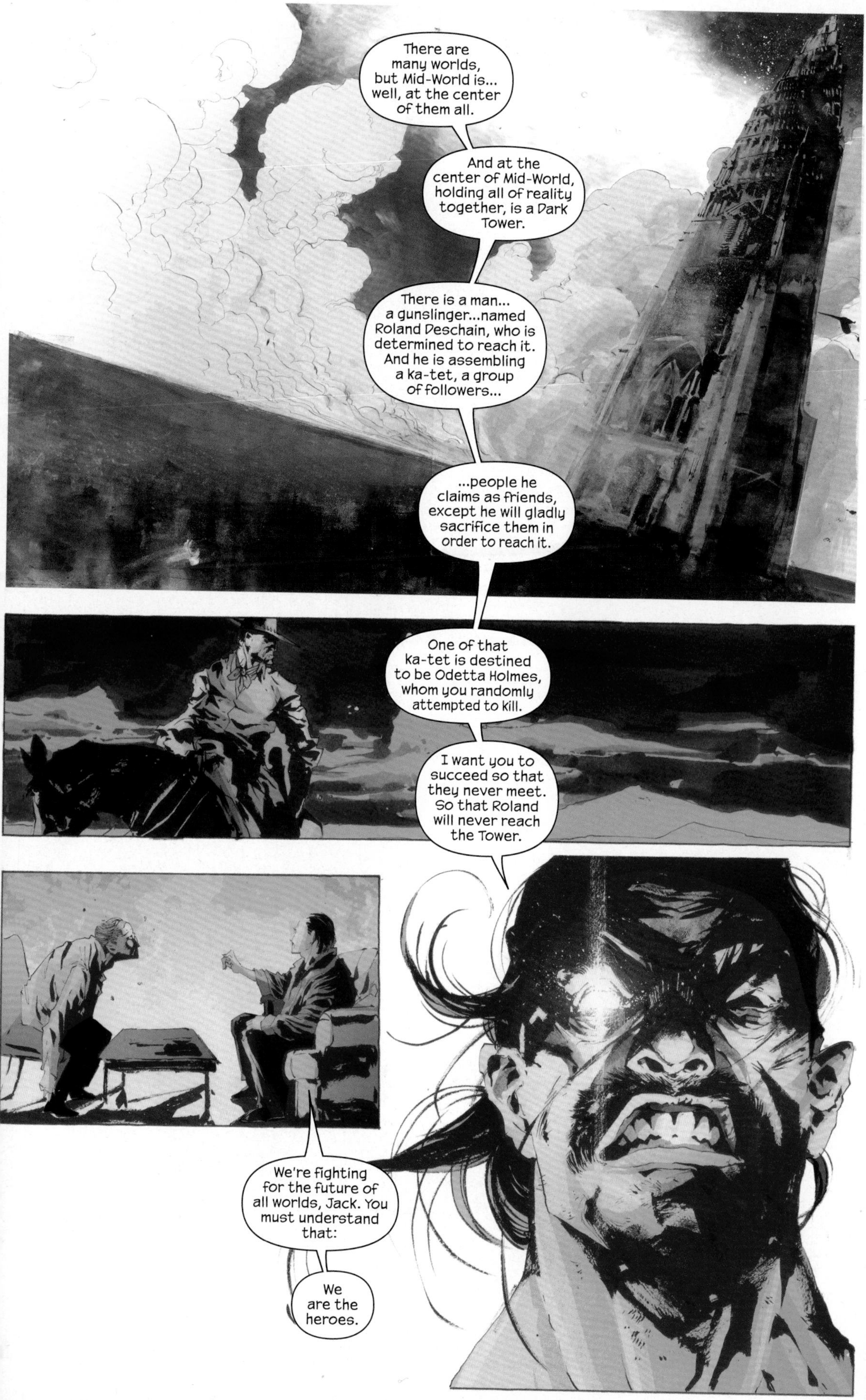
There are many worlds, but Mid-World is... well, at the center of them all.
And at the center of Mid-World, holding all of reality together, is a Dark Tower.
There is a man... a gunslinger...named Roland Deschain, who is determined to reach it. And he is assembling a ka-tet, a group of followers...
...people he claims as friends, except he will gladly sacrifice them in order to reach it.
One of that ka-tet is destined to be Odetta Holmes, whom you randomly attempted to kill.
I want you to succeed so that they never meet. So that Roland will never reach the Tower.
We're fighting for the future of all worlds, Jack. You must understand that:
We are the heroes.

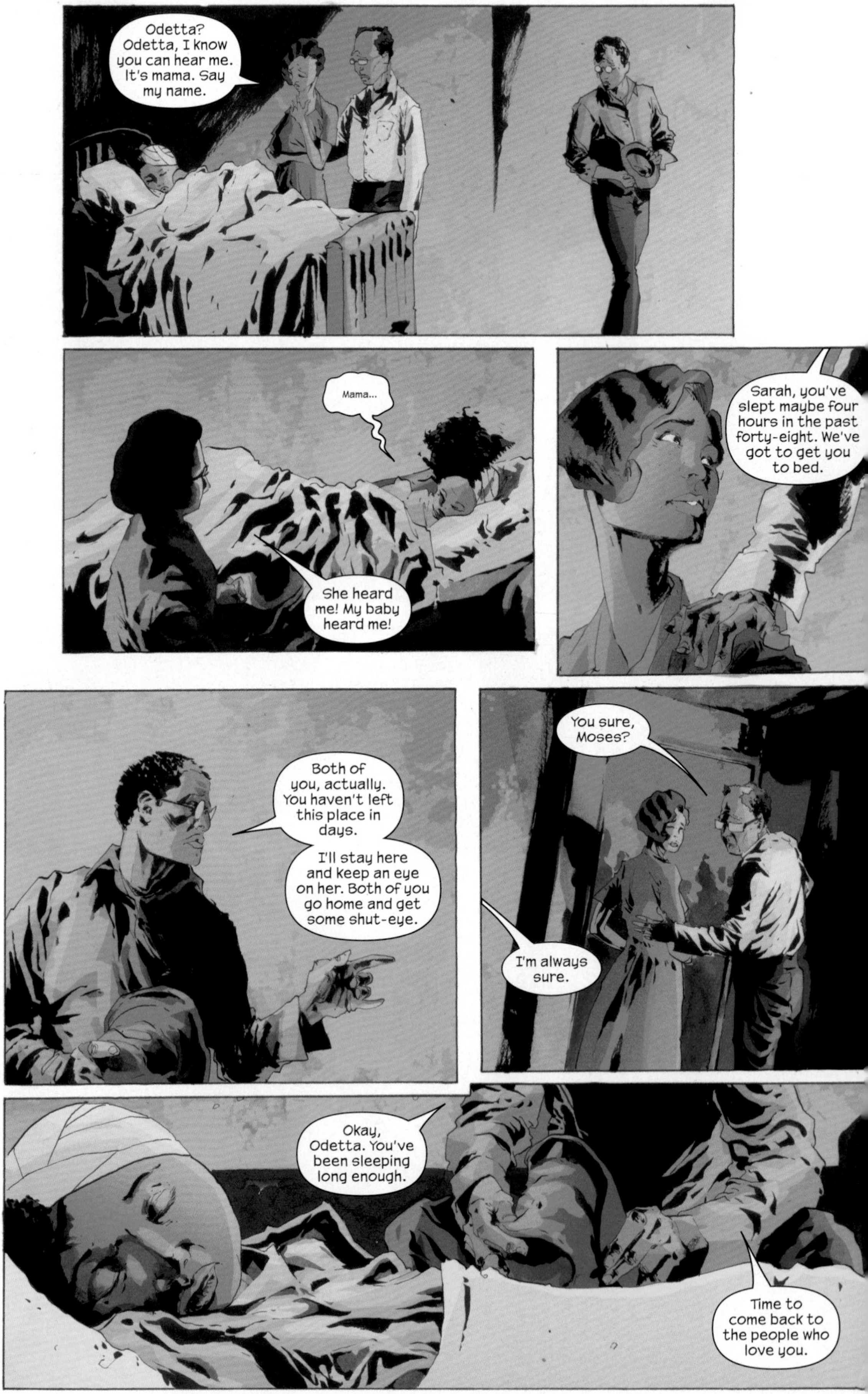
Odetta? Odetta, I know you can hear me. It's mama. Say my name.
Mama...
She heard me! My baby heard me!
Sarah, you've slept maybe four hours in the past forty-eight. We've got to get you to bed.
Both of you, actually. You haven't left this place in days.
I'll stay here and keep an eye on her. Both of you go home and get some shut-eye.
You sure, Moses?
I'm always sure.
Okay, Odetta. You've been sleeping long enough.
Time to come back to the people who love you.

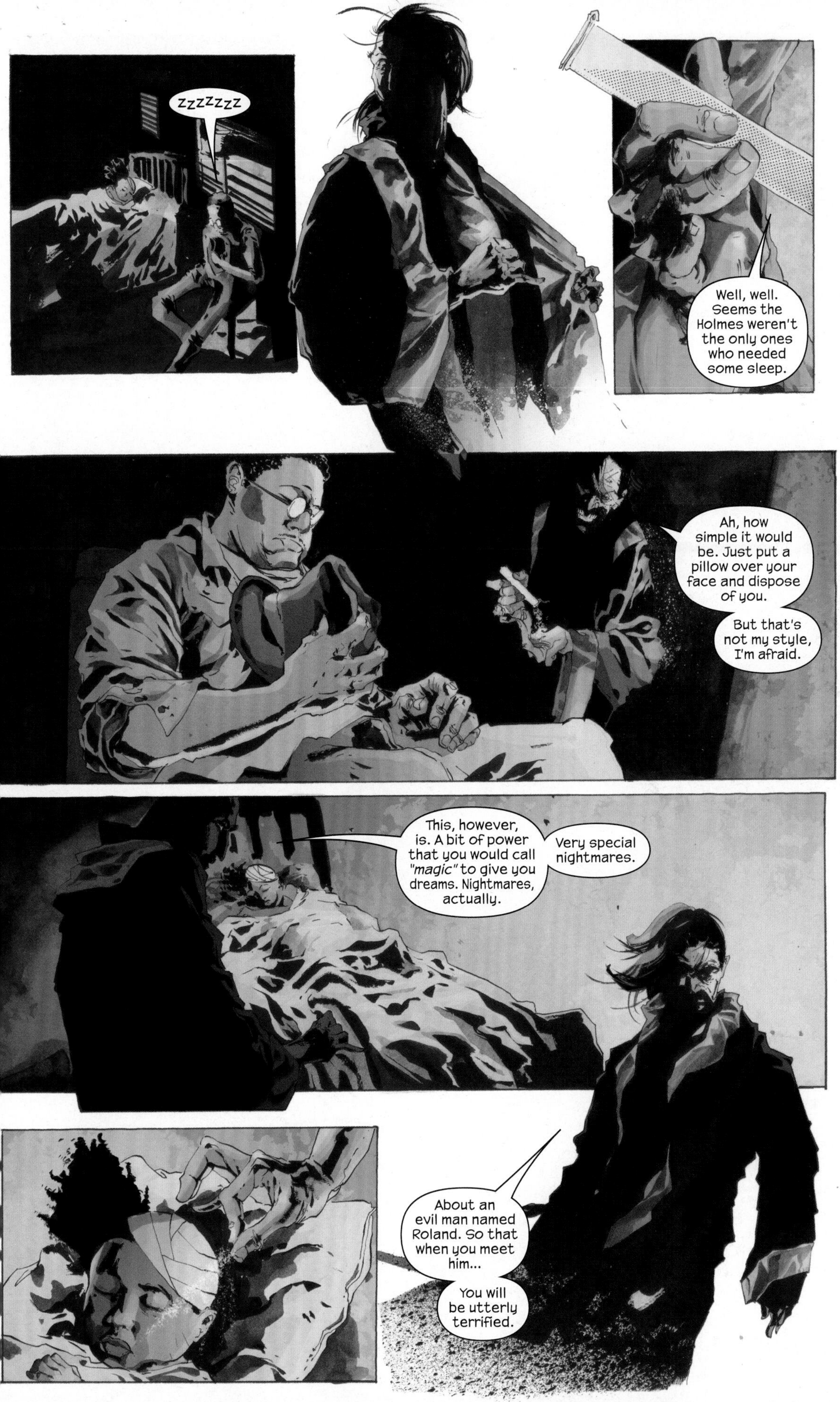

ZZZZZZZ
Well, well. Seems the Holmes weren't the only ones who needed some sleep.
Ah, how simple it would be. Just put a pillow over your face and dispose of you.
But that's not my style, I'm afraid.
This, however, is. A bit of power that you would call *"magic"* to give you dreams. Nightmares, actually.
Very special nightmares.
About an evil man named Roland. So that when you meet him...
You will be utterly terrified.

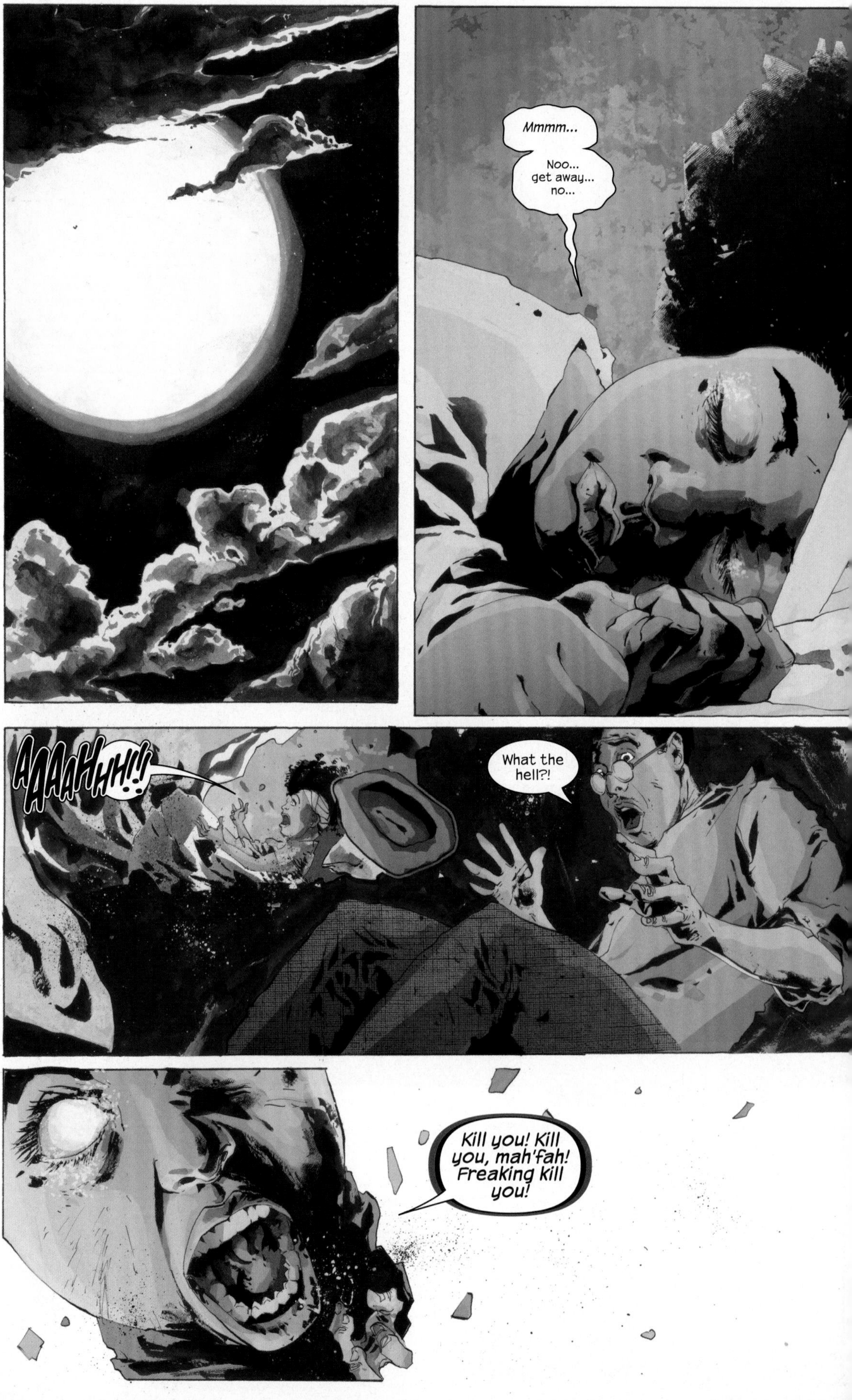
Mmmm...
Noo... get away... no...
AAAAHHH!!
What the hell?!
Kill you! Kill you, mah'fah! Freaking kill you!

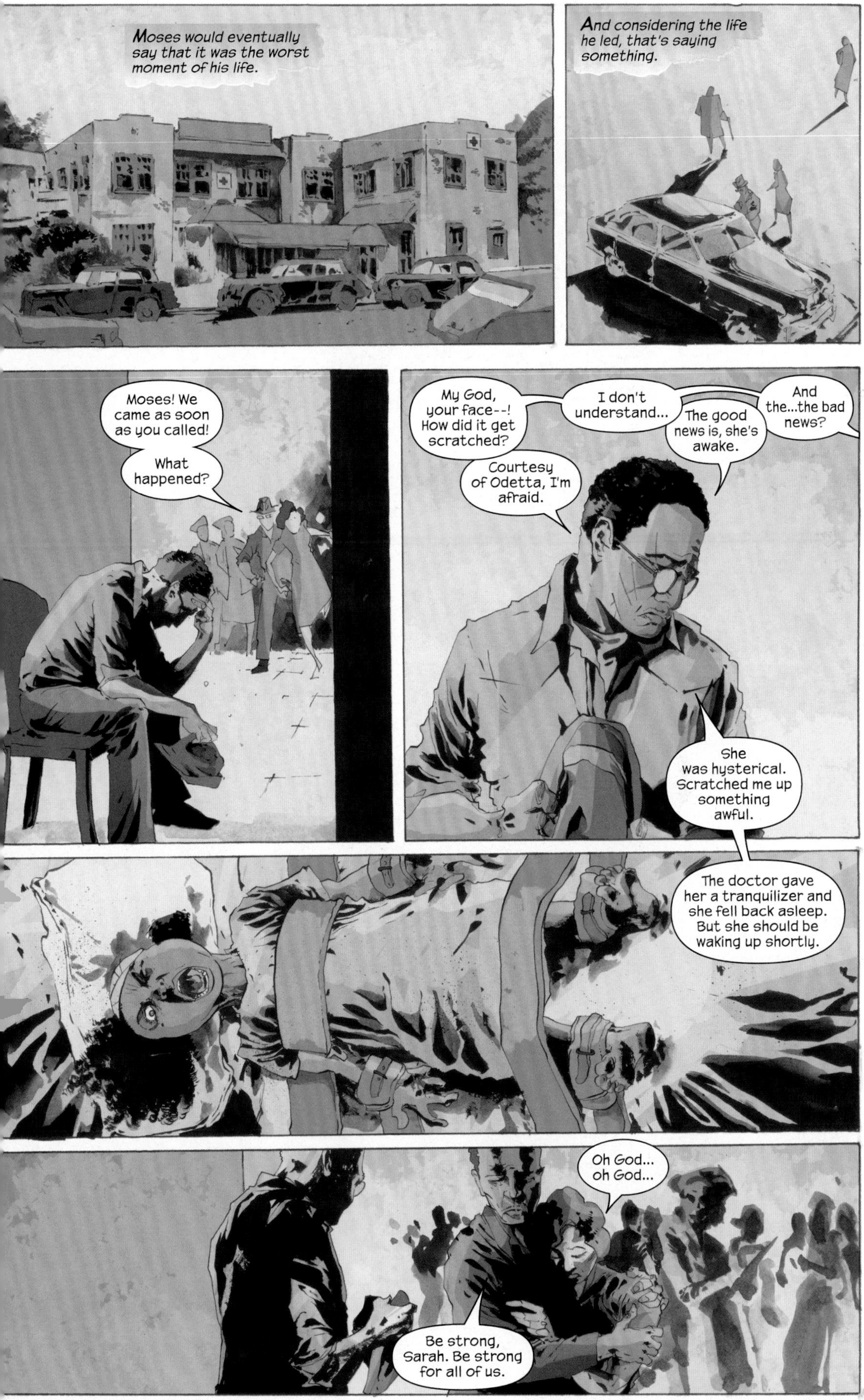
Moses would eventually say that it was the worst moment of his life.
And considering the life he led, that's saying something.
Moses! We came as soon as you called!
What happened?
My God, your face--! How did it get scratched?
Courtesy of Odetta, I'm afraid.
I don't understand...
The good news is, she's awake.
And the...the bad news?
She was hysterical. Scratched me up something awful.
The doctor gave her a tranquilizer and she fell back asleep. But she should be waking up shortly.
Oh God... oh God...
Be strong, Sarah. Be strong for all of us.

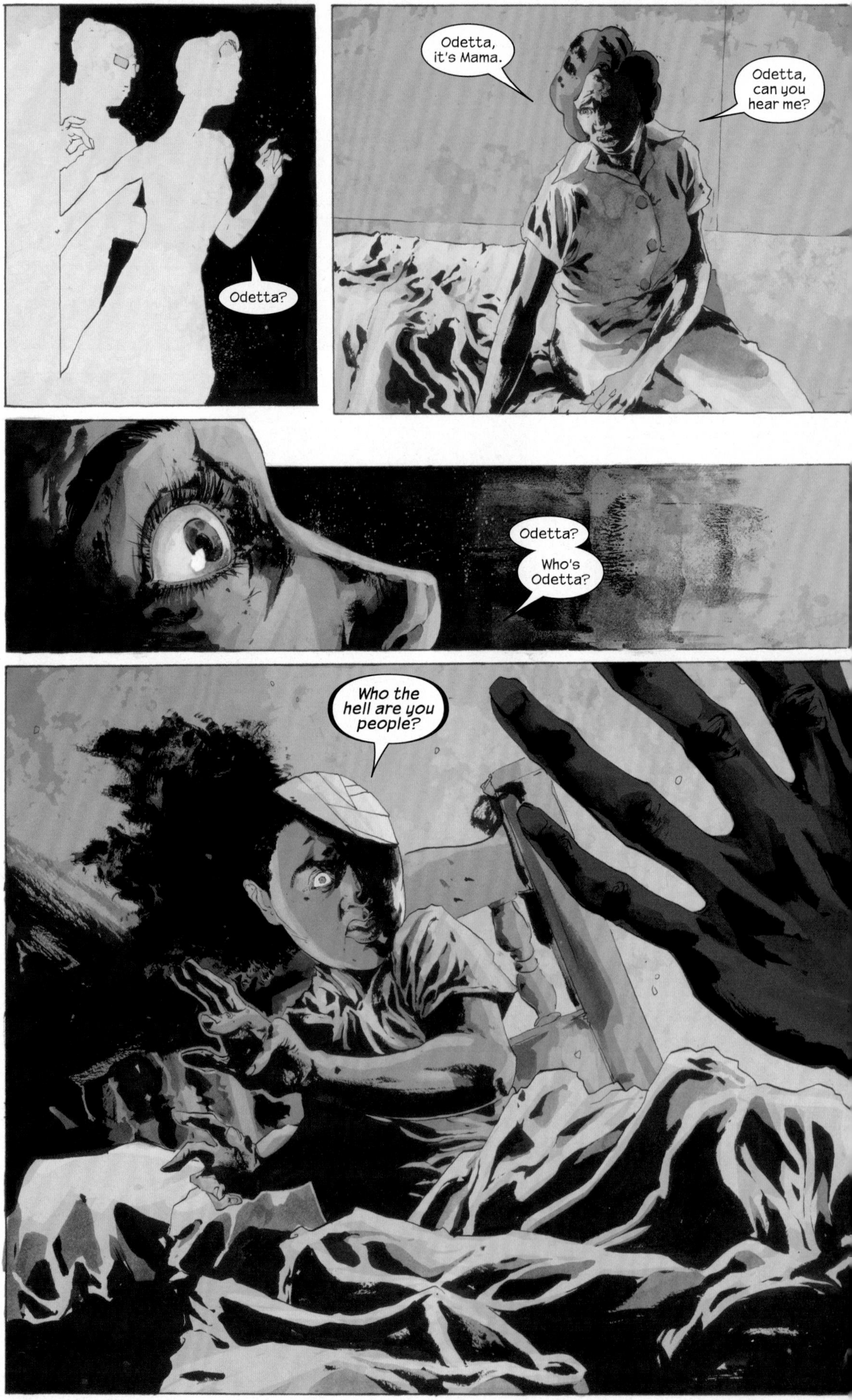
Odetta?
Odetta, it's Mama.
Odetta, can you hear me?
Odetta?
Who's Odetta?
Who the hell are you people?

THE DARK TOWER
THE DRAWING OF THE THREE
STEPHEN KING

THE LADY OF SHADOWS
CHAPTER THREE

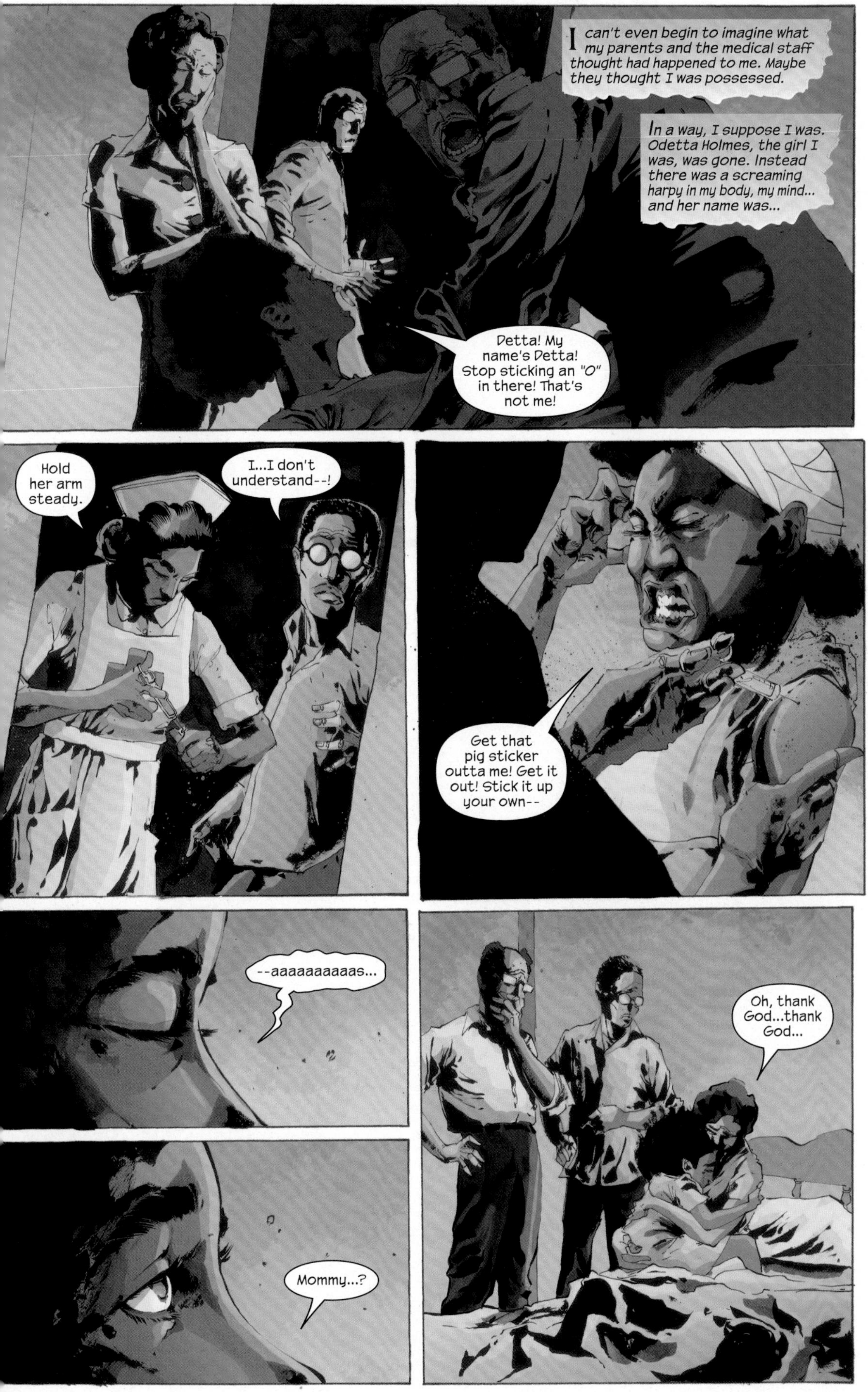
I can't even begin to imagine what my parents and the medical staff thought had happened to me. Maybe they thought I was possessed.
In a way, I suppose I was. Odetta Holmes, the girl I was, was gone. Instead there was a screaming harpy in my body, my mind... and her name was...
Detta! My name's Detta! Stop sticking an "O" in there! That's not me!
Hold her arm steady.
I...I don't understand--!
Get that pig sticker outta me! Get it out! Stick it up your own--
--aaaaaaaaaas...
Mommy...?
Oh, thank God...thank God...

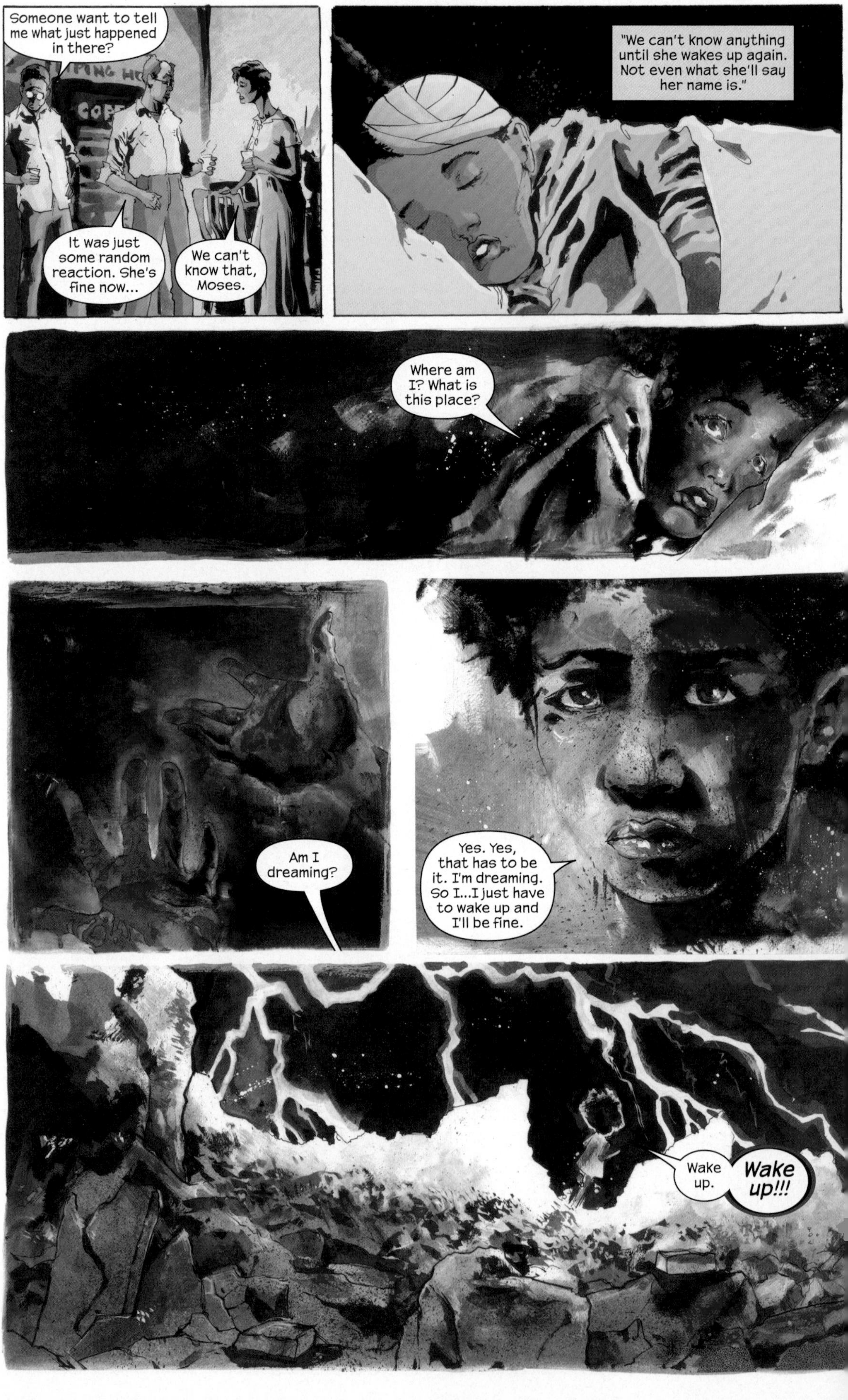

Someone want to tell me what just happened in there?
It was just some random reaction. She's fine now...
We can't know that, Moses.
"We can't know anything until she wakes up again. Not even what she'll say her name is."
Where am I? What is this place?
Am I dreaming?
Yes. Yes, that has to be it. I'm dreaming. So I...I just have to wake up and I'll be fine.
Wake up.
Wake up!!!

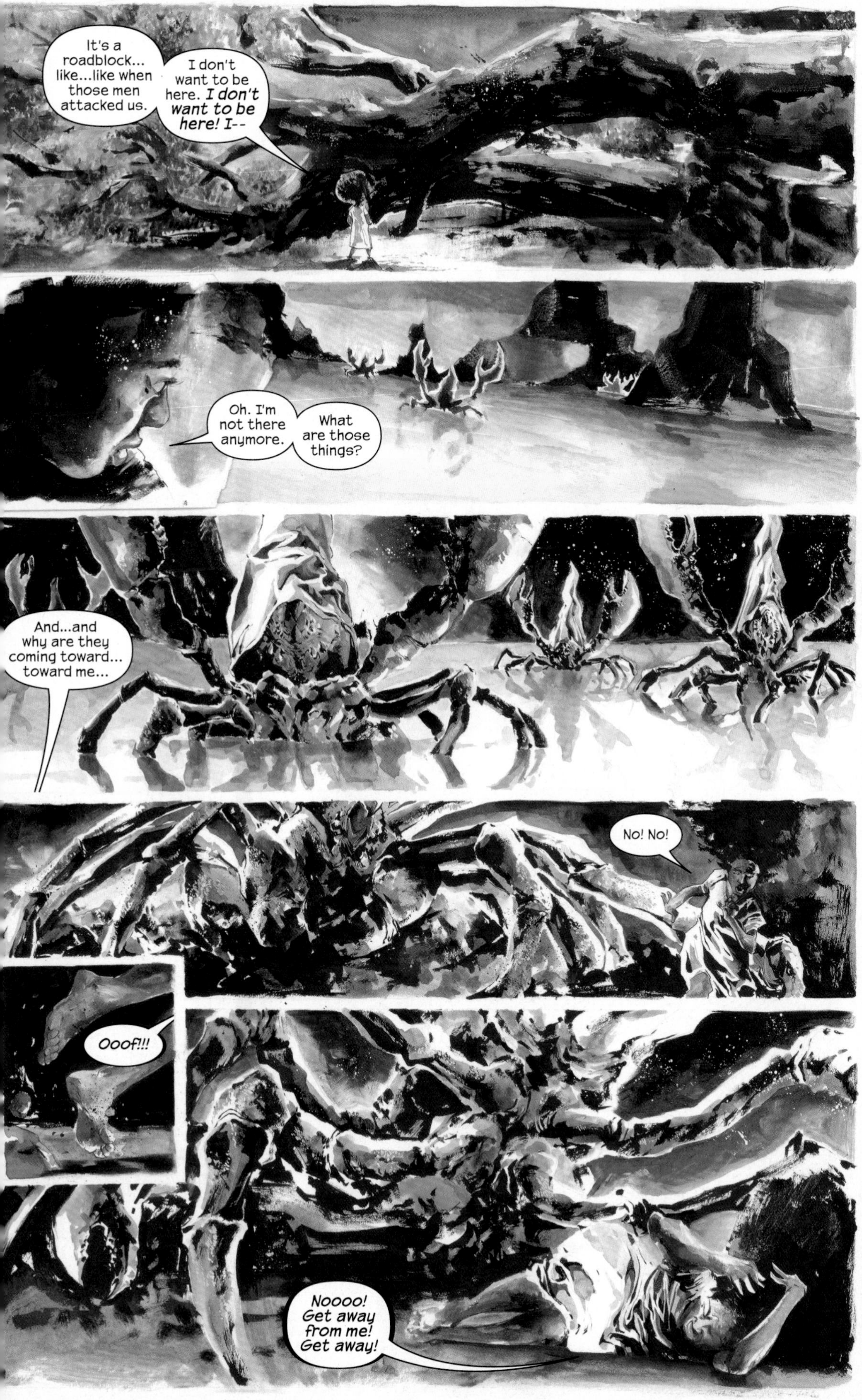
It's a roadblock... like...like when those men attacked us.
I don't want to be here. *I don't want to be here!* I--
Oh. I'm not there anymore.
What are those things?
And...and why are they coming toward... toward me...
No! No!
Ooof!!!
Noooo! Get away from me! Get away!

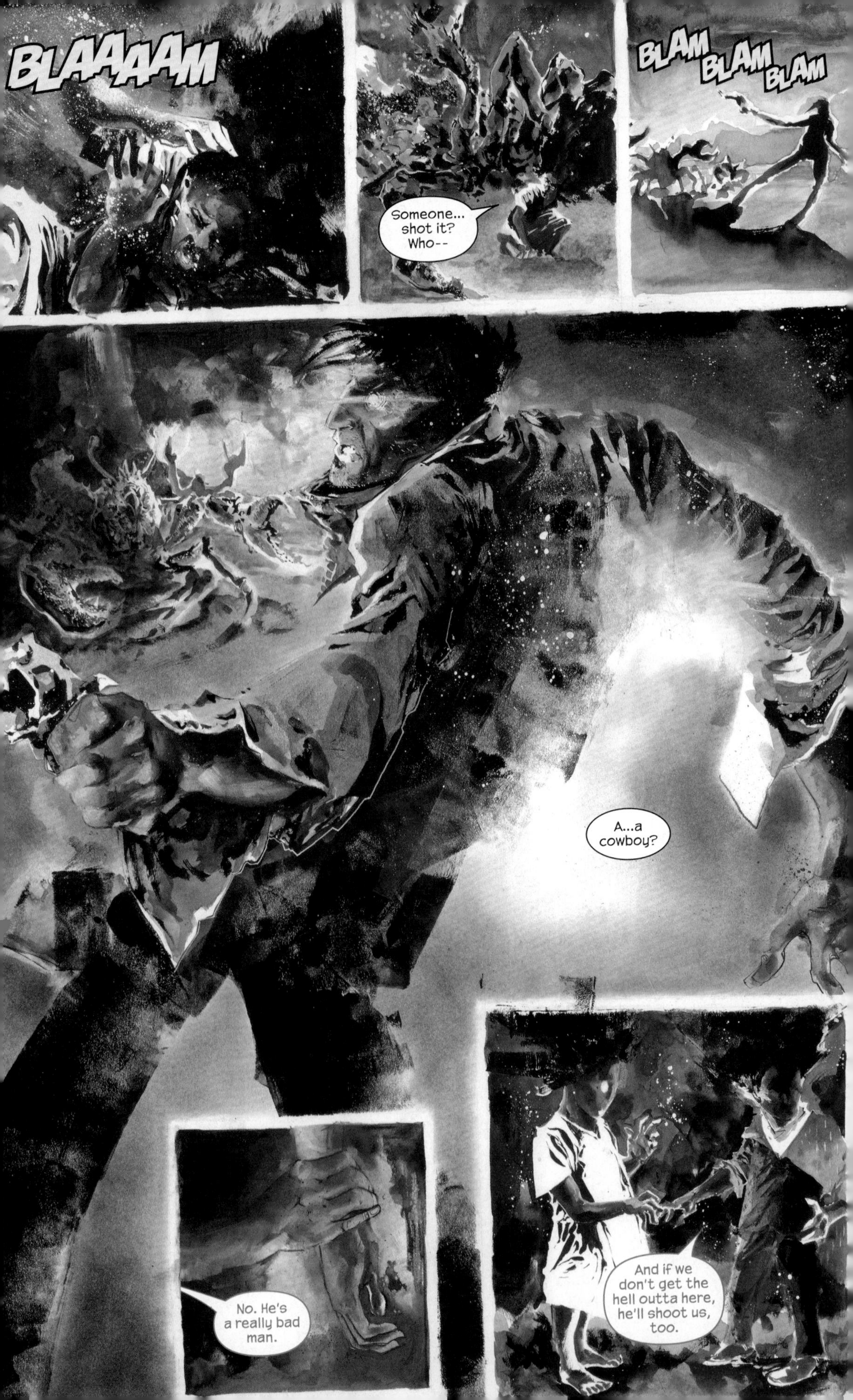
BLAAAAM
Someone... shot it? Who--
BLAM BLAM BLAM
A...a cowboy?
No. He's a really bad man.
And if we don't get the hell outta here, he'll shoot us, too.

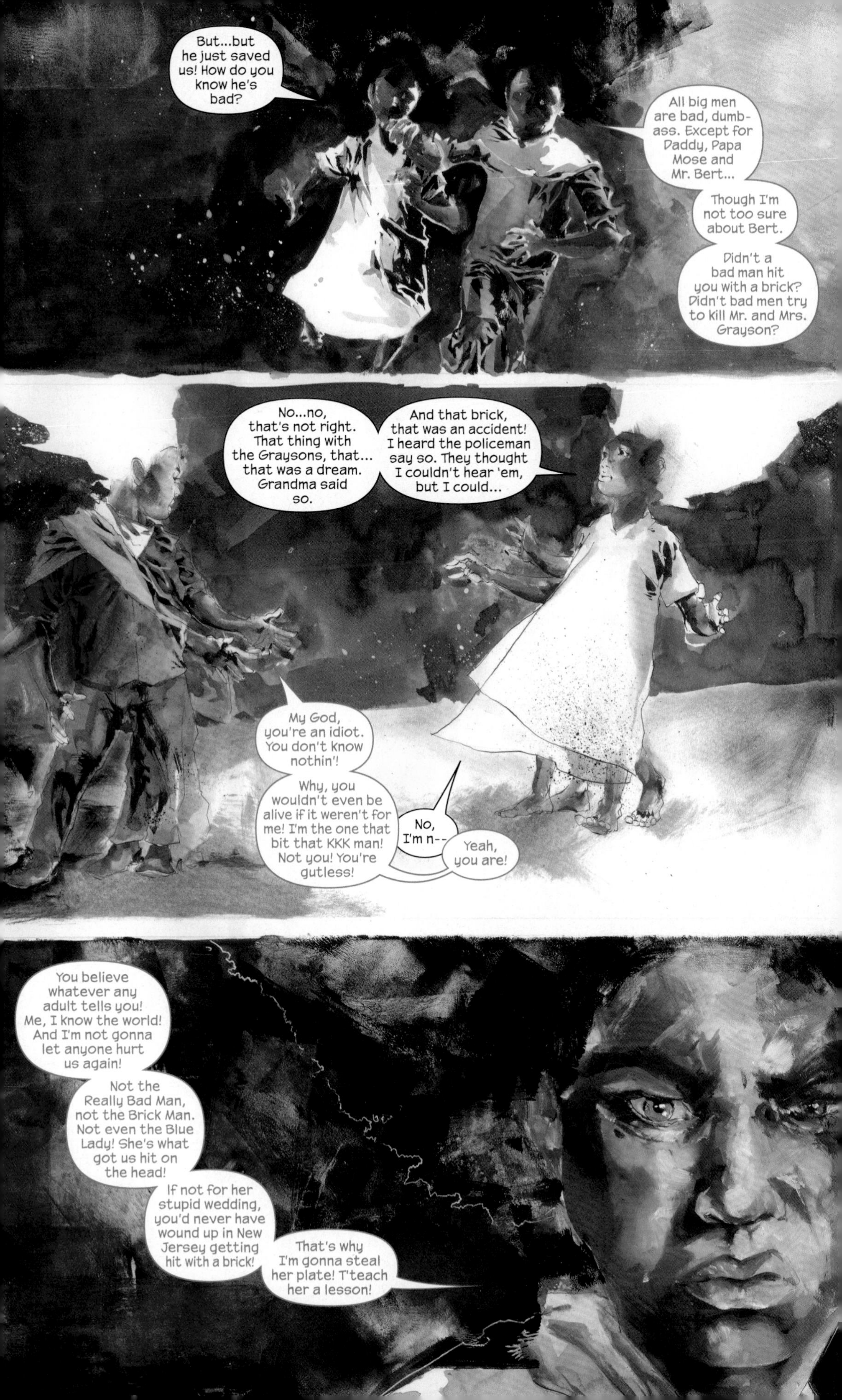

But...but he just saved us! How do you know he's bad?
All big men are bad, dumb-ass. Except for Daddy, Papa Mose and Mr. Bert...
Though I'm not too sure about Bert.
Didn't a bad man hit you with a brick? Didn't bad men try to kill Mr. and Mrs. Grayson?
No...no, that's not right. That thing with the Graysons, that... that was a dream. Grandma said so.
And that brick, that was an accident! I heard the policeman say so. They thought I couldn't hear 'em, but I could...
My God, you're an idiot. You don't know nothin'!
Why, you wouldn't even be alive if it weren't for me! I'm the one that bit that KKK man! Not you! You're gutless!
No, I'm n--
Yeah, you are!
You believe whatever any adult tells you! Me, I know the world! And I'm not gonna let anyone hurt us again!
Not the Really Bad Man, not the Brick Man. Not even the Blue Lady! She's what got us hit on the head!
If not for her stupid wedding, you'd never have wound up in New Jersey getting hit with a brick!
That's why I'm gonna steal her plate! T'teach her a lesson!

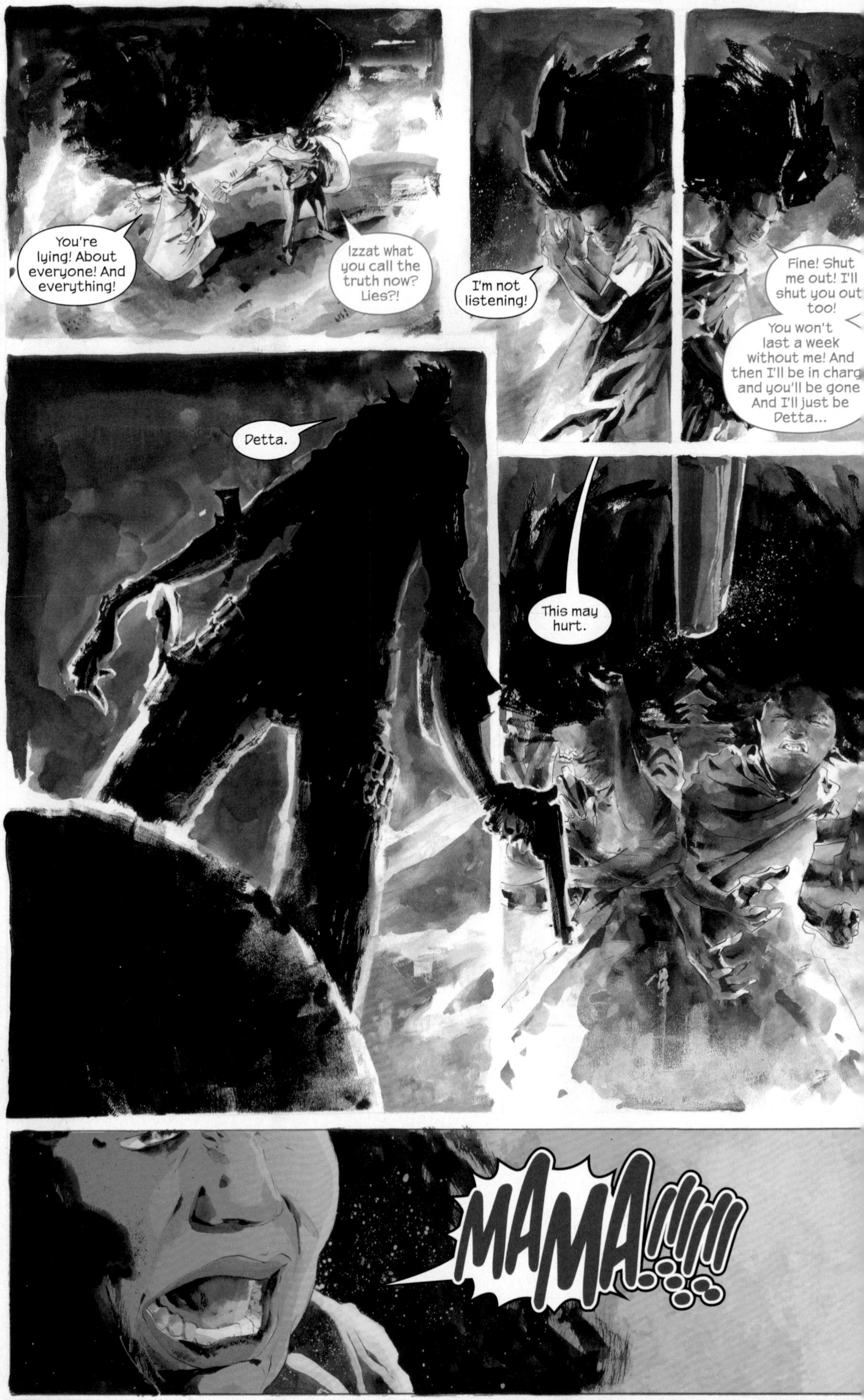
You're lying! About everyone! And everything!
Izzat what you call the truth now? Lies?!
I'm not listening!
Fine! Shut me out! I'll shut you out too!
You won't last a week without me! And then I'll be in charg and you'll be gone And I'll just be Detta...
Detta.
This may hurt.
MAMA!!!!!!

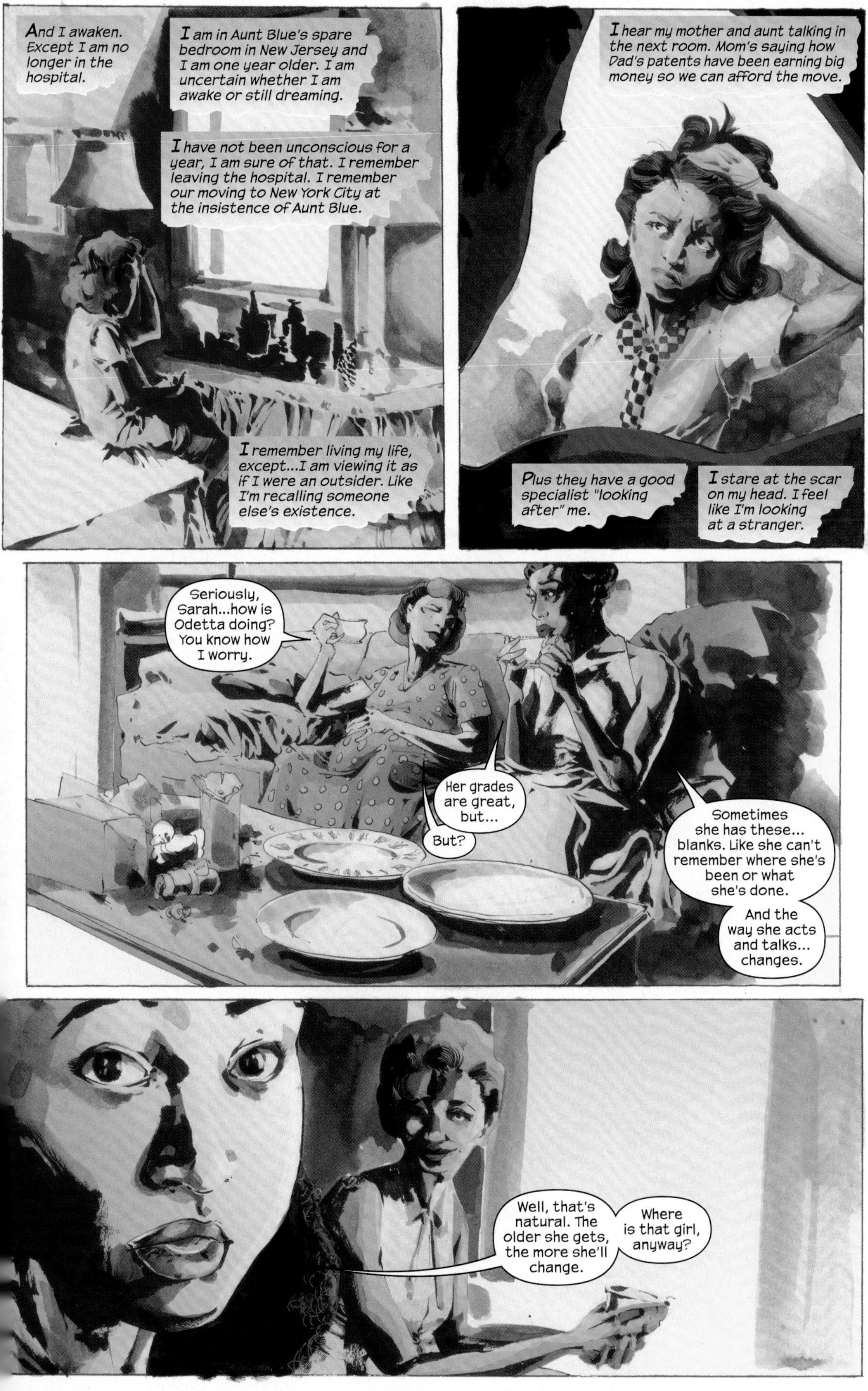
And I awaken. Except I am no longer in the hospital.
I am in Aunt Blue's spare bedroom in New Jersey and I am one year older. I am uncertain whether I am awake or still dreaming.
I have not been unconscious for a year, I am sure of that. I remember leaving the hospital. I remember our moving to New York City at the insistence of Aunt Blue.
I remember living my life, except...I am viewing it as if I were an outsider. Like I'm recalling someone else's existence.
I hear my mother and aunt talking in the next room. Mom's saying how Dad's patents have been earning big money so we can afford the move.
Plus they have a good specialist "looking after" me.
I stare at the scar on my head. I feel like I'm looking at a stranger.
Seriously, Sarah...how is Odetta doing? You know how I worry.
Her grades are great, but...
But?
Sometimes she has these... blanks. Like she can't remember where she's been or what she's done.
And the way she acts and talks... changes.
Well, that's natural. The older she gets, the more she'll change.
Where is that girl, anyway?

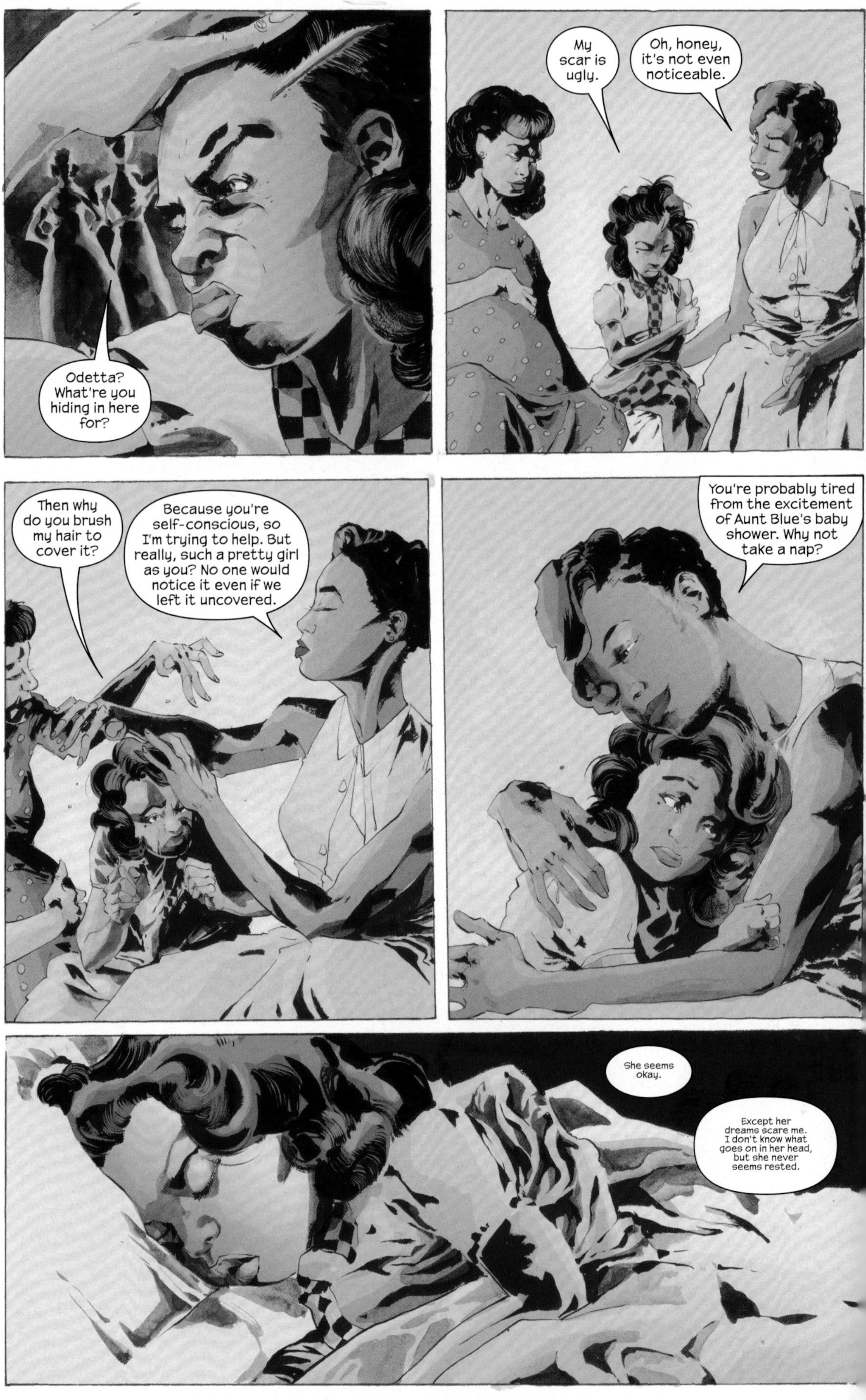
Odetta? What're you hiding in here for?
My scar is ugly.
Oh, honey, it's not even noticeable.
Then why do you brush my hair to cover it?
Because you're self-conscious, so I'm trying to help. But really, such a pretty girl as you? No one would notice it even if we left it uncovered.
You're probably tired from the excitement of Aunt Blue's baby shower. Why not take a nap?
She seems okay.
Except her dreams scare me. I don't know what goes on in her head, but she never seems rested.

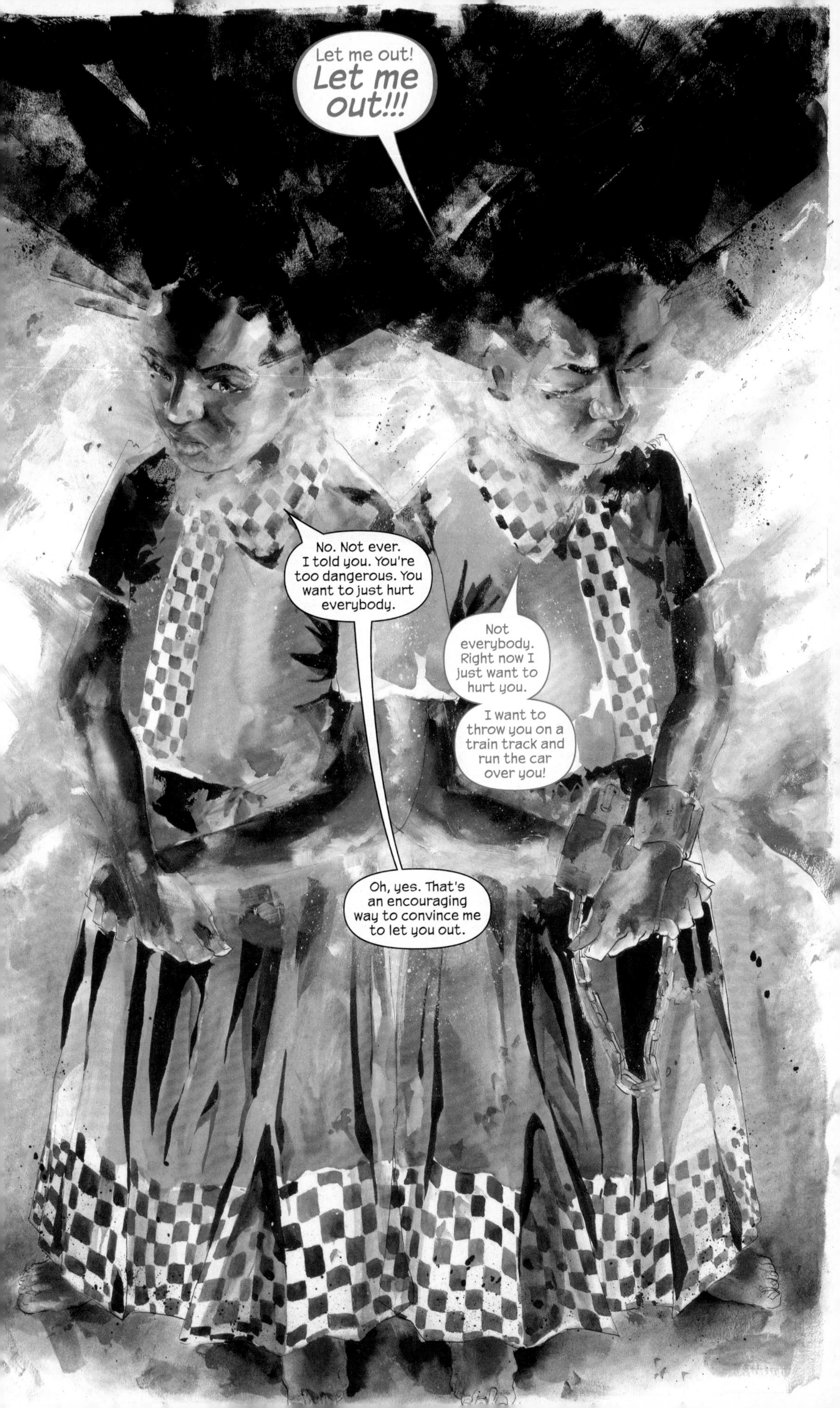
Let me out! Let me out!!!
No. Not ever. I told you. You're too dangerous. You want to just hurt everybody.
Not everybody. Right now I just want to hurt you.
I want to throw you on a train track and run the car over you!
Oh, yes. That's an encouraging way to convince me to let you out.

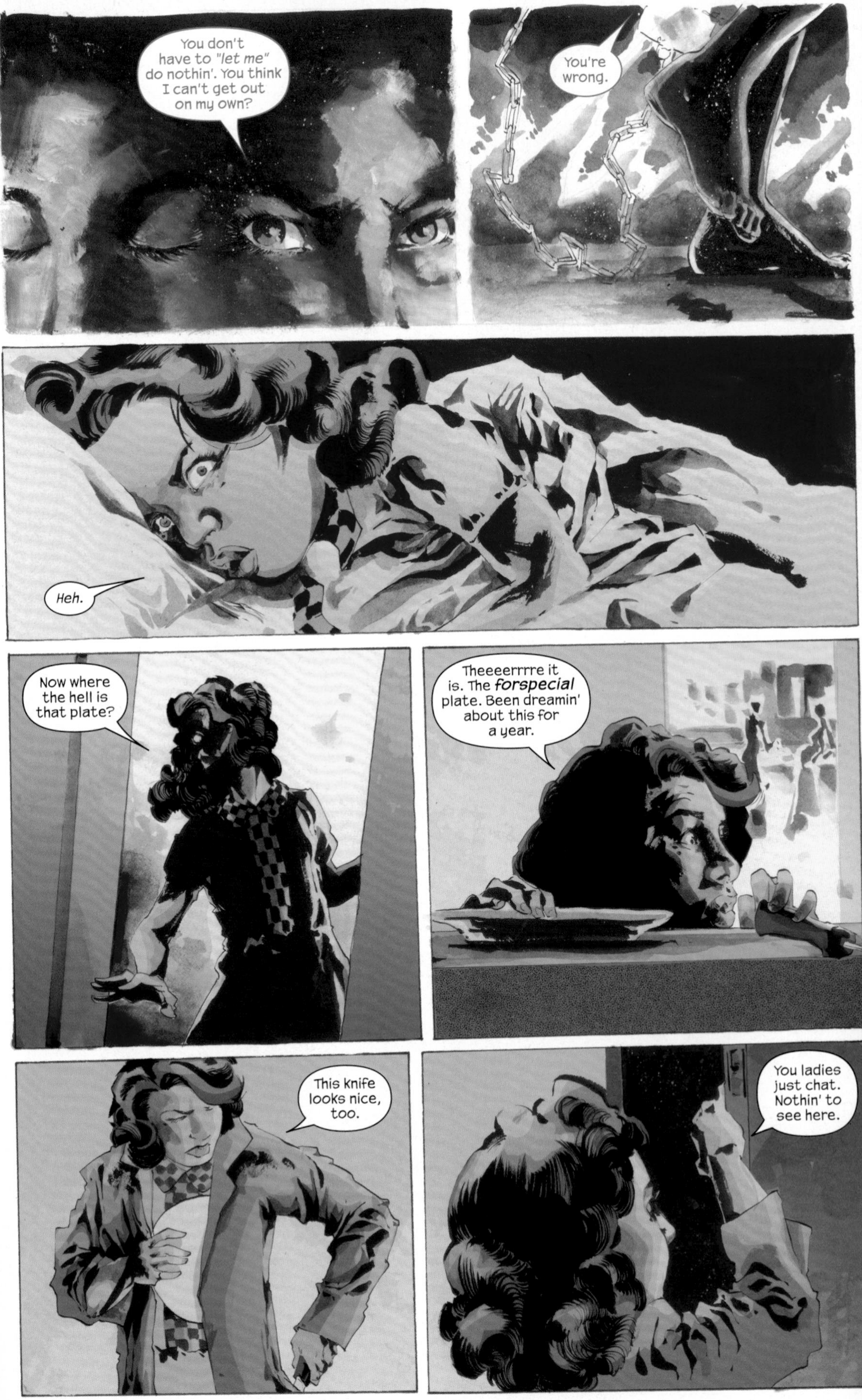

You don't have to "let me" do nothin'. You think I can't get out on my own?
You're wrong.
Heh.
Now where the hell is that plate?
Theeeerrrre it is. The *forspecial* plate. Been dreamin' about this for a year.
This knife looks nice, too.
You ladies just chat. Nothin' to see here.

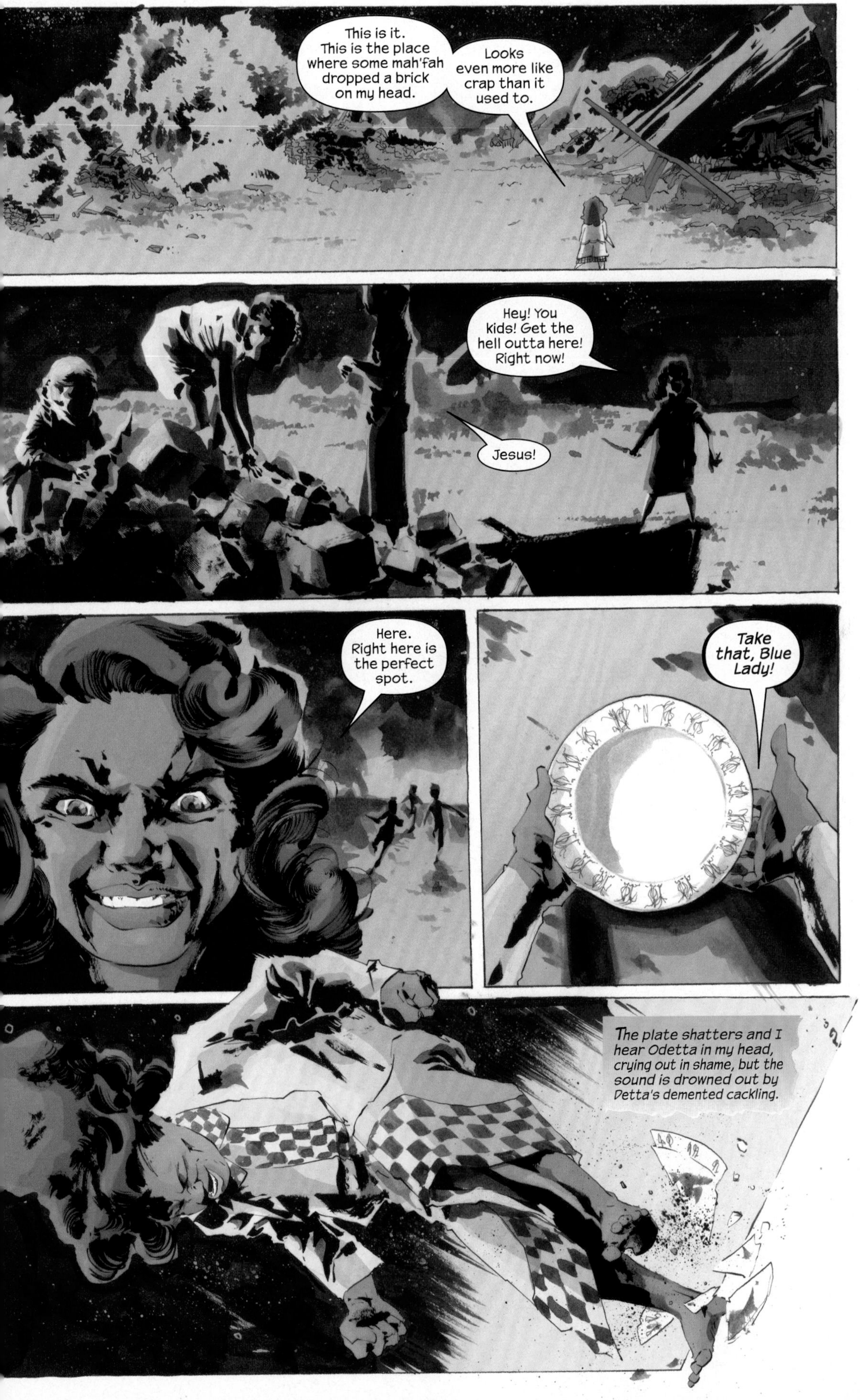
This is it. This is the place where some mah'fah dropped a brick on my head.
Looks even more like crap than it used to.
Hey! You kids! Get the hell outta here! Right now!
Jesus!
Here. Right here is the perfect spot.
Take that, Blue Lady!
The plate shatters and I hear Odetta in my head, crying out in shame, but the sound is drowned out by Detta's demented cackling.

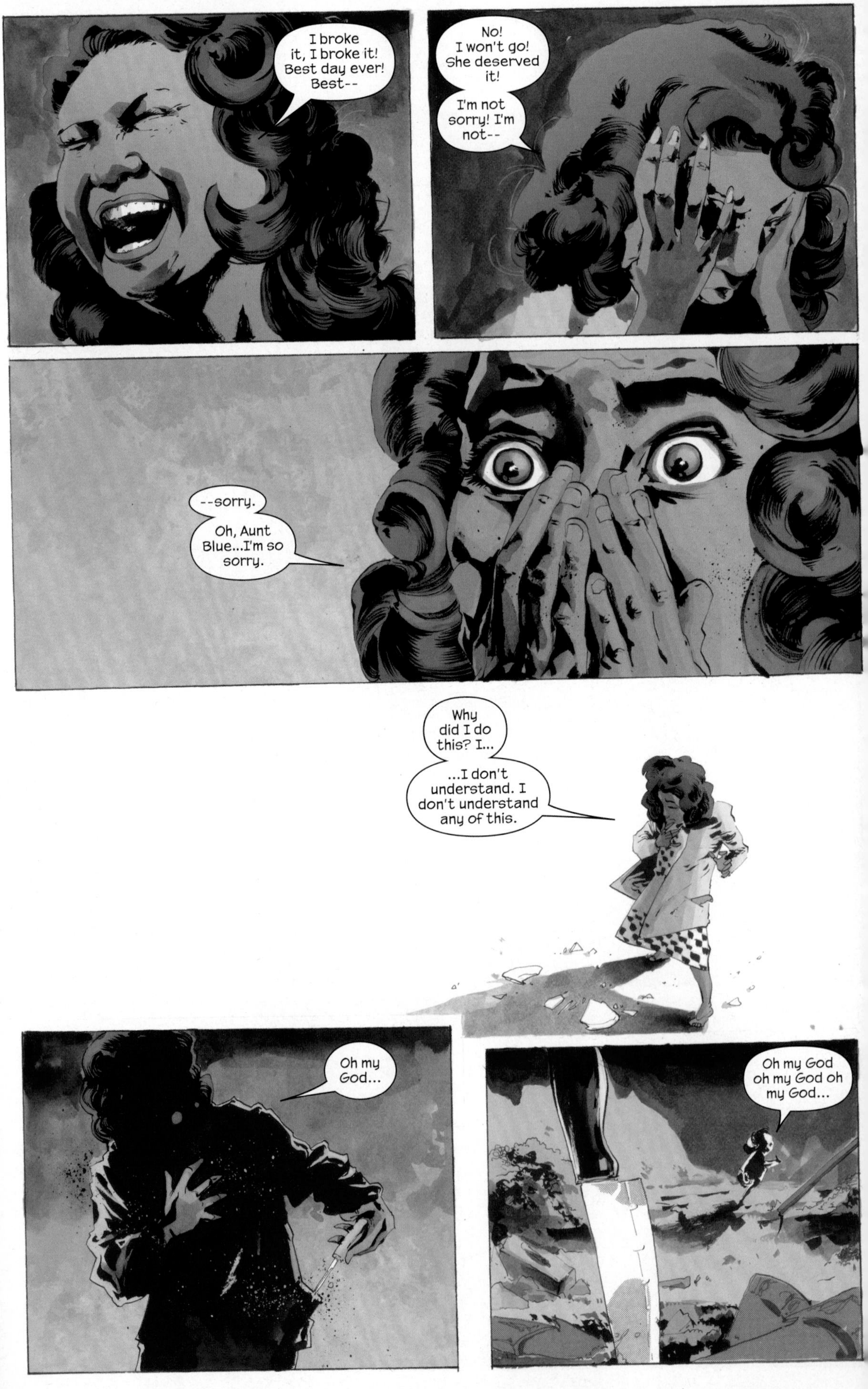
I broke it, I broke it! Best day ever! Best--
No! I won't go! She deserved it!
I'm not sorry! I'm not--
--sorry.
Oh, Aunt Blue...I'm so sorry.
Why did I do this? I...
...I don't understand. I don't understand any of this.
Oh my God...
Oh my God oh my God oh my God...

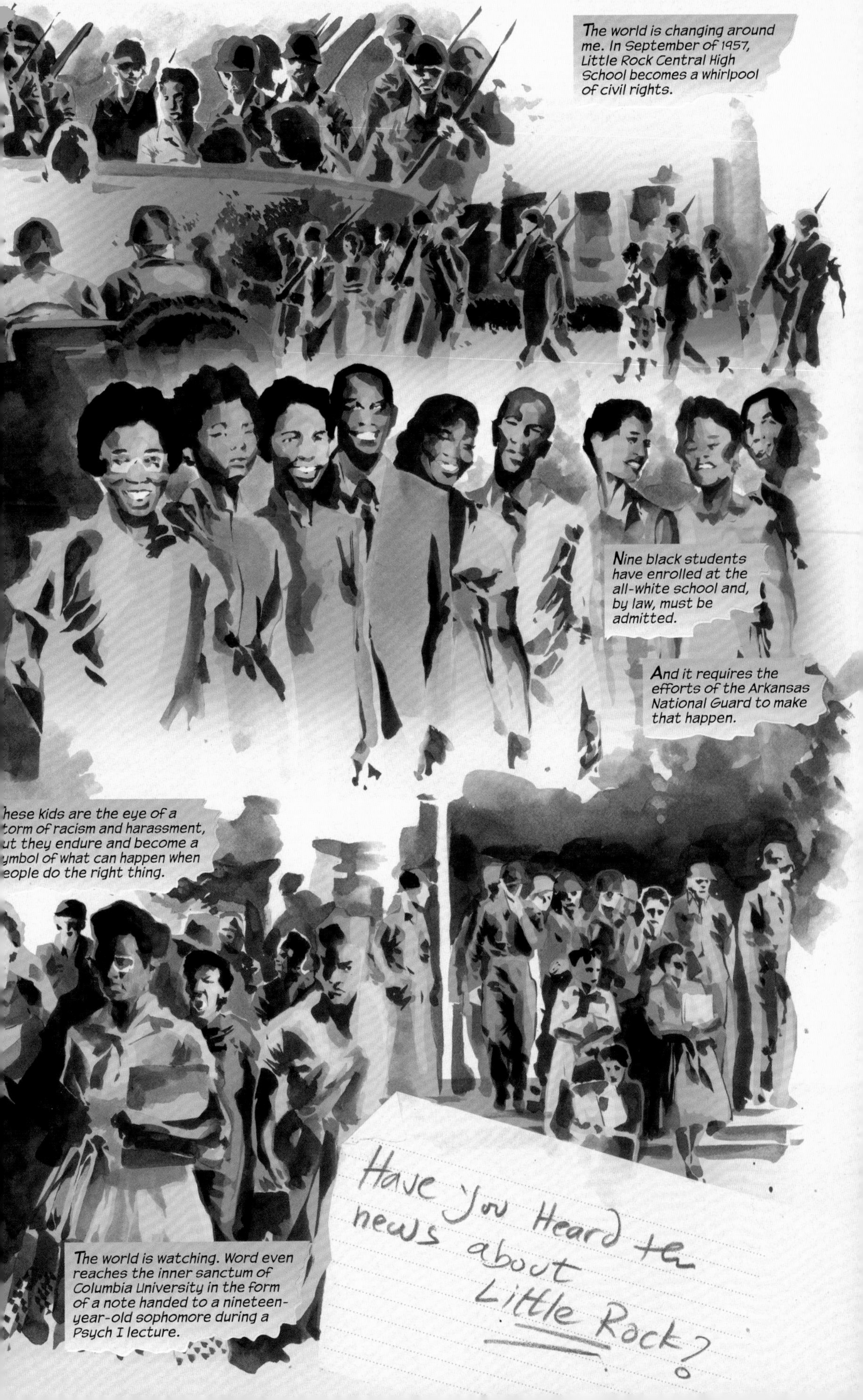
The world is changing around me. In September of 1957, Little Rock Central High School becomes a whirlpool of civil rights.
Nine black students have enrolled at the all-white school and, by law, must be admitted.
And it requires the efforts of the Arkansas National Guard to make that happen.
hese kids are the eye of a torm of racism and harassment, ut they endure and become a ymbol of what can happen when eople do the right thing.
The world is watching. Word even reaches the inner sanctum of Columbia University in the form of a note handed to a nineteen-year-old sophomore during a Psych I lecture.
Have you Heard the news about Little Rock?

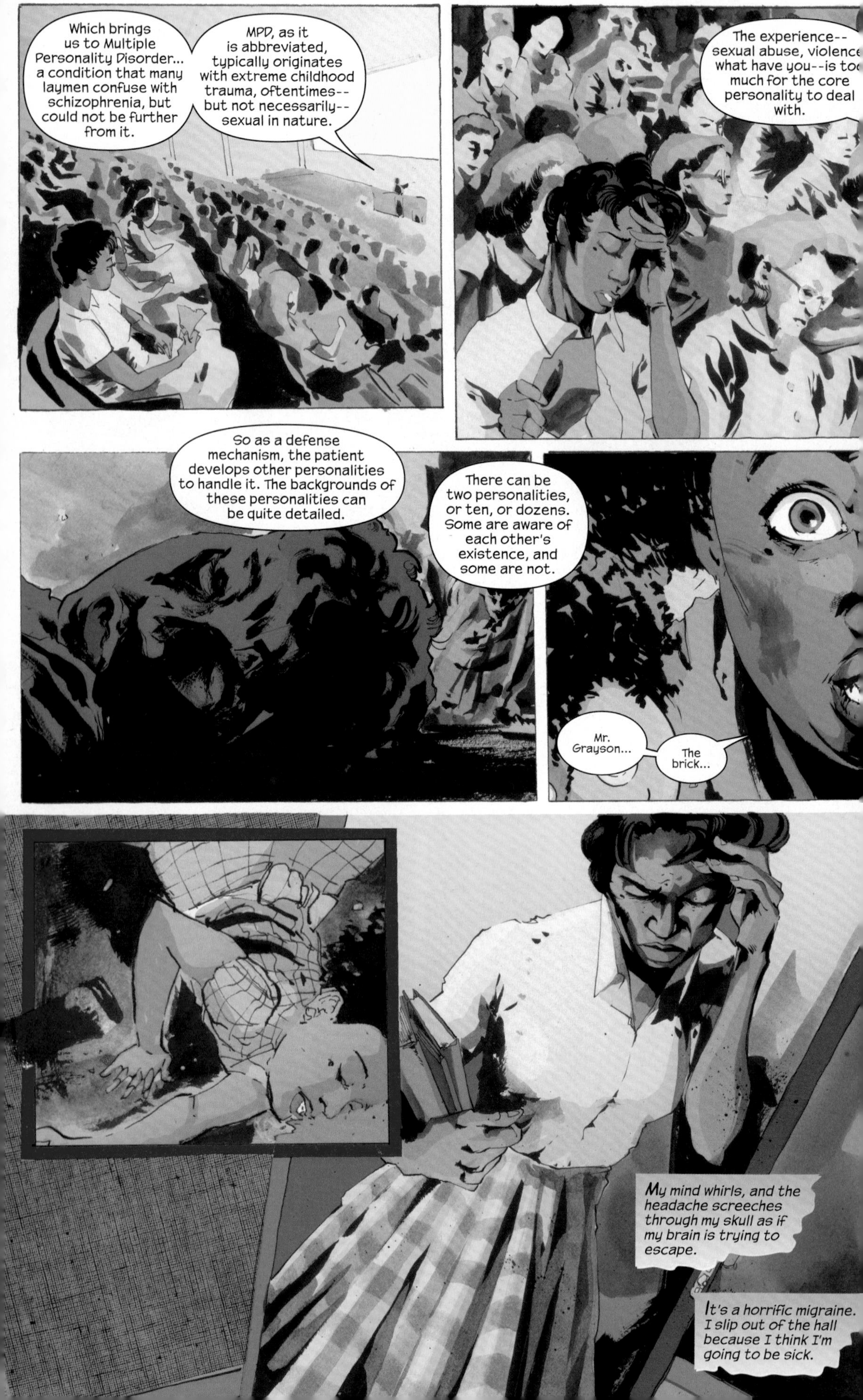
Which brings us to Multiple Personality Disorder... a condition that many laymen confuse with schizophrenia, but could not be further from it.
MPD, as it is abbreviated, typically originates with extreme childhood trauma, oftentimes--but not necessarily--sexual in nature.
The experience--sexual abuse, violence, what have you--is too much for the core personality to deal with.
So as a defense mechanism, the patient develops other personalities to handle it. The backgrounds of these personalities can be quite detailed.
There can be two personalities, or ten, or dozens. Some are aware of each other's existence, and some are not.
Mr. Grayson...
The brick...
My mind whirls, and the headache screeches through my skull as if my brain is trying to escape.
It's a horrific migraine. I slip out of the hall because I think I'm going to be sick.

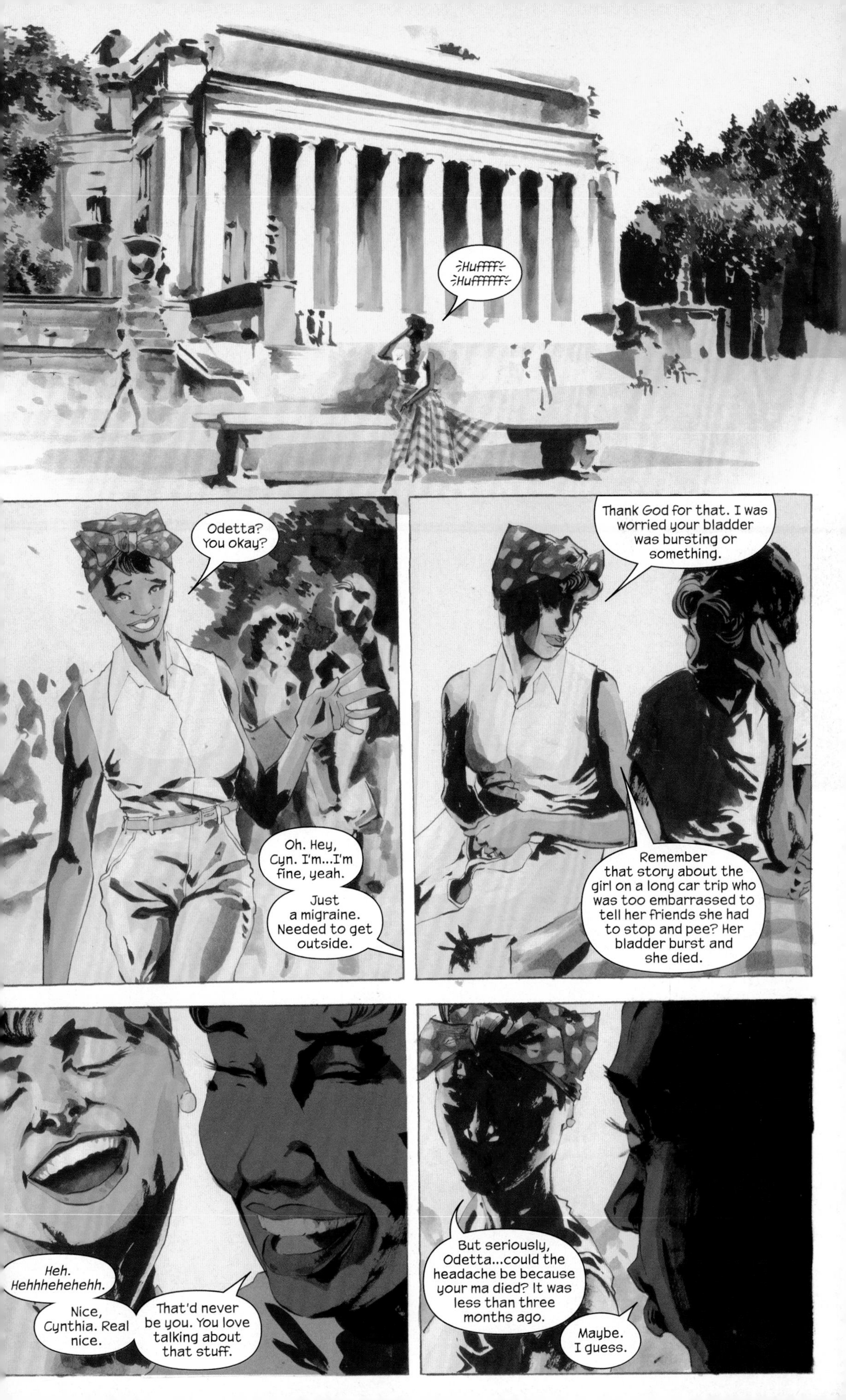

Hufffff
Hufffffff
Odetta? You okay?
Oh. Hey, Cyn. I'm...I'm fine, yeah.
Just a migraine. Needed to get outside.
Thank God for that. I was worried your bladder was bursting or something.
Remember that story about the girl on a long car trip who was too embarrassed to tell her friends she had to stop and pee? Her bladder burst and she died.
Heh. Hehhhehehehh.
Nice, Cynthia. Real nice.
That'd never be you. You love talking about that stuff.
But seriously, Odetta...could the headache be because your ma died? It was less than three months ago.
Maybe. I guess.

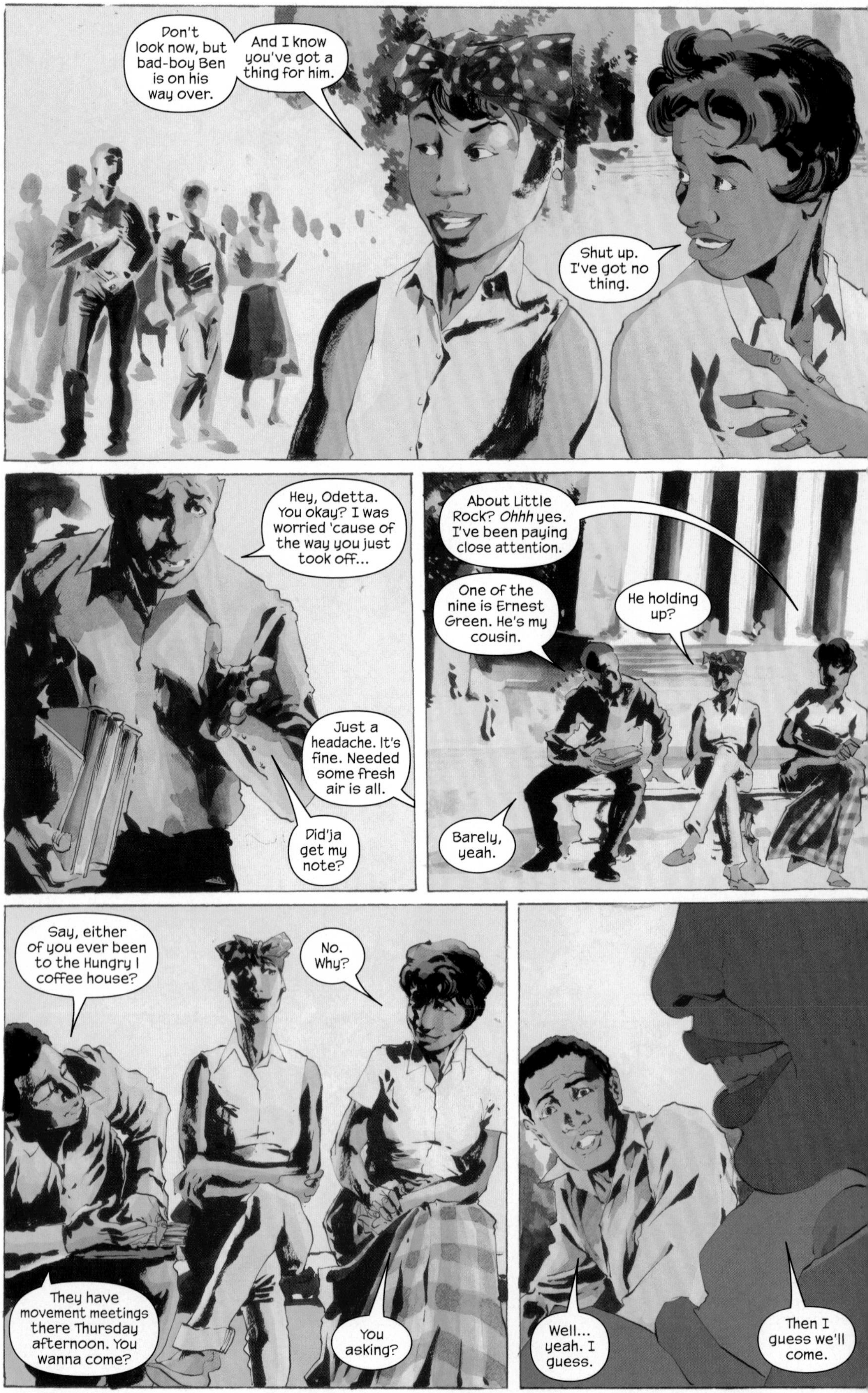

Don't look now, but bad-boy Ben is on his way over.
And I know you've got a thing for him.
Shut up. I've got no thing.
Hey, Odetta. You okay? I was worried 'cause of the way you just took off...
Just a headache. It's fine. Needed some fresh air is all.
Did'ja get my note?
About Little Rock? *Ohhh* yes. I've been paying close attention.
One of the nine is Ernest Green. He's my cousin.
He holding up?
Barely, yeah.
Say, either of you ever been to the Hungry I coffee house?
No. Why?
They have movement meetings there Thursday afternoon. You wanna come?
You asking?
Well... yeah. I guess.
Then I guess we'll come.

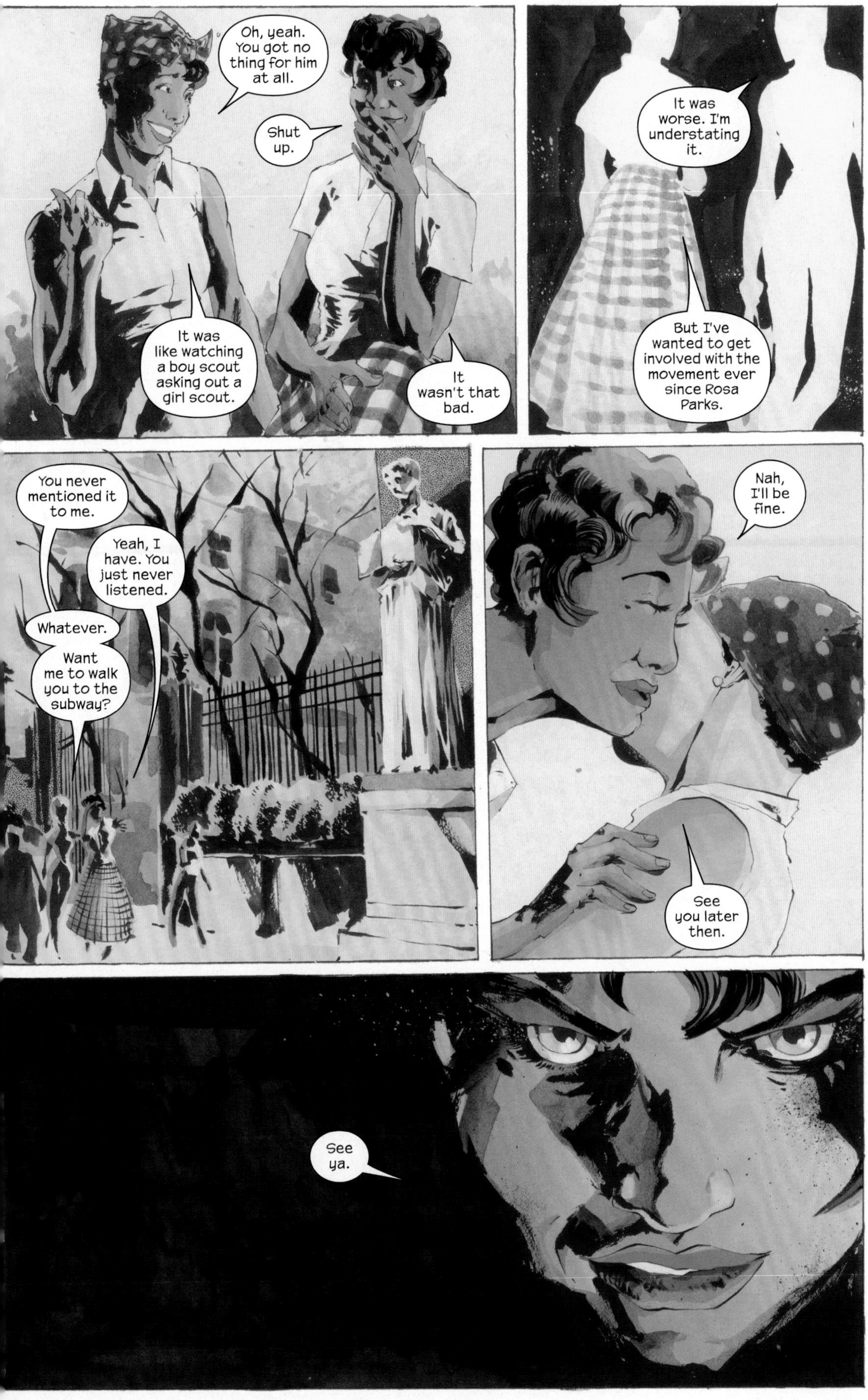

Oh, yeah. You got no thing for him at all.
Shut up.
It was like watching a boy scout asking out a girl scout.
It wasn't that bad.
It was worse. I'm understating it.
But I've wanted to get involved with the movement ever since Rosa Parks.
You never mentioned it to me.
Yeah, I have. You just never listened.
Whatever.
Want me to walk you to the subway?
Nah, I'll be fine.
See you later then.
See ya.

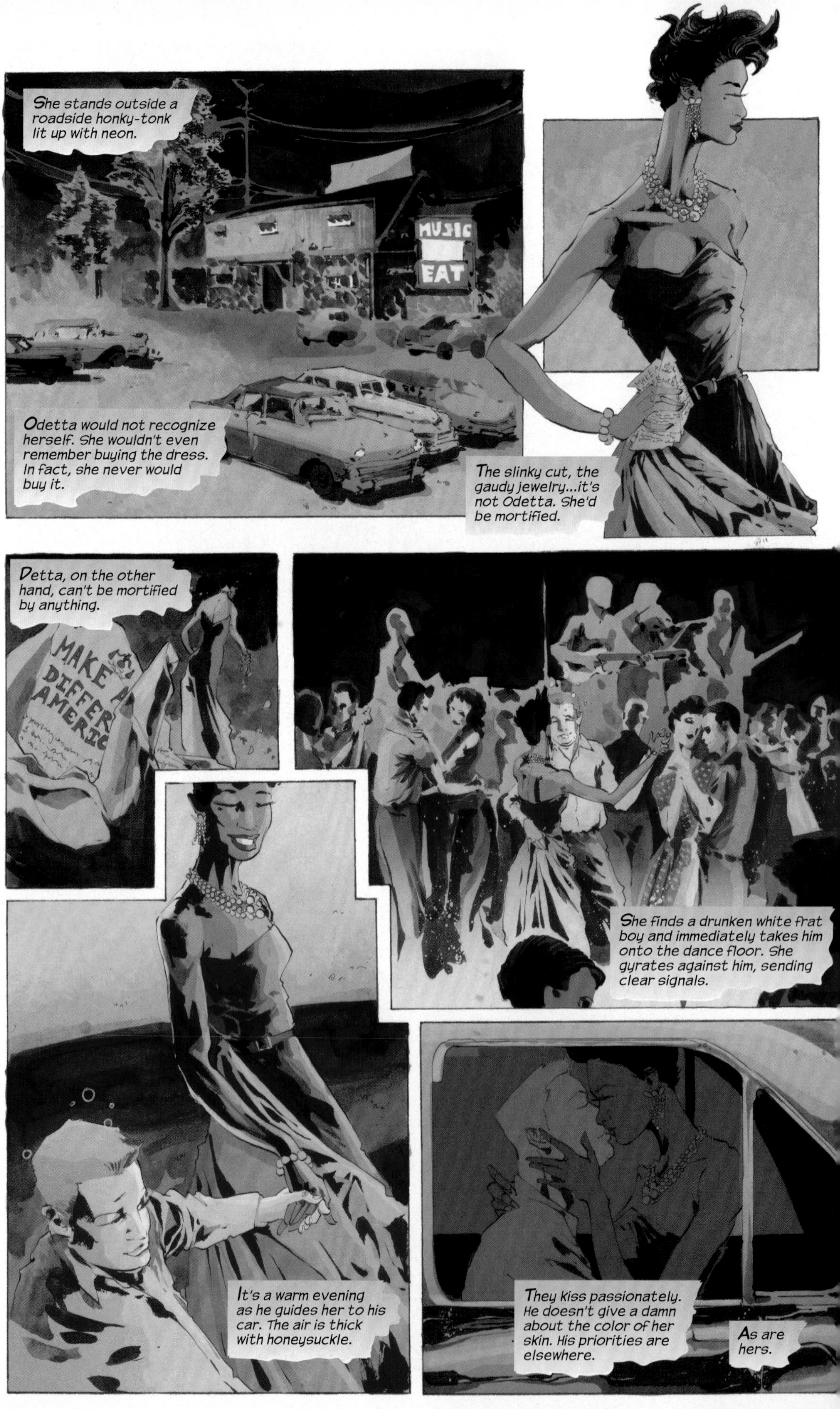
She stands outside a roadside honky-tonk lit up with neon.
MUSIC
EAT
Odetta would not recognize herself. She wouldn't even remember buying the dress. In fact, she never would buy it.
The slinky cut, the gaudy jewelry...it's not Odetta. She'd be mortified.
Detta, on the other hand, can't be mortified by anything.
She finds a drunken white frat boy and immediately takes him onto the dance floor. She gyrates against him, sending clear signals.
It's a warm evening as he guides her to his car. The air is thick with honeysuckle.
They kiss passionately. He doesn't give a damn about the color of her skin. His priorities are elsewhere.
As are hers.

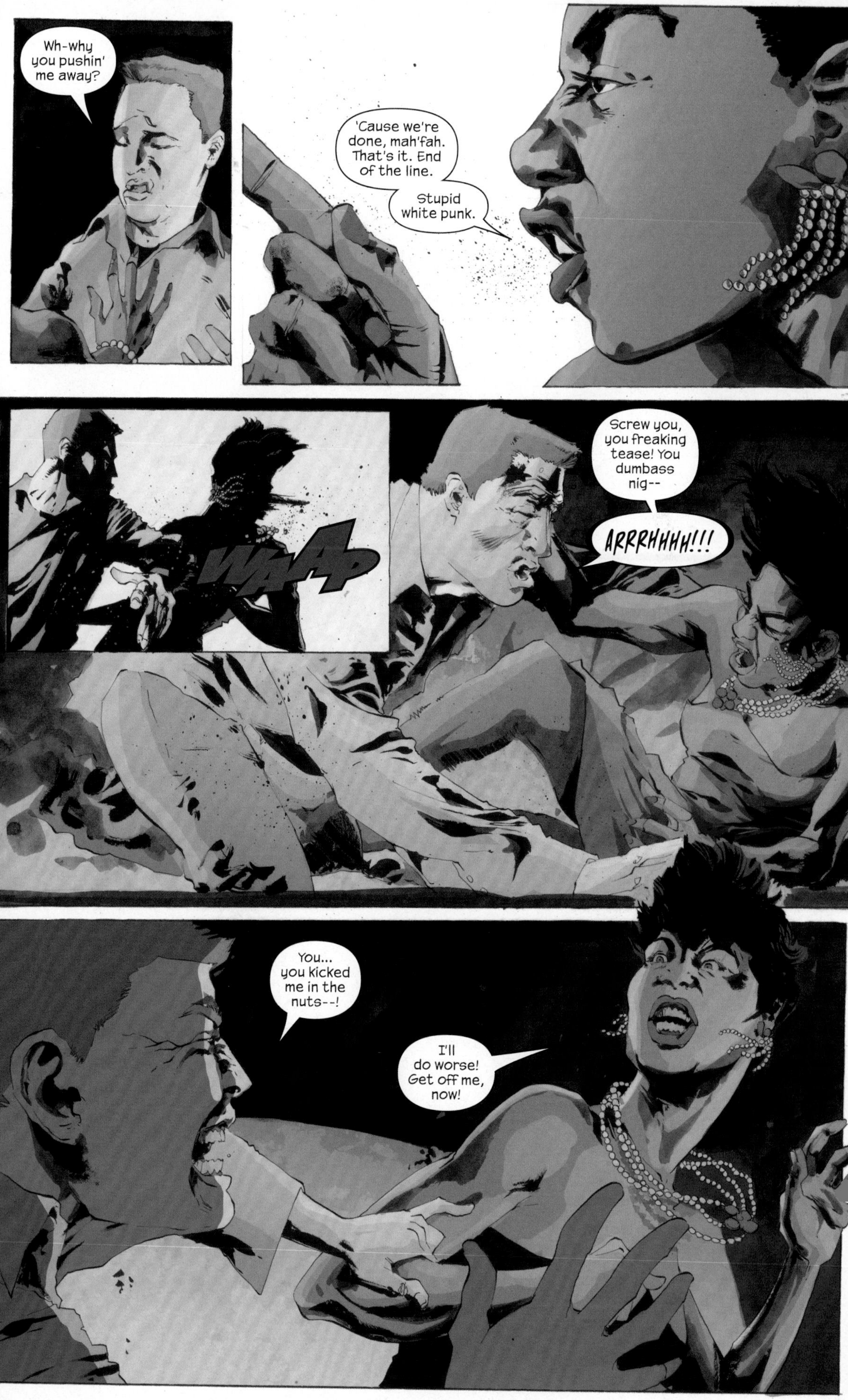
Wh-why you pushin' me away?
'Cause we're done, mah'fah. That's it. End of the line.
Stupid white punk.
WAAP
Screw you, you freaking tease! You dumbass nig--
ARRRHHHH!!!
You... you kicked me in the nuts--!
I'll do worse! Get off me, now!

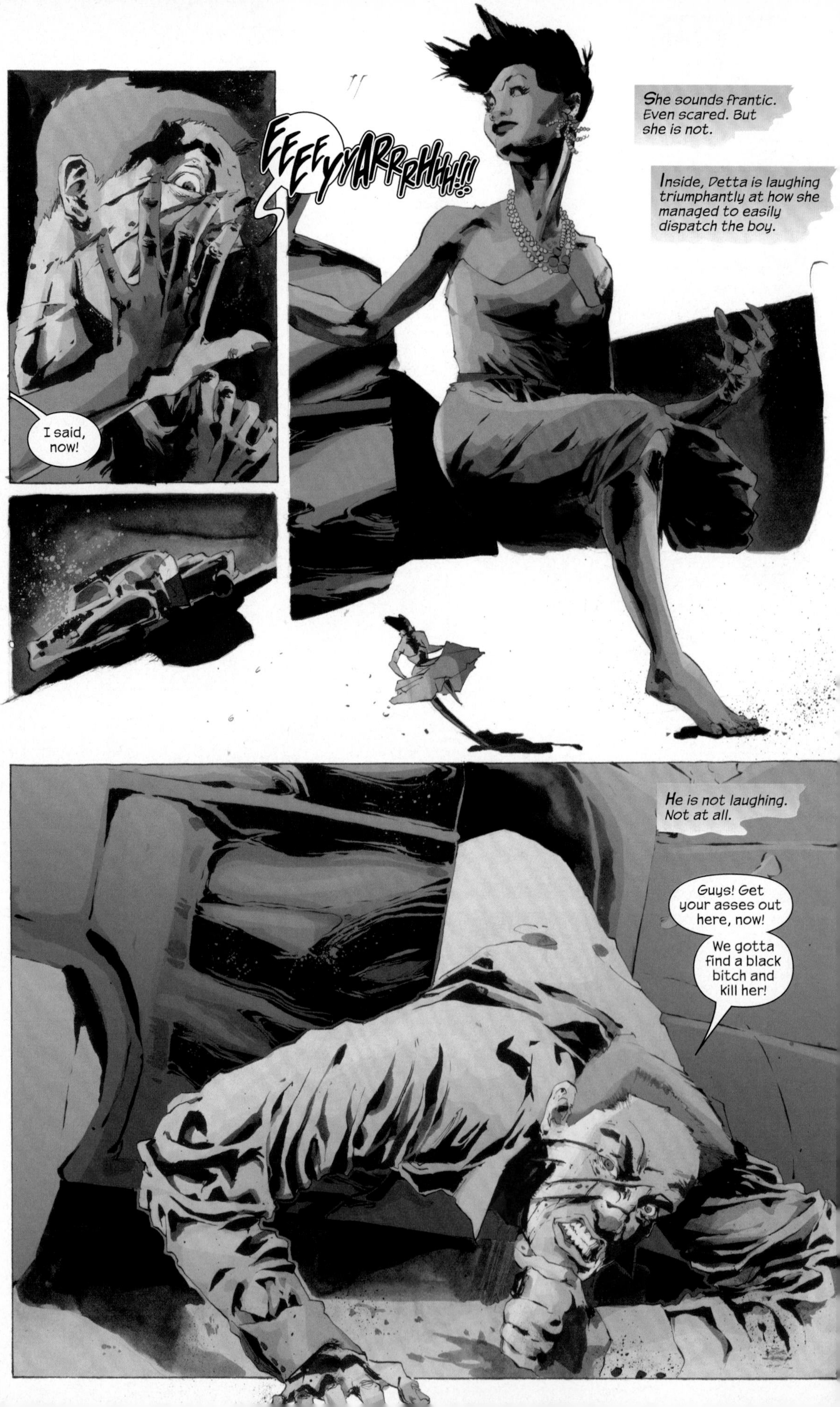
EEEEYYARRRHHH!!!
She sounds frantic. Even scared. But she is not.
Inside, Detta is laughing triumphantly at how she managed to easily dispatch the boy.
I said, now!
He is not laughing. Not at all.
Guys! Get your asses out here, now!
We gotta find a black bitch and kill her!

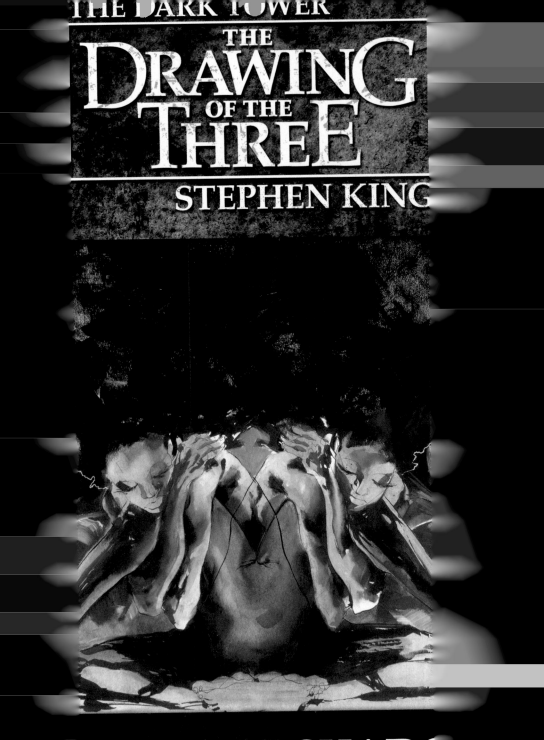

THE DARK TOWER
THE DRAWING OF THE THREE
STEPHEN KING

LADY OF SHADO
CHAPTER FOUR

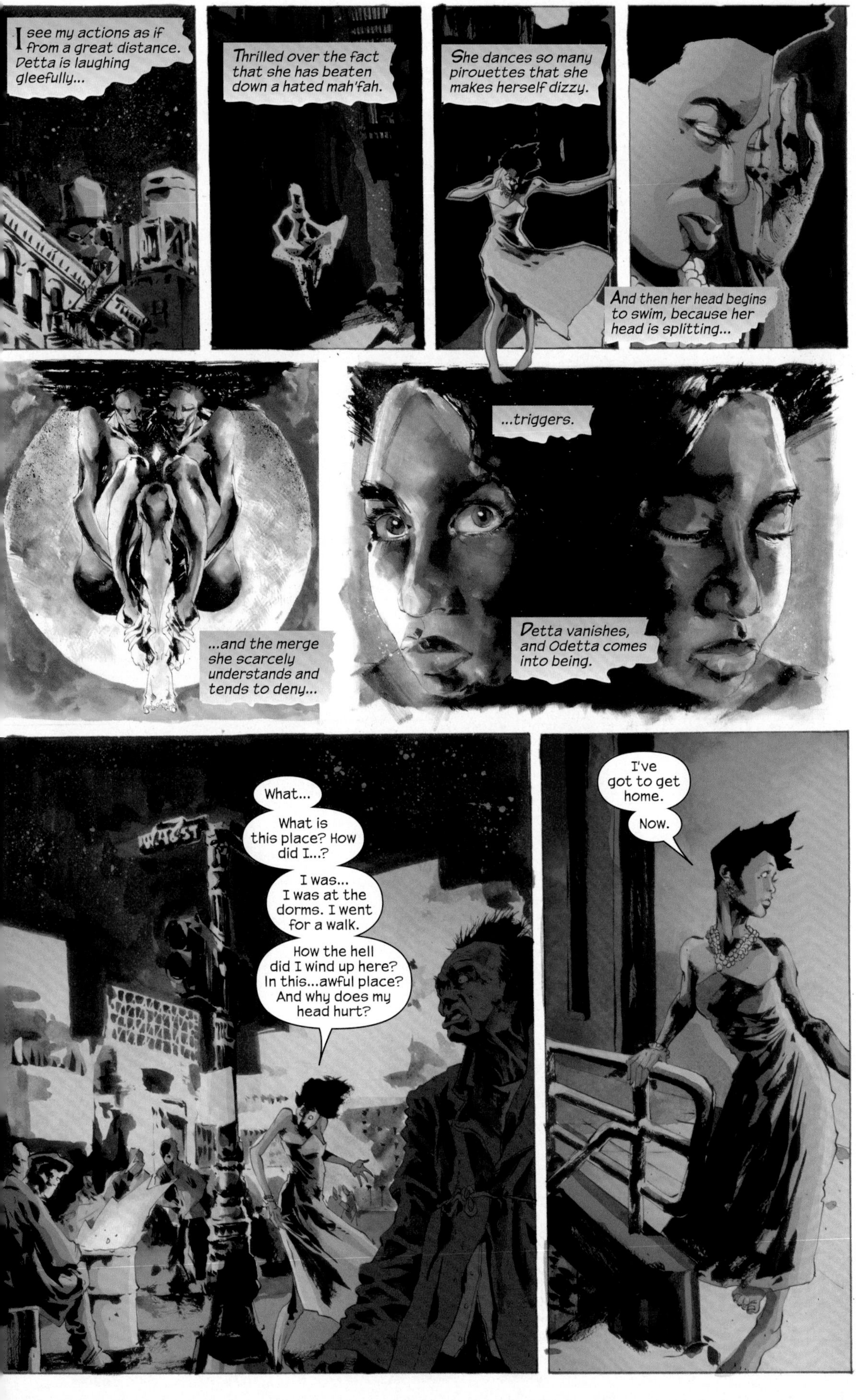
I see my actions as if from a great distance. Detta is laughing gleefully...
Thrilled over the fact that she has beaten down a hated mah'fah.
She dances so many pirouettes that she makes herself dizzy.
And then her head begins to swim, because her head is splitting...
...and the merge she scarcely understands and tends to deny...
...triggers.
Detta vanishes, and Odetta comes into being.
W. 46 ST
What...
What is this place? How did I...?
I was... I was at the dorms. I went for a walk.
How the hell did I wind up here? In this...awful place? And why does my head hurt?
I've got to get home.
Now.

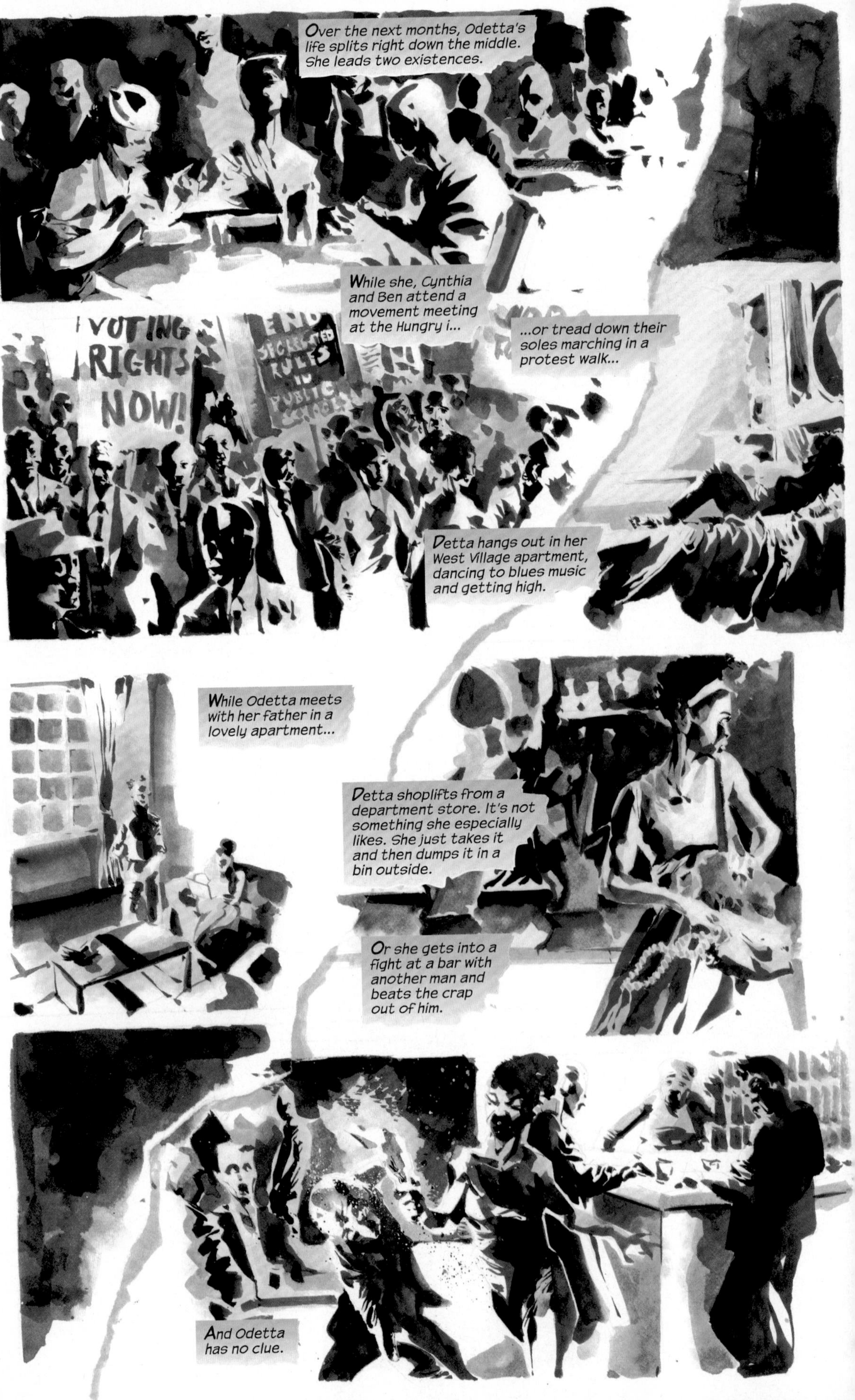
Over the next months, Odetta's life splits right down the middle. She leads two existences.
While she, Cynthia and Ben attend a movement meeting at the Hungry i...
VOTING RIGHTS NOW!
...or tread down their soles marching in a protest walk...
Detta hangs out in her West Village apartment, dancing to blues music and getting high.
While Odetta meets with her father in a lovely apartment...
Detta shoplifts from a department store. It's not something she especially likes. She just takes it and then dumps it in a bin outside.
Or she gets into a fight at a bar with another man and beats the crap out of him.
And Odetta has no clue.

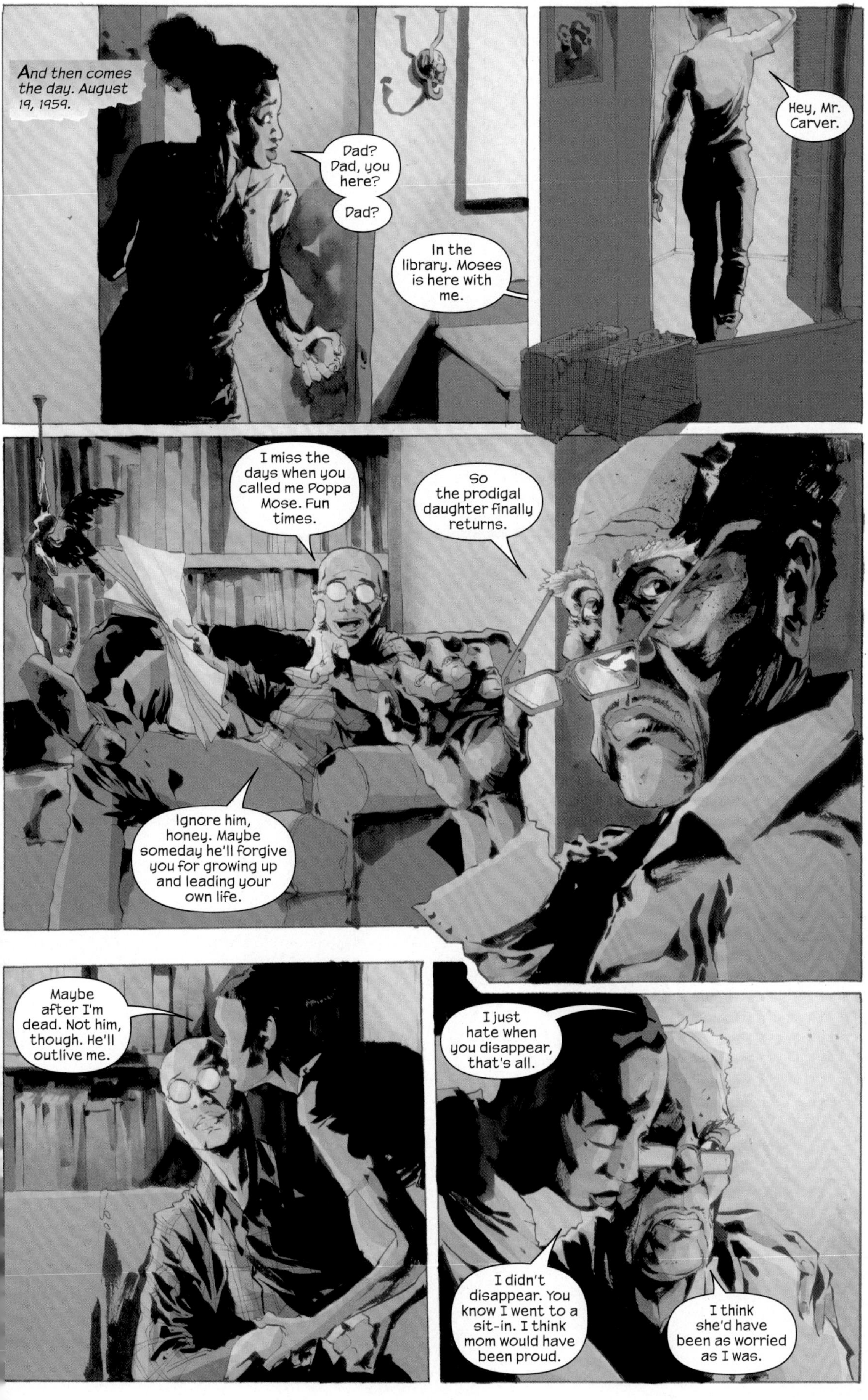

And then comes the day. August 19, 1959.
Dad? Dad, you here?
Dad?
In the library. Moses is here with me.
Hey, Mr. Carver.
I miss the days when you called me Poppa Mose. Fun times.
So the prodigal daughter finally returns.
Ignore him, honey. Maybe someday he'll forgive you for growing up and leading your own life.
Maybe after I'm dead. Not him, though. He'll outlive me.
I just hate when you disappear, that's all.
I didn't disappear. You know I went to a sit-in. I think mom would have been proud.
I think she'd have been as worried as I was.

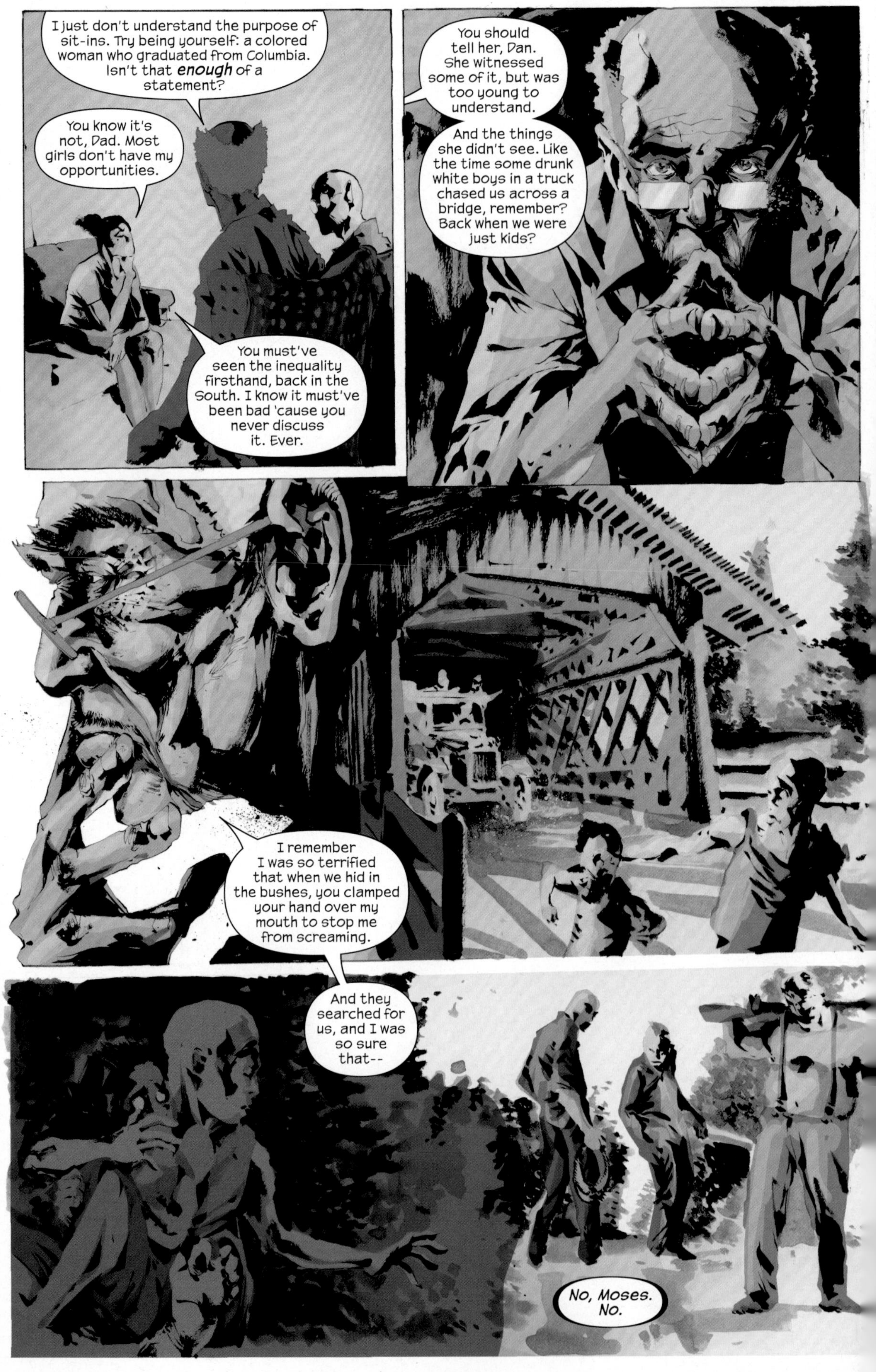
I just don't understand the purpose of sit-ins. Try being yourself: a colored woman who graduated from Columbia. Isn't that ***enough*** of a statement?
You know it's not, Dad. Most girls don't have my opportunities.
You must've seen the inequality firsthand, back in the South. I know it must've been bad 'cause you never discuss it. Ever.
You should tell her, Dan. She witnessed some of it, but was too young to understand.
And the things she didn't see. Like the time some drunk white boys in a truck chased us across a bridge, remember? Back when we were just kids?
I remember I was so terrified that when we hid in the bushes, you clamped your hand over my mouth to stop me from screaming.
And they searched for us, and I was so sure that--
No, Moses. No.

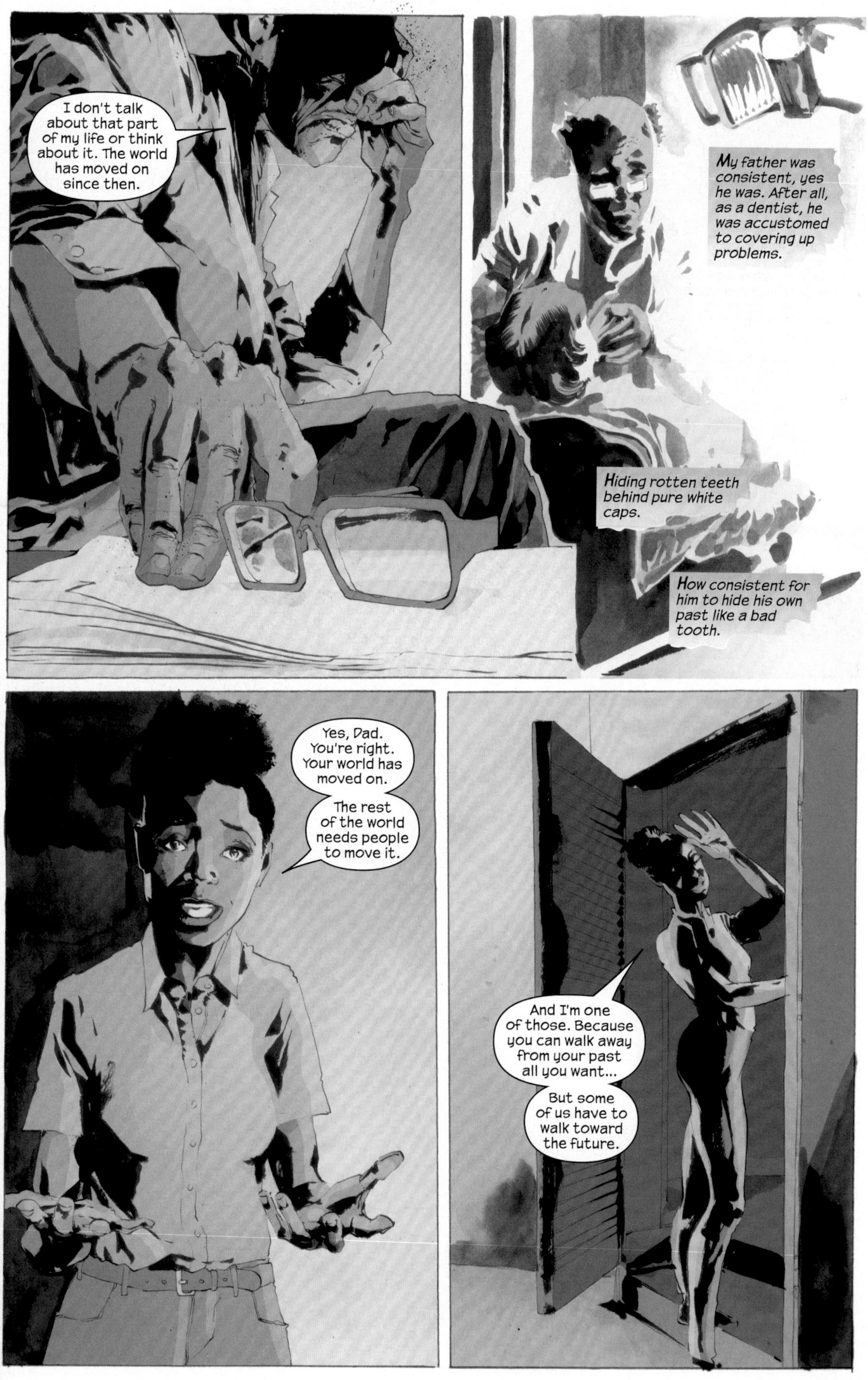
I don't talk about that part of my life or think about it. The world has moved on since then.
My father was consistent, yes he was. After all, as a dentist, he was accustomed to covering up problems.
Hiding rotten teeth behind pure white caps.
How consistent for him to hide his own past like a bad tooth.
Yes, Dad. You're right. Your world has moved on.
The rest of the world needs people to move it.
And I'm one of those. Because you can walk away from your past all you want...
But some of us have to walk toward the future.

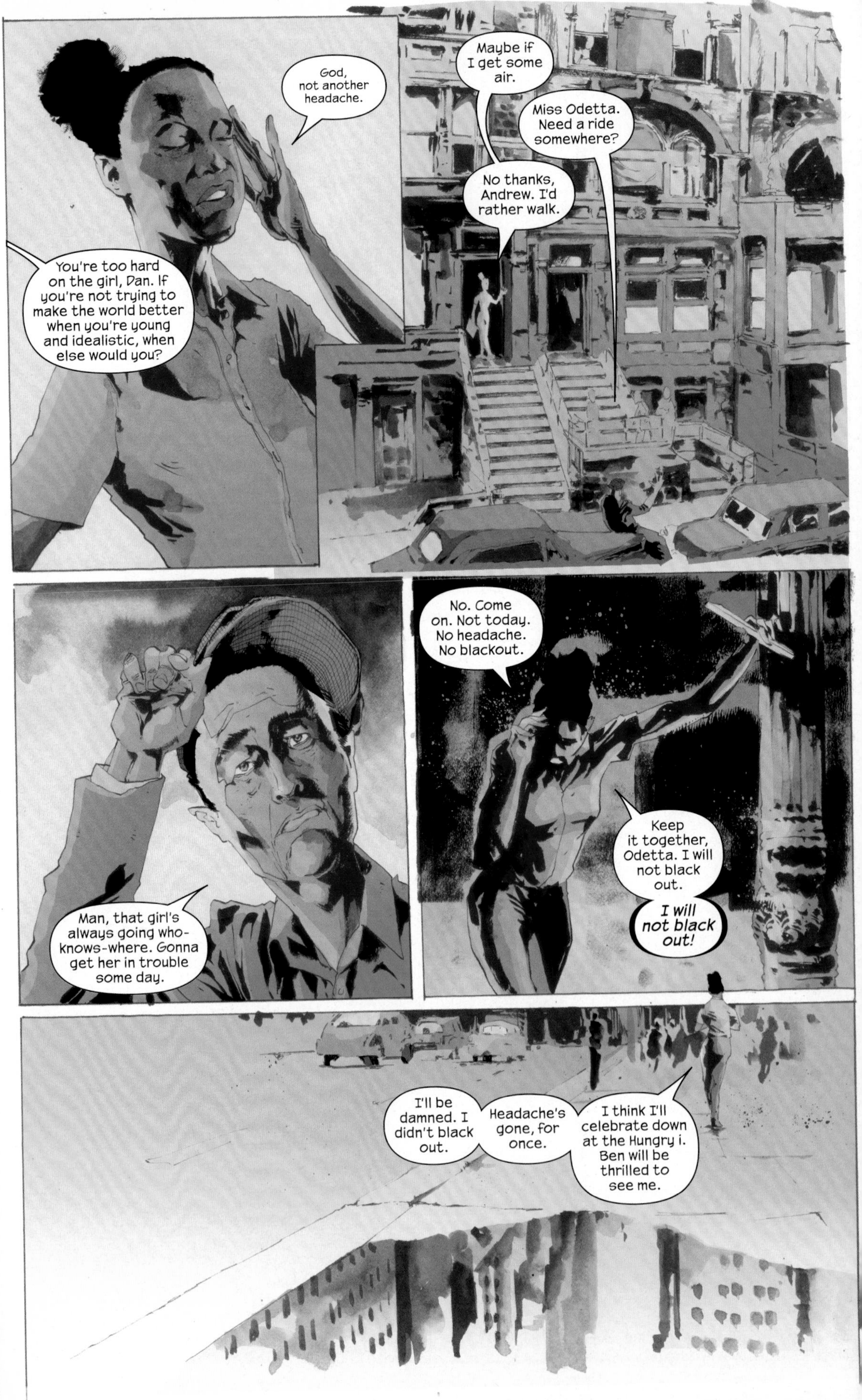
God, not another headache.
You're too hard on the girl, Dan. If you're not trying to make the world better when you're young and idealistic, when else would you?
Maybe if I get some air.
Miss Odetta. Need a ride somewhere?
No thanks, Andrew. I'd rather walk.
Man, that girl's always going who-knows-where. Gonna get her in trouble some day.
No. Come on. Not today. No headache. No blackout.
Keep it together, Odetta. I will not black out.
I will not black out!
I'll be damned. I didn't black out.
Headache's gone, for once.
I think I'll celebrate down at the Hungry i. Ben will be thrilled to see me.

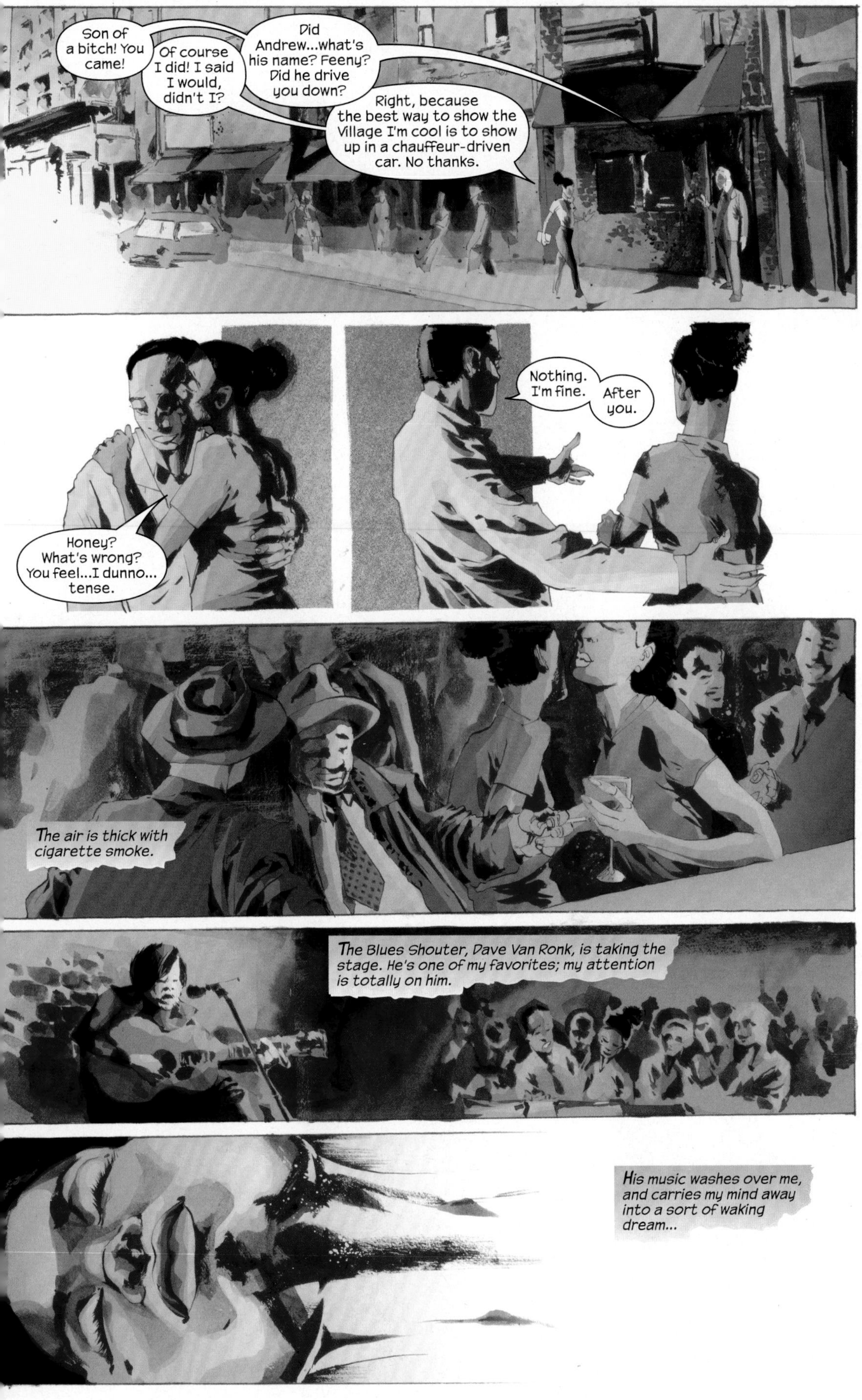

Son of a bitch! You came!
Of course I did! I said I would, didn't I?
Did Andrew...what's his name? Feeny? Did he drive you down?
Right, because the best way to show the Village I'm cool is to show up in a chauffeur-driven car. No thanks.
Honey? What's wrong? You feel...I dunno... tense.
Nothing. I'm fine.
After you.
The air is thick with cigarette smoke.
The Blues Shouter, Dave Van Ronk, is taking the stage. He's one of my favorites; my attention is totally on him.
His music washes over me, and carries my mind away into a sort of waking dream...

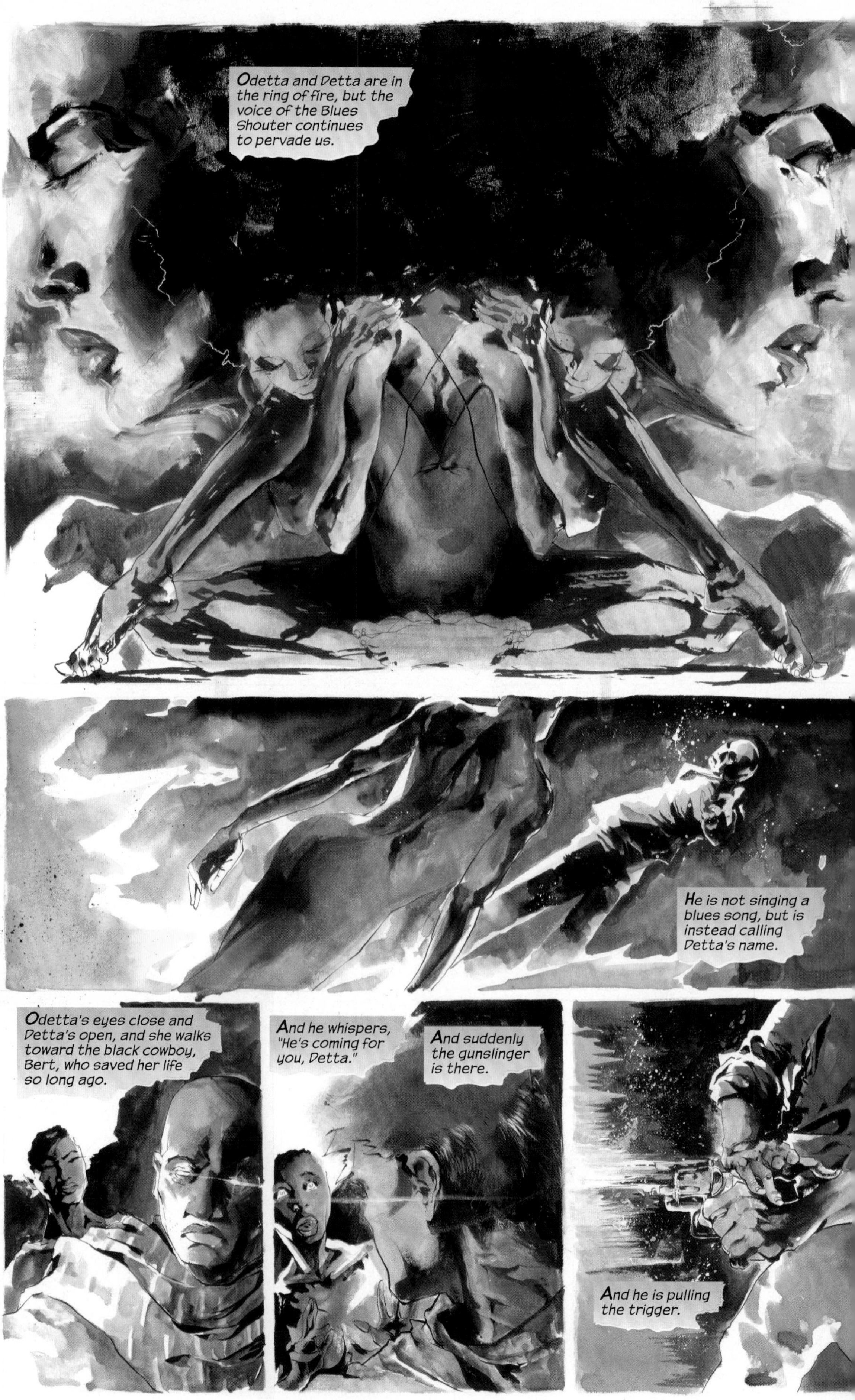
Odetta and Detta are in the ring of fire, but the voice of the Blues Shouter continues to pervade us.
He is not singing a blues song, but is instead calling Detta's name.
Odetta's eyes close and Detta's open, and she walks toward the black cowboy, Bert, who saved her life so long ago.
And he whispers, "He's coming for you, Detta."
And suddenly the gunslinger is there.
And he is pulling the trigger.

Less than an hour later, we say farewell to some friends. Then it's just us.

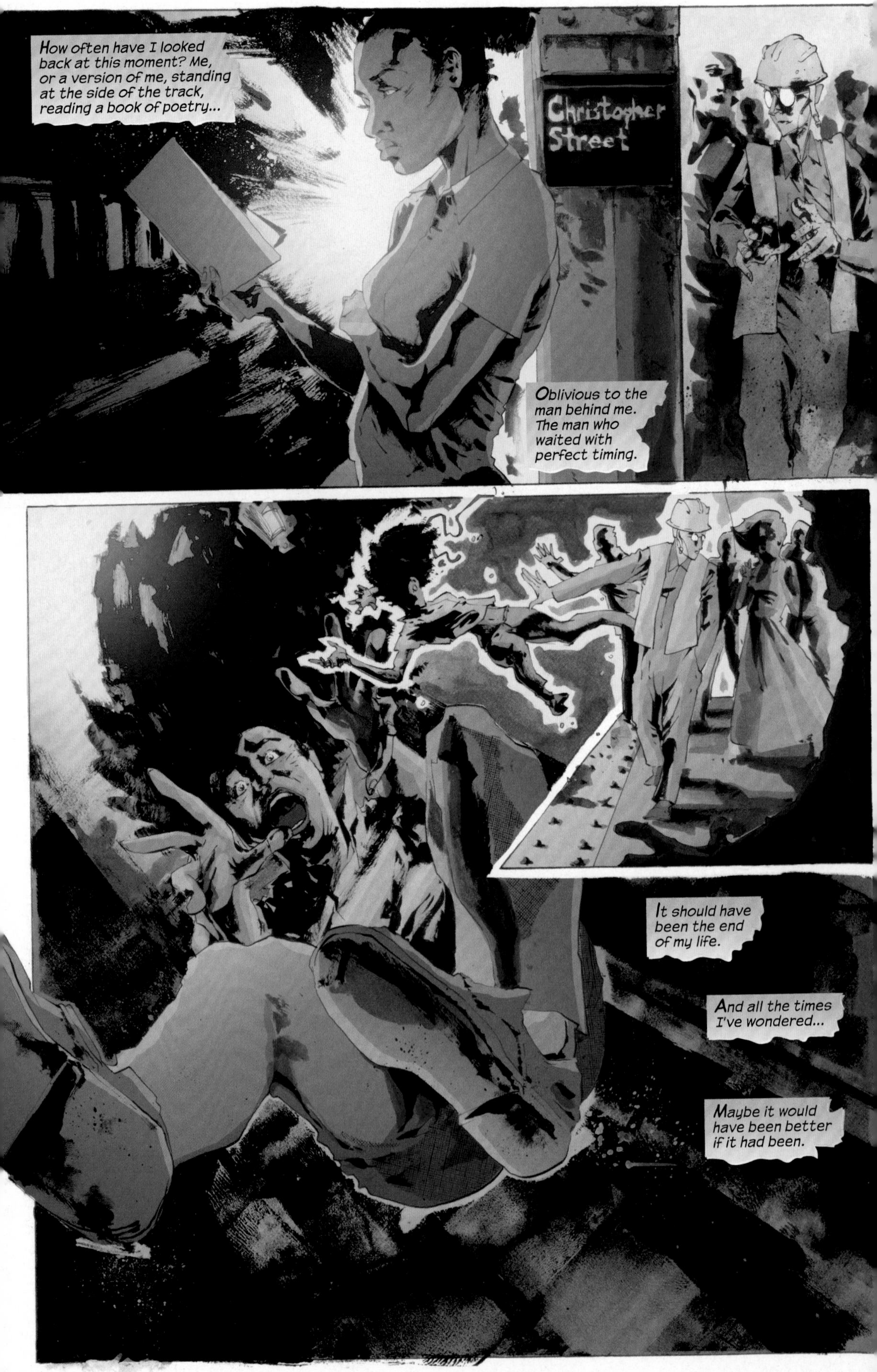
How often have I looked back at this moment? Me, or a version of me, standing at the side of the track, reading a book of poetry...
Christopher Street
Oblivious to the man behind me. The man who waited with perfect timing.
It should have been the end of my life.
And all the times I've wondered...
Maybe it would have been better if it had been.

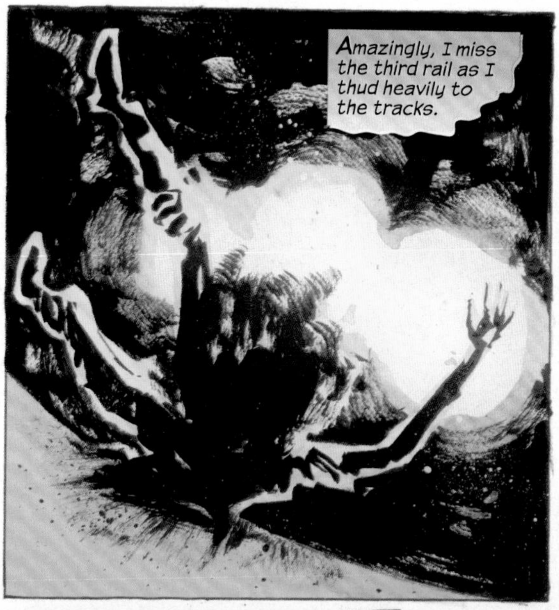
Amazingly, I miss the third rail as I thud heavily to the tracks.

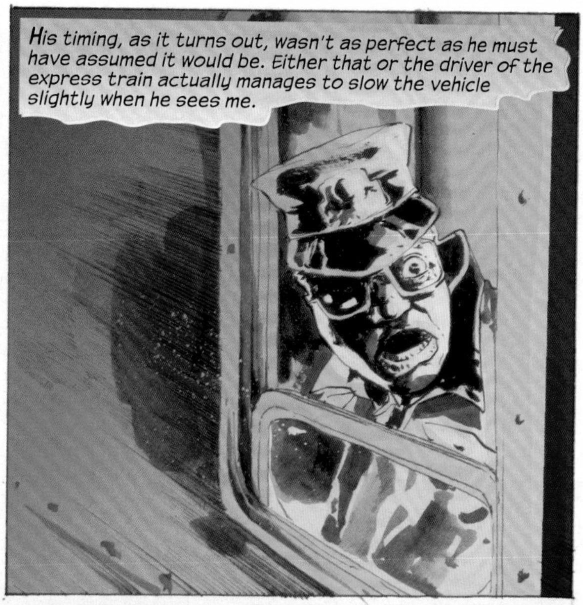
His timing, as it turns out, wasn't as perfect as he must have assumed it would be. Either that or the driver of the express train actually manages to slow the vehicle slightly when he sees me.

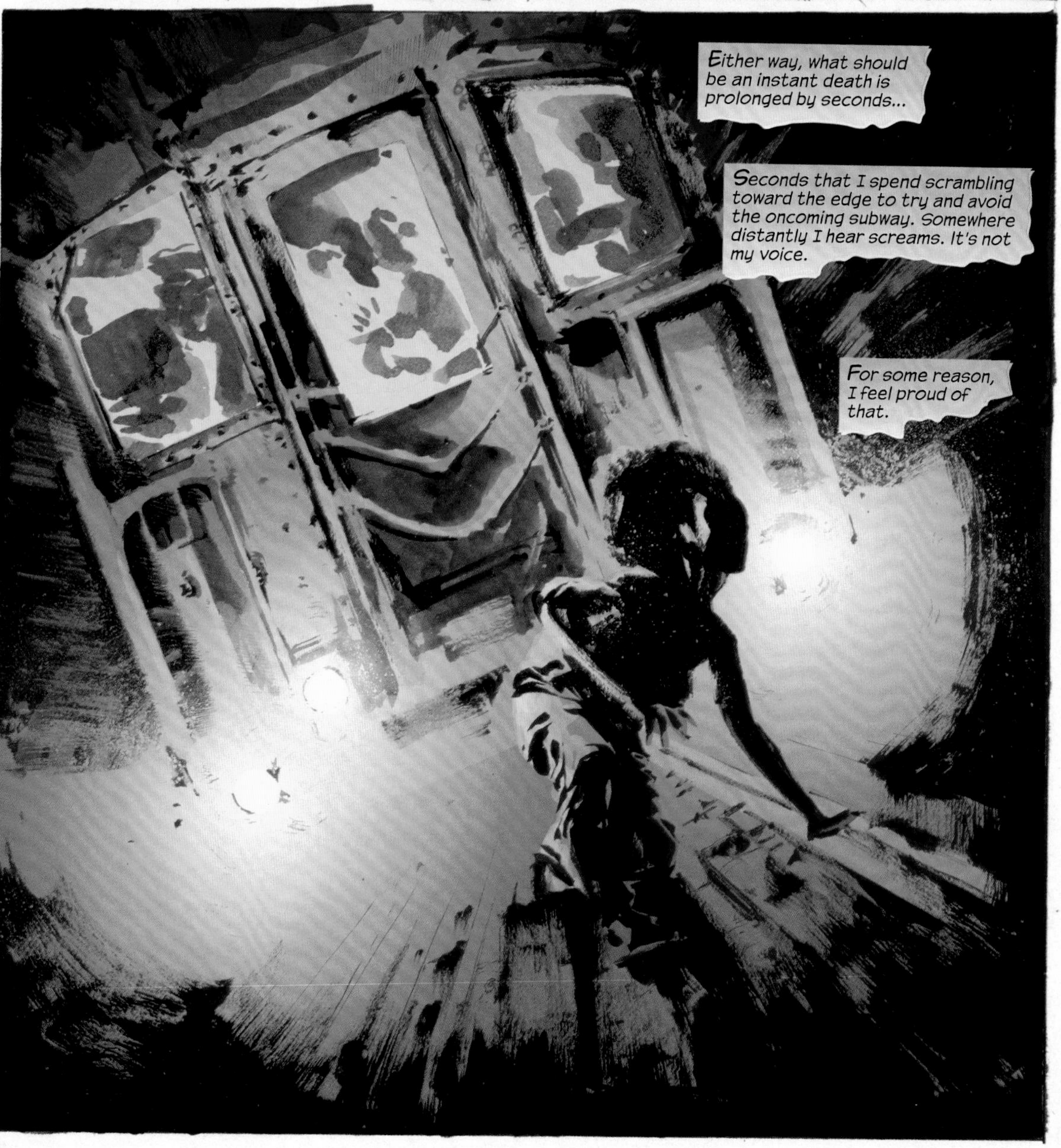
Either way, what should be an instant death is prolonged by seconds...
Seconds that I spend scrambling toward the edge to try and avoid the oncoming subway. Somewhere distantly I hear screams. It's not my voice.
For some reason, I feel proud of that.

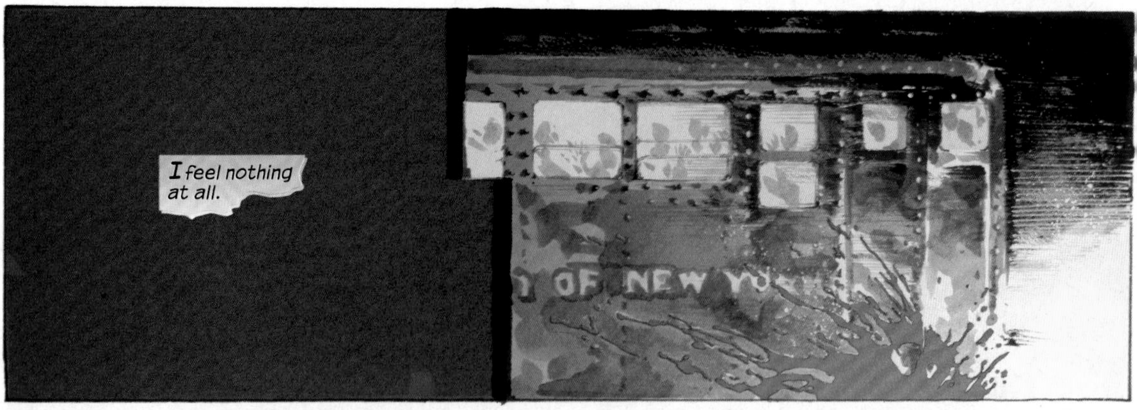
I feel nothing at all.
OF NEW YO

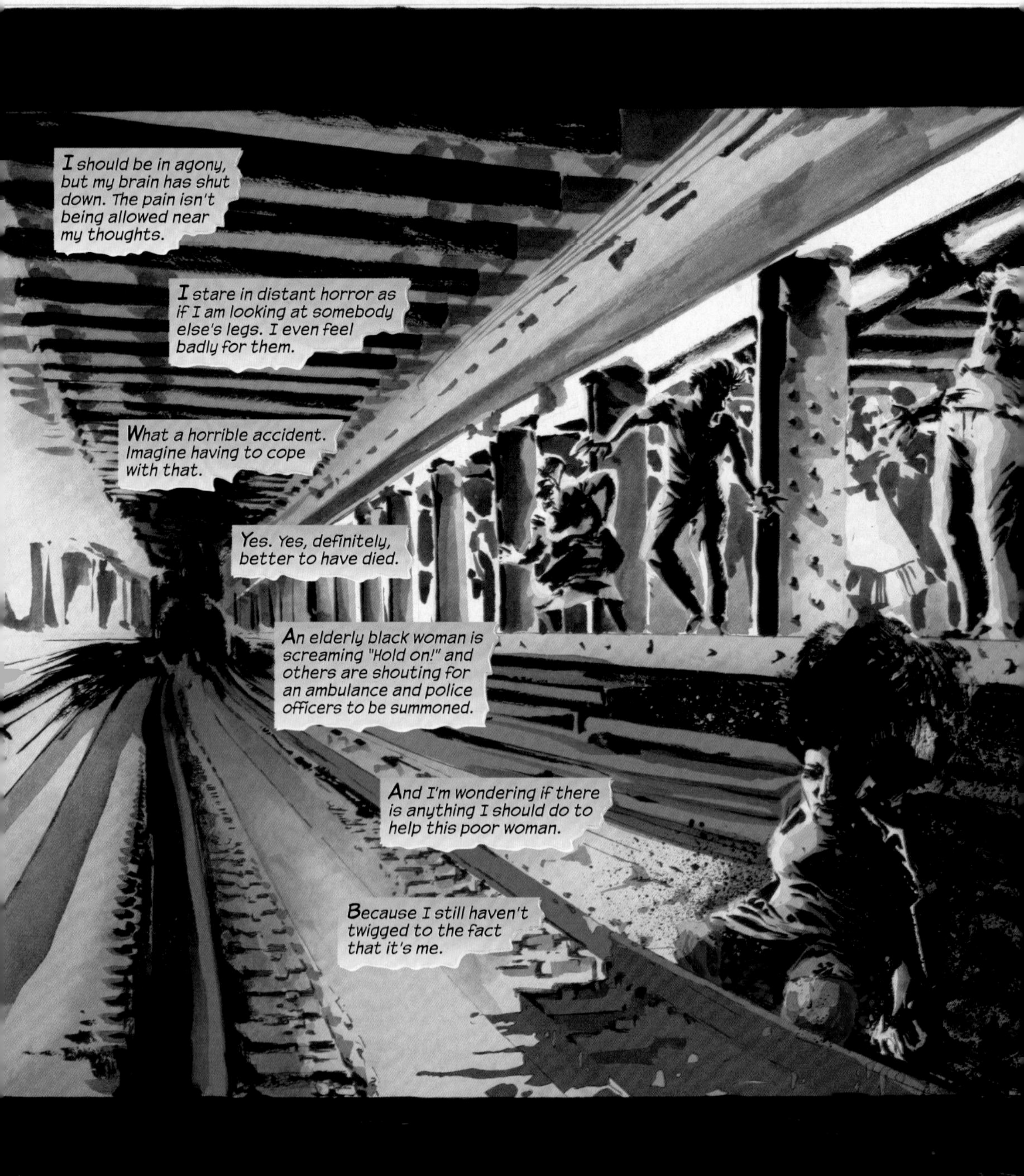
I should be in agony, but my brain has shut down. The pain isn't being allowed near my thoughts.
I stare in distant horror as if I am looking at somebody else's legs. I even feel badly for them.
What a horrible accident. Imagine having to cope with that.
Yes. Yes, definitely, better to have died.
An elderly black woman is screaming "Hold on!" and others are shouting for an ambulance and police officers to be summoned.
And I'm wondering if there is anything I should do to help this poor woman.
Because I still haven't twigged to the fact that it's me.

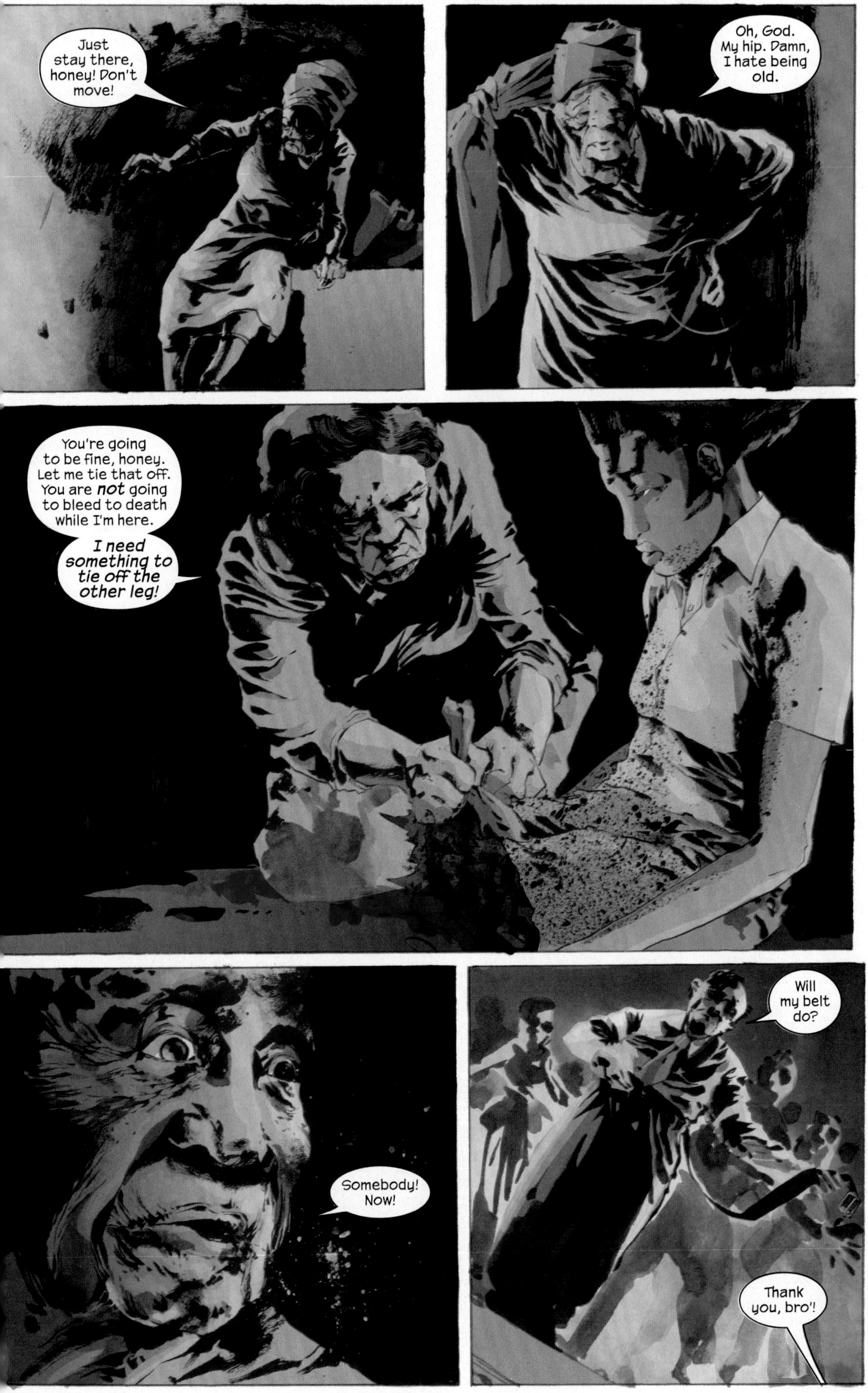
Just stay there, honey! Don't move!
Oh, God. My hip. Damn, I hate being old.
You're going to be fine, honey. Let me tie that off. You are **not** going to bleed to death while I'm here.
I need something to tie off the other leg!
Somebody! Now!
Will my belt do?
Thank you, bro'!

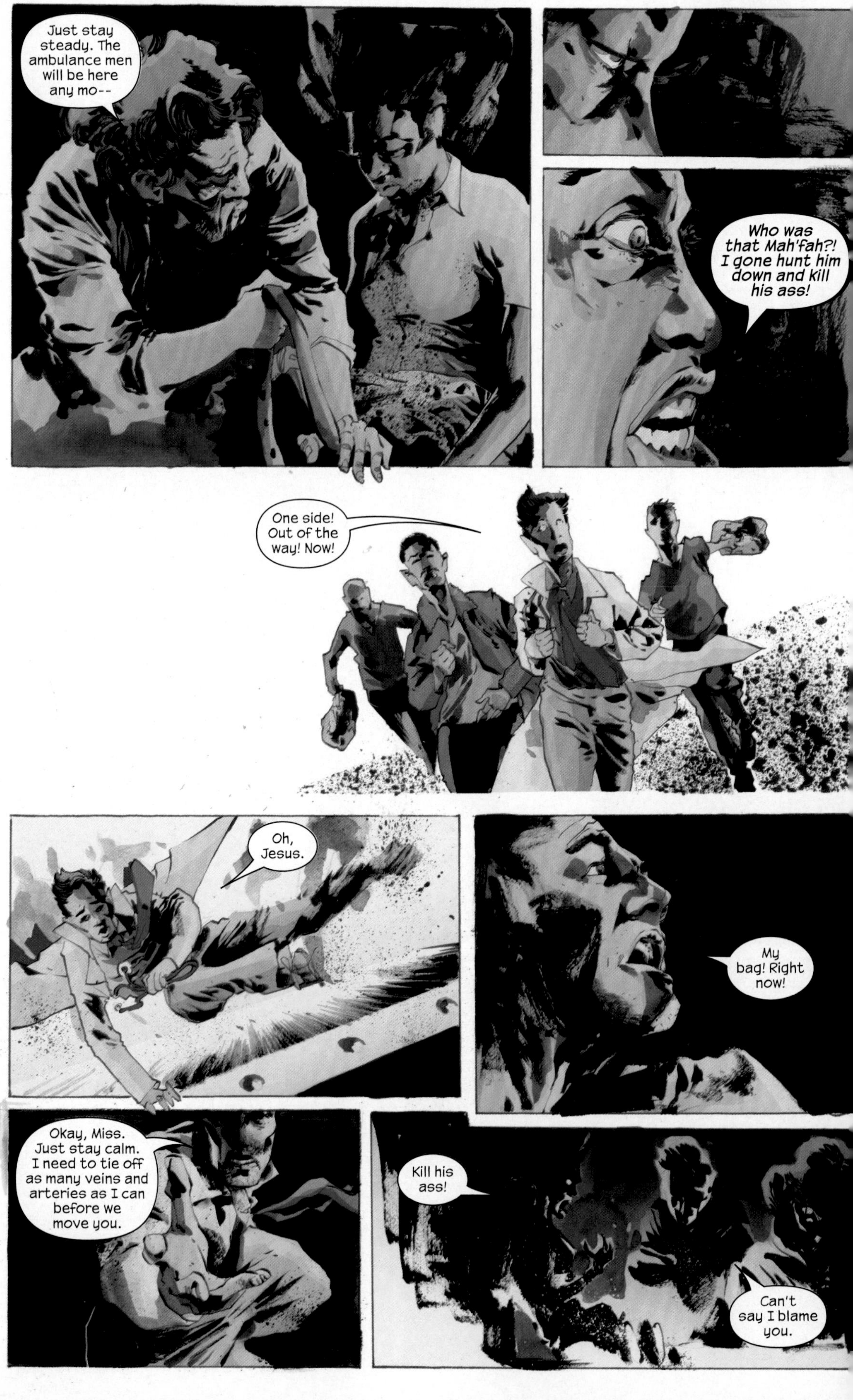
Just stay steady. The ambulance men will be here any mo--
Who was that Mah'fah?! I gone hunt him down and kill his ass!
One side! Out of the way! Now!
Oh, Jesus.
My bag! Right now!
Okay, Miss. Just stay calm. I need to tie off as many veins and arteries as I can before we move you.
Kill his ass!
Can't say I blame you.

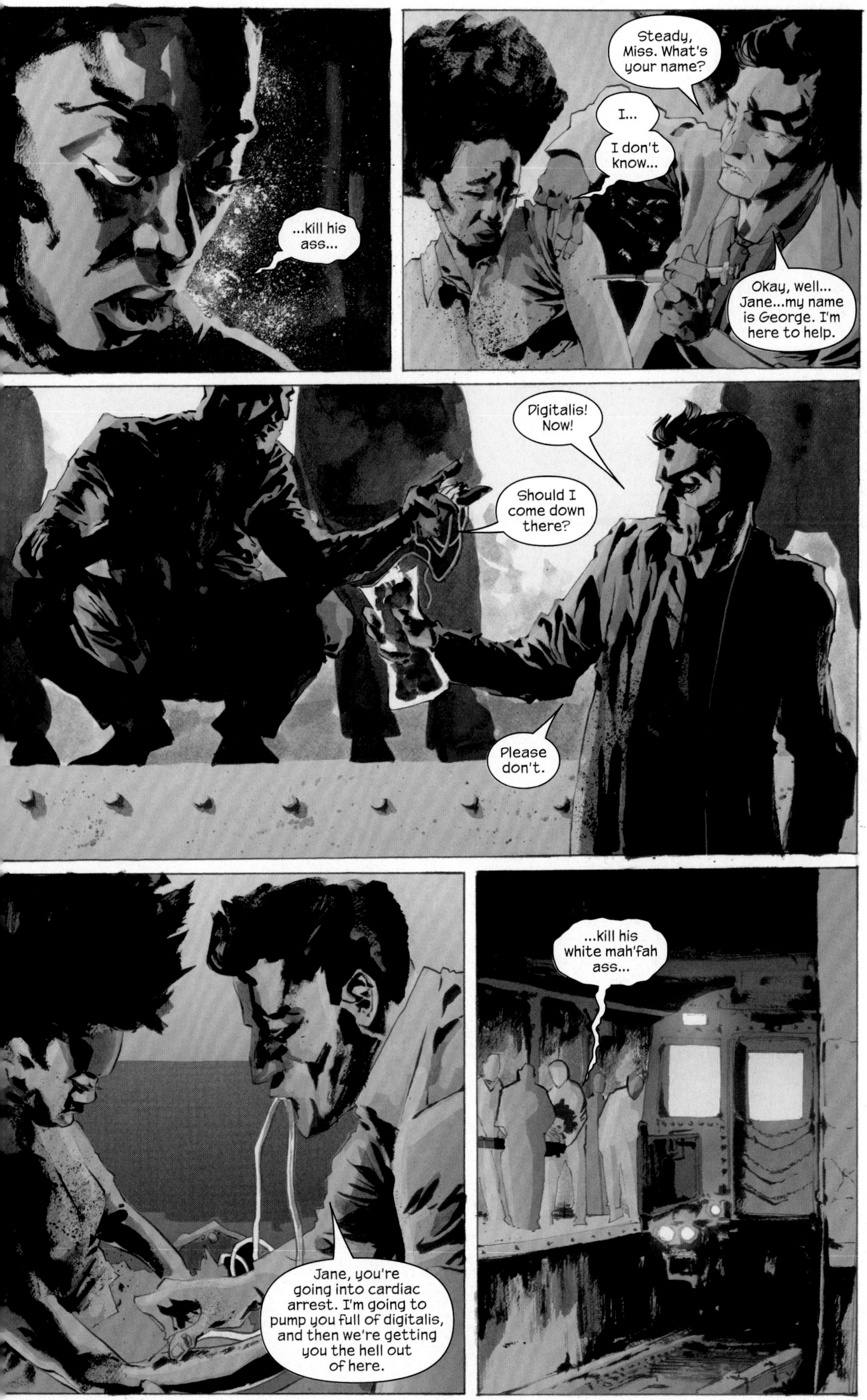
...kill his ass...
Steady, Miss. What's your name?
I...
I don't know...
Okay, well... Jane...my name is George. I'm here to help.
Digitalis! Now!
Should I come down there?
Please don't.
Jane, you're going into cardiac arrest. I'm going to pump you full of digitalis, and then we're getting you the hell out of here.
...kill his white mah'fah ass...

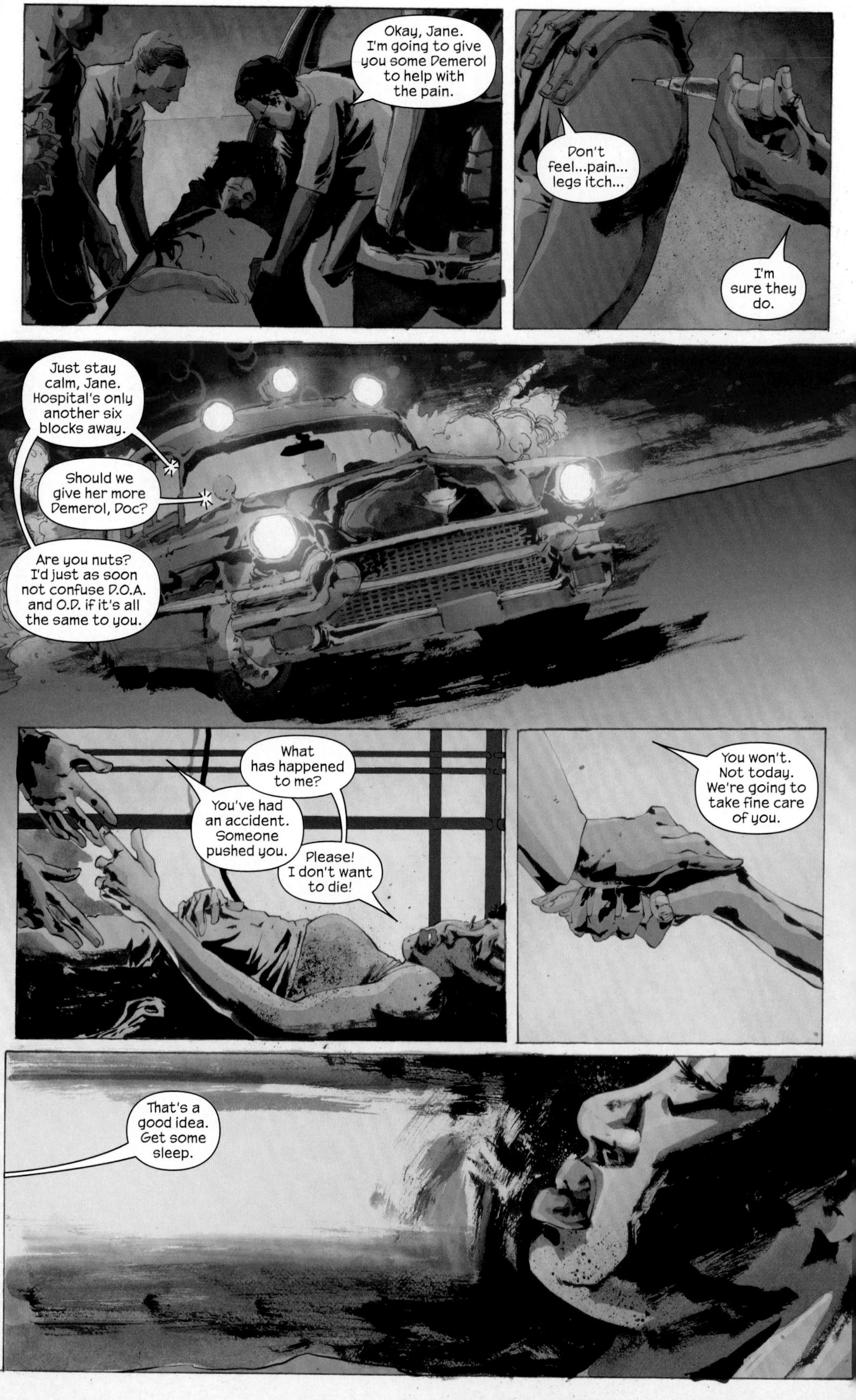

Okay, Jane. I'm going to give you some Demerol to help with the pain.
Don't feel...pain... legs itch...
I'm sure they do.
Just stay calm, Jane. Hospital's only another six blocks away.
Should we give her more Demerol, Doc?
Are you nuts? I'd just as soon not confuse D.O.A. and O.D. if it's all the same to you.
What has happened to me?
You've had an accident. Someone pushed you.
Please! I don't want to die!
You won't. Not today. We're going to take fine care of you.
That's a good idea. Get some sleep.

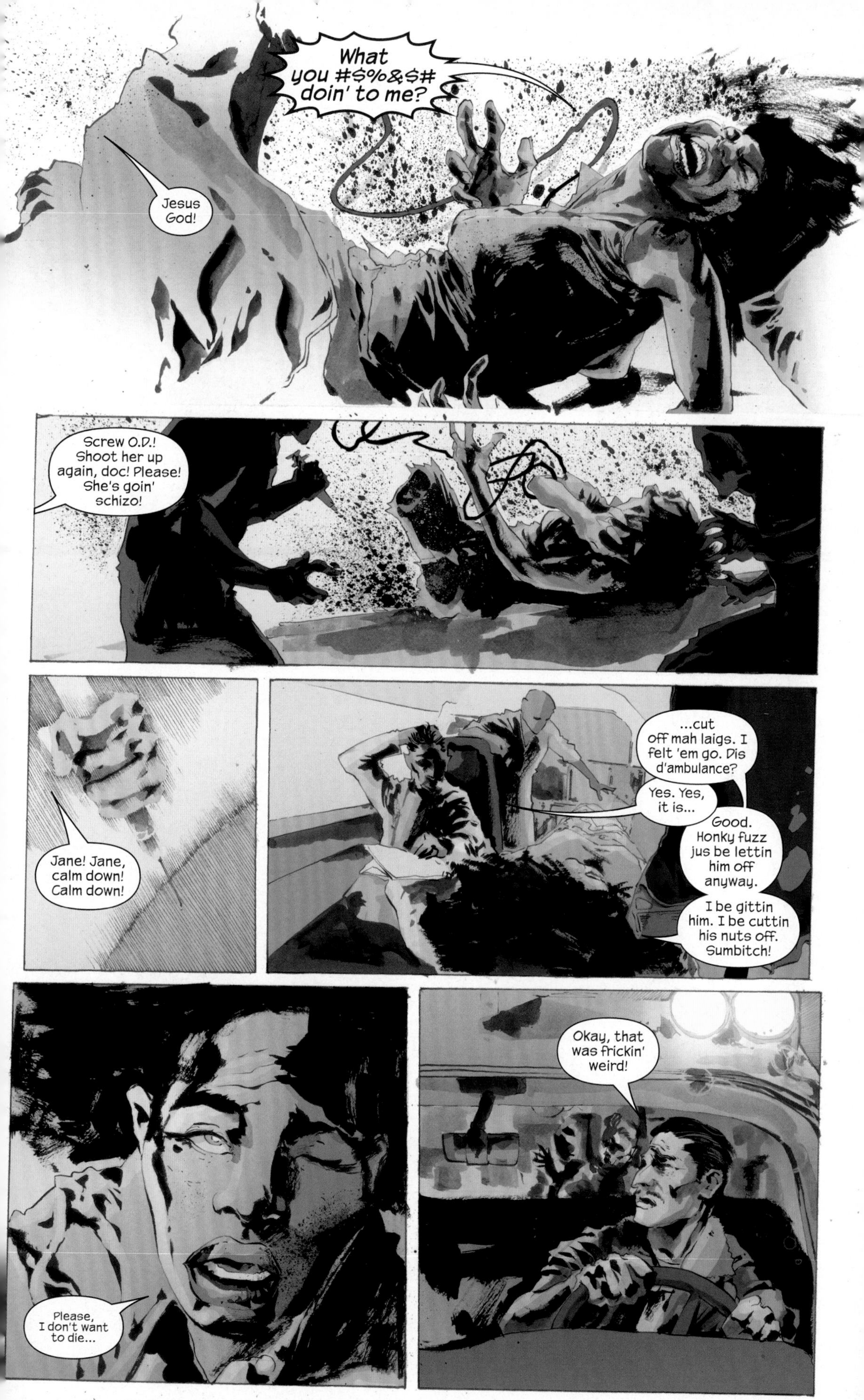
What you #$%&$# doin' to me?
Jesus God!
Screw O.D.! Shoot her up again, doc! Please! She's goin' schizo!
Jane! Jane, calm down! Calm down!
...cut off mah laigs. I felt 'em go. Dis d'ambulance?
Yes. Yes, it is...
Good. Honky fuzz jus be lettin him off anyway.
I be gittin him. I be cuttin his nuts off. Sumbitch!
Please, I don't want to die...
Okay, that was frickin' weird!

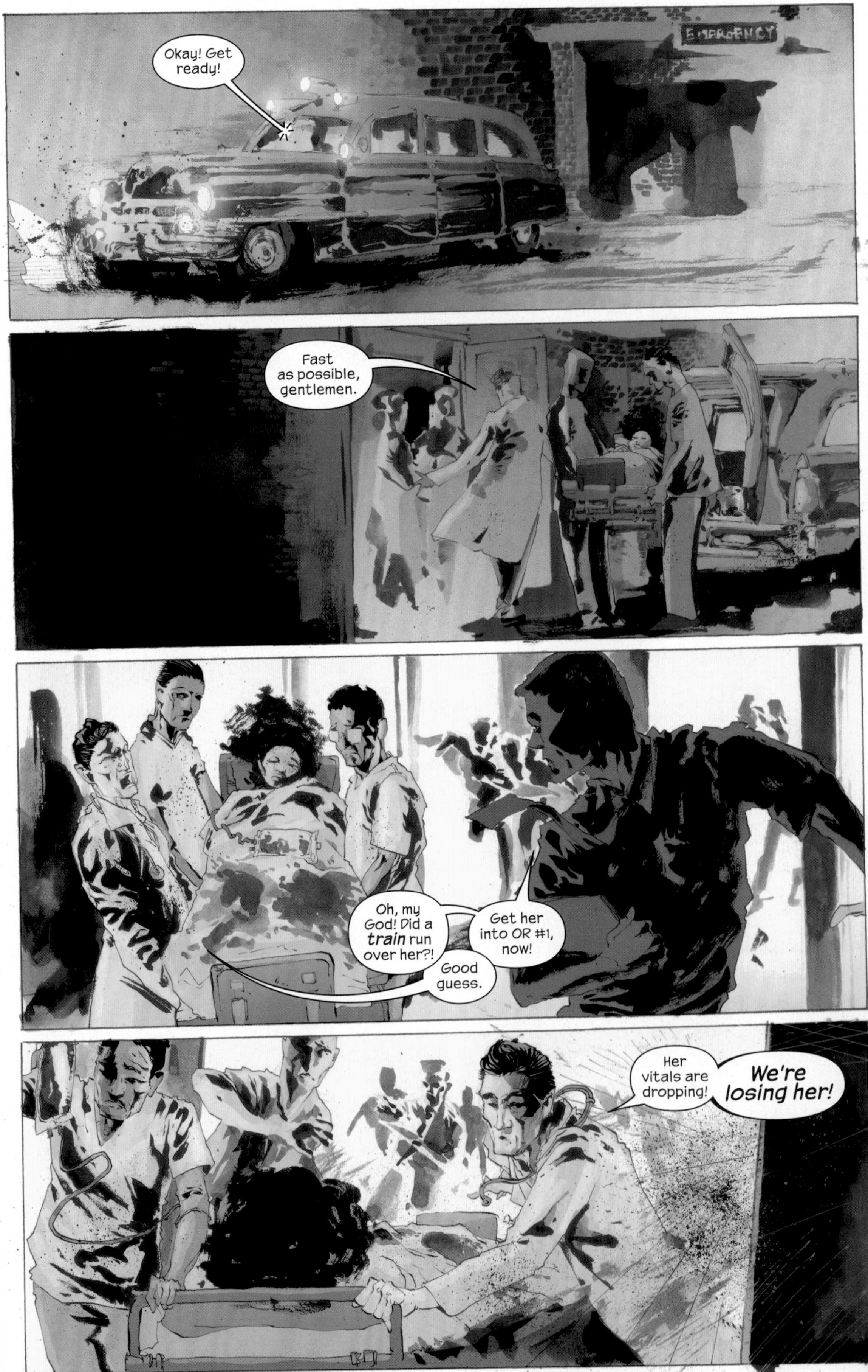
EMERGENCY
Okay! Get ready!
Fast as possible, gentlemen.
Oh, my God! Did a *train* run over her?!
Get her into OR #1, now!
Good guess.
Her vitals are dropping!
We're losing her!

THE DARK TOWER
THE DRAWING OF THE THREE
STEPHEN KING

THE LADY OF SHADOWS
CHAPTER FIVE

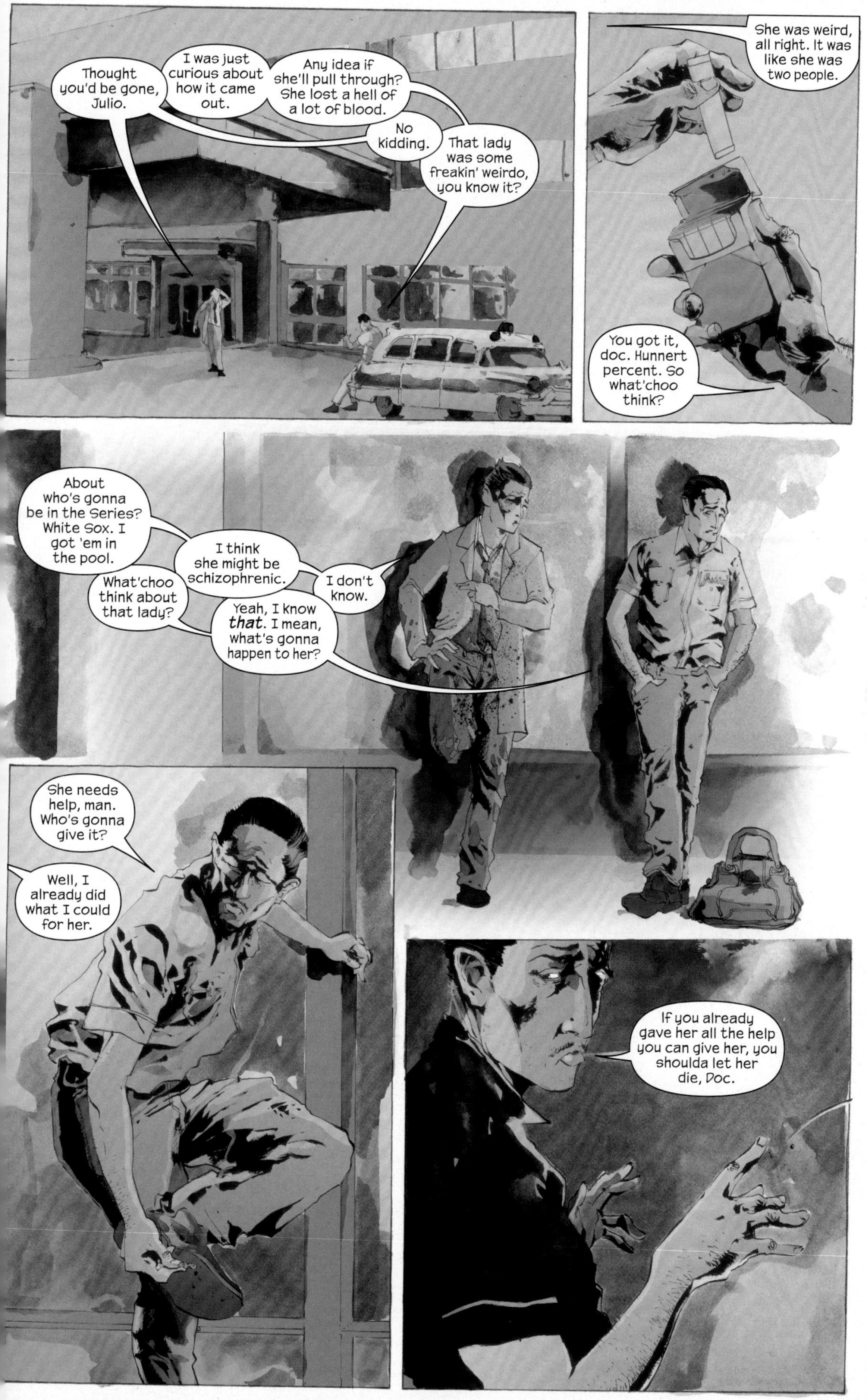
Thought you'd be gone, Julio.
I was just curious about how it came out.
Any idea if she'll pull through? She lost a hell of a lot of blood.
No kidding.
That lady was some freakin' weirdo, you know it?
She was weird, all right. It was like she was two people.
You got it, doc. Hunnert percent. So what'choo think?
About who's gonna be in the Series? White Sox. I got 'em in the pool.
I think she might be schizophrenic.
I don't know.
What'choo think about that lady?
Yeah, I know *that*. I mean, what's gonna happen to her?
She needs help, man. Who's gonna give it?
Well, I already did what I could for her.
If you already gave her all the help you can give her, you shoulda let her die, Doc.

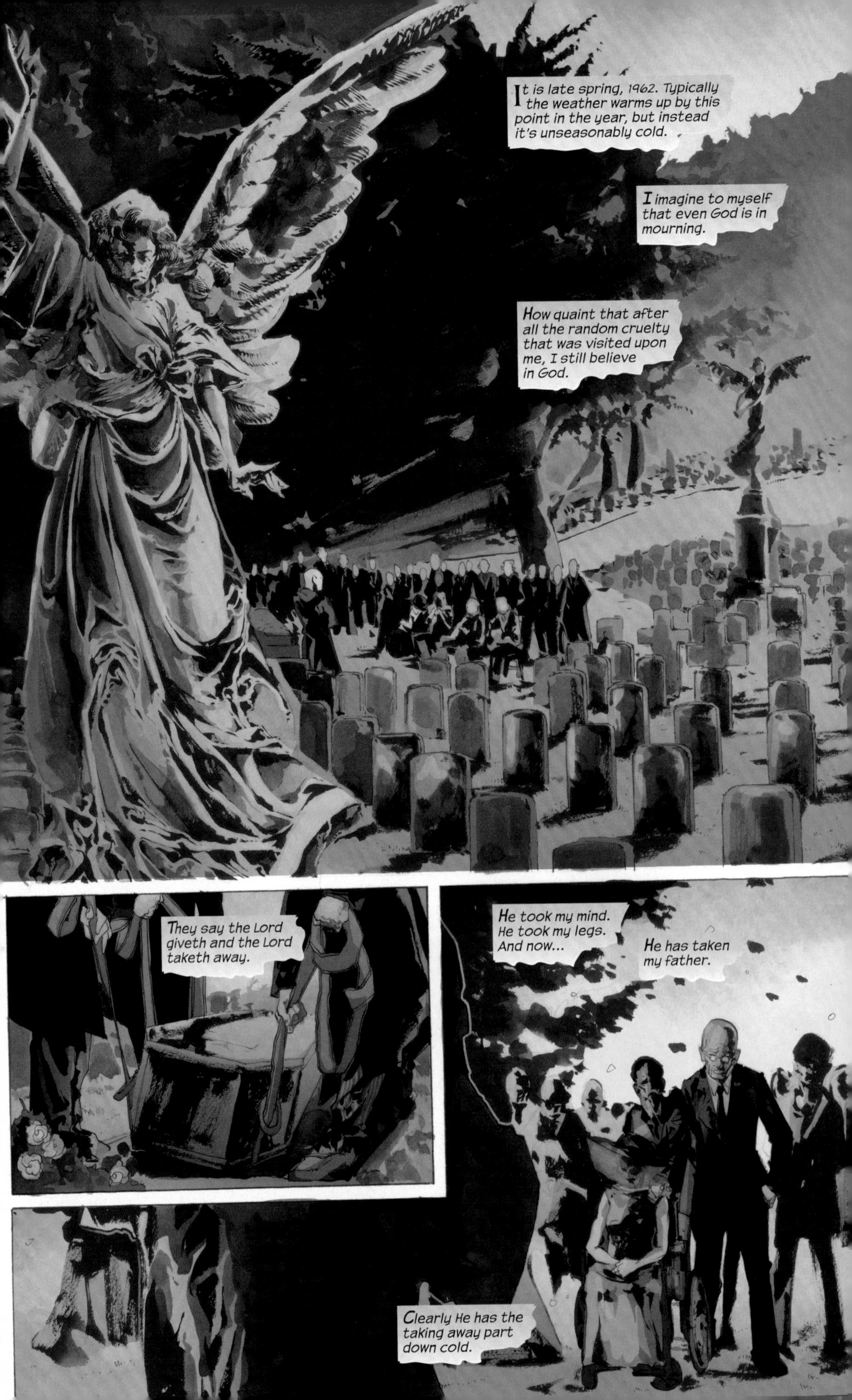
It is late spring, 1962. Typically the weather warms up by this point in the year, but instead it's unseasonably cold.
I imagine to myself that even God is in mourning.
How quaint that after all the random cruelty that was visited upon me, I still believe in God.
They say the Lord giveth and the Lord taketh away.
He took my mind. He took my legs. And now...
He has taken my father.
Clearly He has the taking away part down cold.

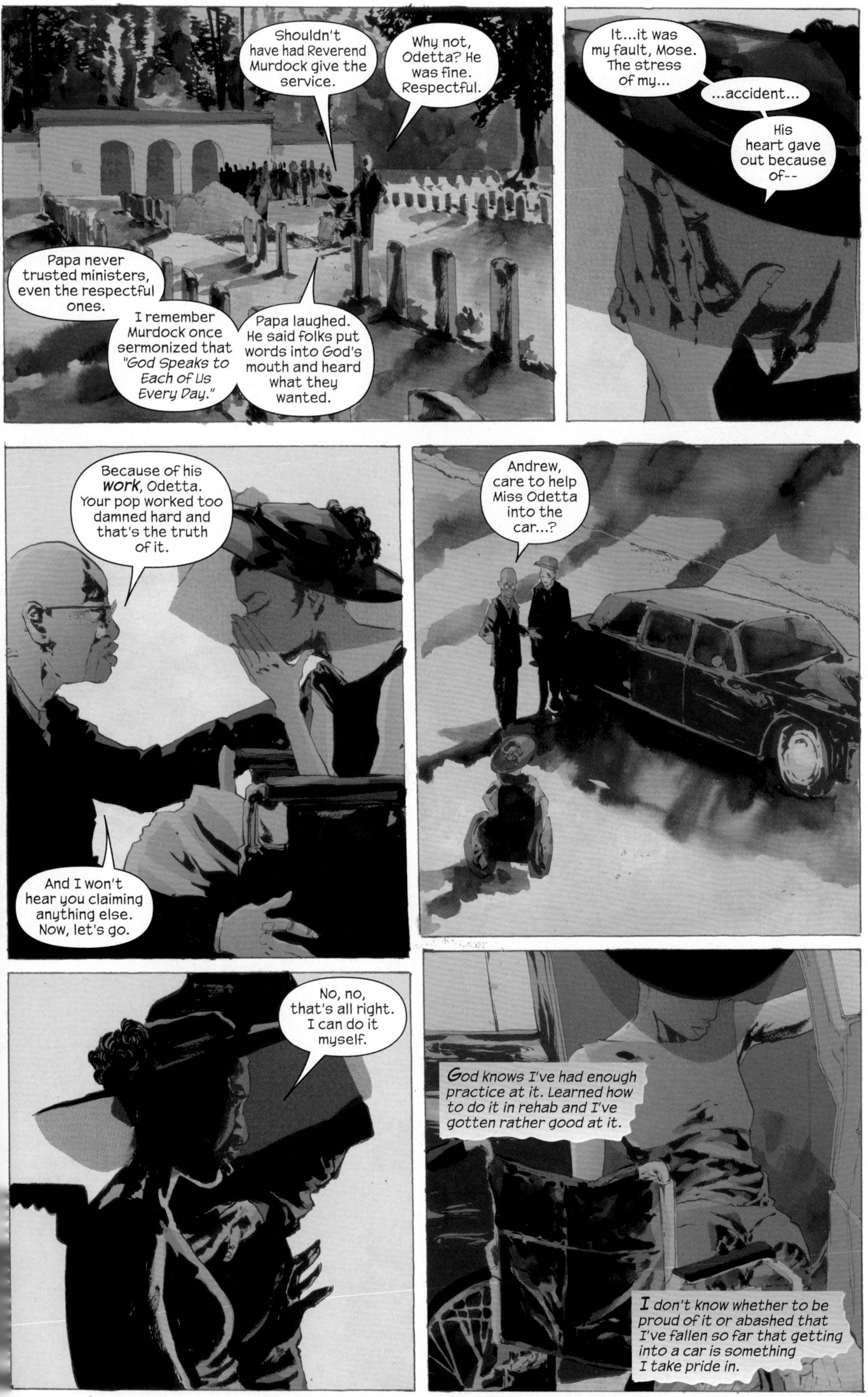
Shouldn't have had Reverend Murdock give the service.
Why not, Odetta? He was fine. Respectful.
Papa never trusted ministers, even the respectful ones.
I remember Murdock once sermonized that "God Speaks to Each of Us Every Day."
Papa laughed. He said folks put words into God's mouth and heard what they wanted.
It...it was my fault, Mose. The stress of my...
...accident...
His heart gave out because of--
Because of his work, Odetta. Your pop worked too damned hard and that's the truth of it.
And I won't hear you claiming anything else. Now, let's go.
Andrew, care to help Miss Odetta into the car...?
No, no, that's all right. I can do it myself.
God knows I've had enough practice at it. Learned how to do it in rehab and I've gotten rather good at it.
I don't know whether to be proud of it or abashed that I've fallen so far that getting into a car is something I take pride in.

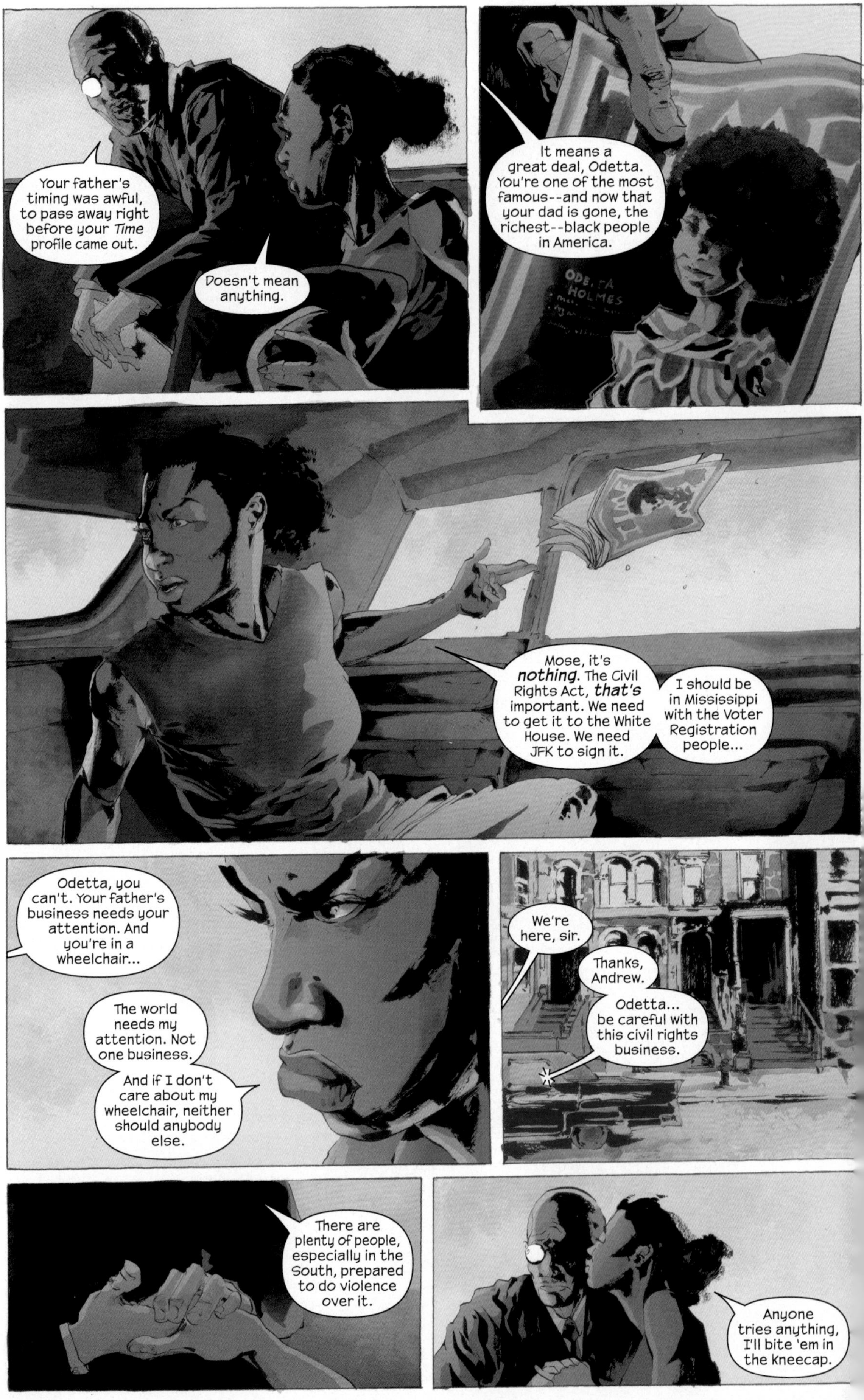
Your father's timing was awful, to pass away right before your *Time* profile came out.
Doesn't mean anything.
It means a great deal, Odetta. You're one of the most famous--and now that your dad is gone, the richest--black people in America.
Mose, it's ***nothing***. The Civil Rights Act, ***that's*** important. We need to get it to the White House. We need JFK to sign it.
I should be in Mississippi with the Voter Registration people...
Odetta, you can't. Your father's business needs your attention. And you're in a wheelchair...
The world needs my attention. Not one business.
And if I don't care about my wheelchair, neither should anybody else.
We're here, sir.
Thanks, Andrew.
Odetta... be careful with this civil rights business.
There are plenty of people, especially in the South, prepared to do violence over it.
Anyone tries anything, I'll bite 'em in the kneecap.

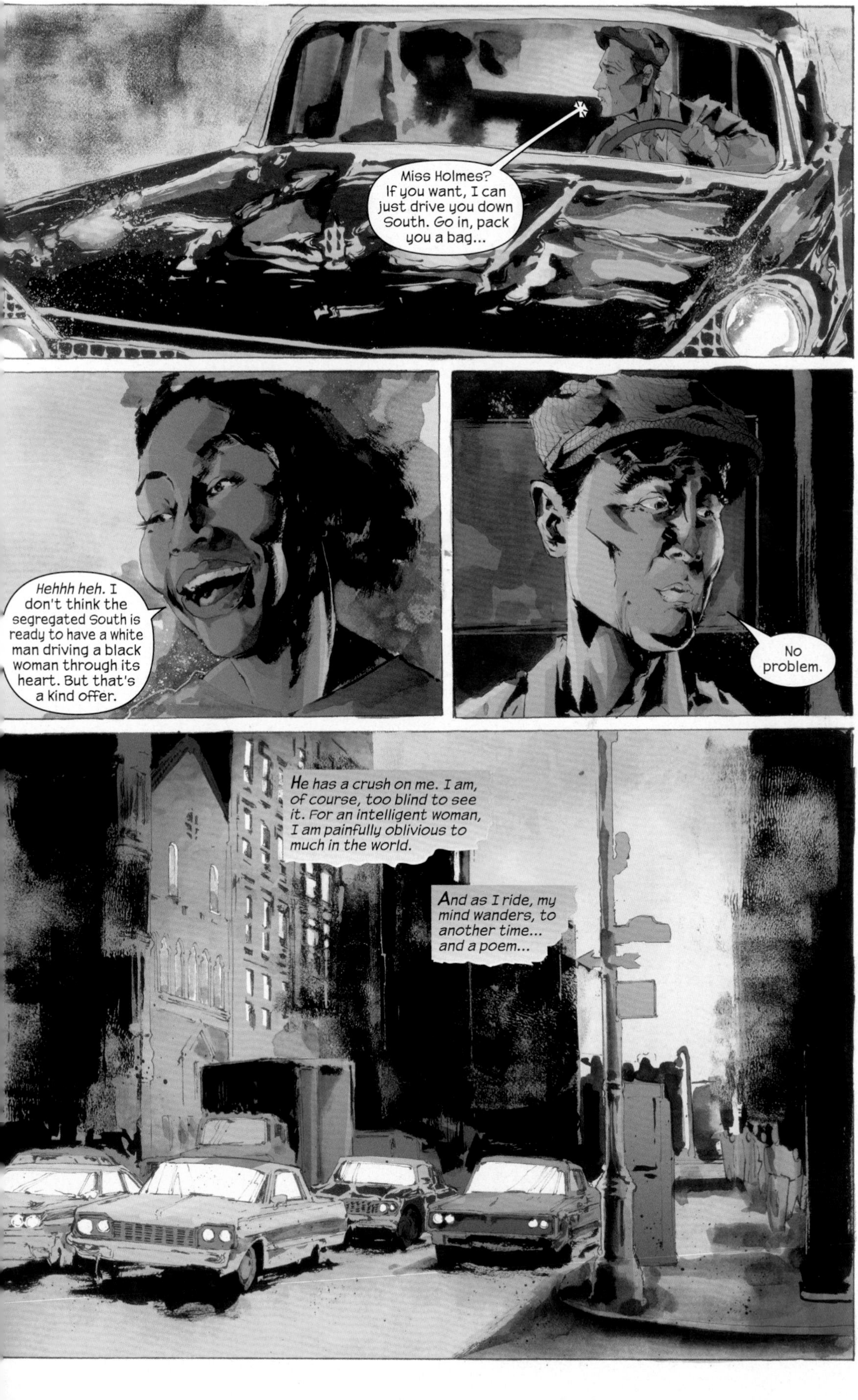

Miss Holmes? If you want, I can just drive you down South. Go in, pack you a bag...
Hehhh heh. I don't think the segregated South is ready to have a white man driving a black woman through its heart. But that's a kind offer.
No problem.
He has a crush on me. I am, of course, too blind to see it. For an intelligent woman, I am painfully oblivious to much in the world.
And as I ride, my mind wanders, to another time... and a poem...

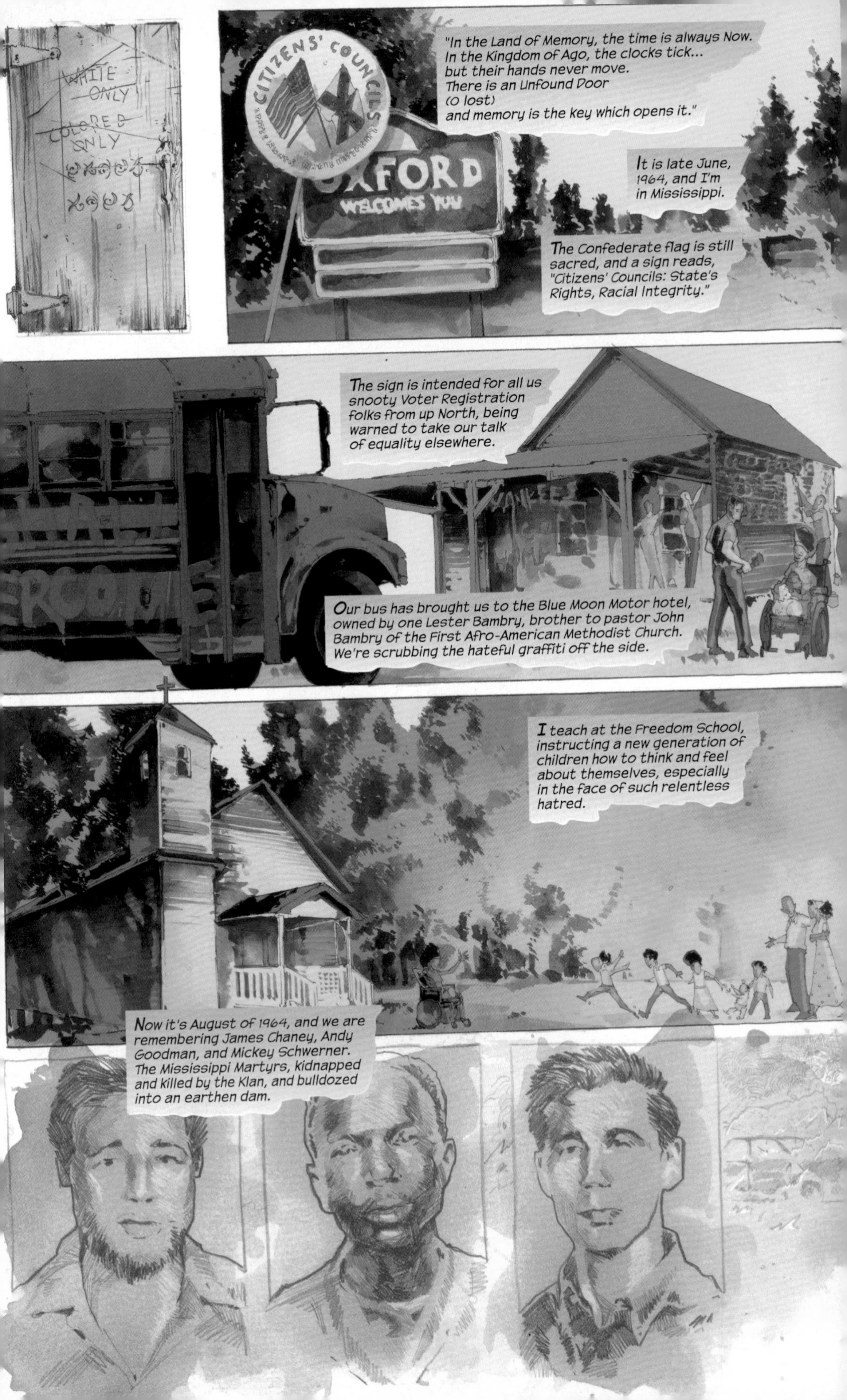
WHITE ONLY
COLORED ONLY
CITIZENS' COUNCILS
OXFORD WELCOMES YOU
"In the Land of Memory, the time is always Now. In the Kingdom of Ago, the clocks tick... but their hands never move. There is an Unfound Door (O lost) and memory is the key which opens it."
It is late June, 1964, and I'm in Mississippi.
The Confederate flag is still sacred, and a sign reads, "Citizens' Councils: State's Rights, Racial Integrity."
The sign is intended for all us snooty Voter Registration folks from up North, being warned to take our talk of equality elsewhere.
Our bus has brought us to the Blue Moon Motor hotel, owned by one Lester Bambry, brother to pastor John Bambry of the First Afro-American Methodist Church. We're scrubbing the hateful graffiti off the side.
I teach at the Freedom School, instructing a new generation of children how to think and feel about themselves, especially in the face of such relentless hatred.
Now it's August of 1964, and we are remembering James Chaney, Andy Goodman, and Mickey Schwerner. The Mississippi Martyrs, kidnapped and killed by the Klan, and bulldozed into an earthen dam.

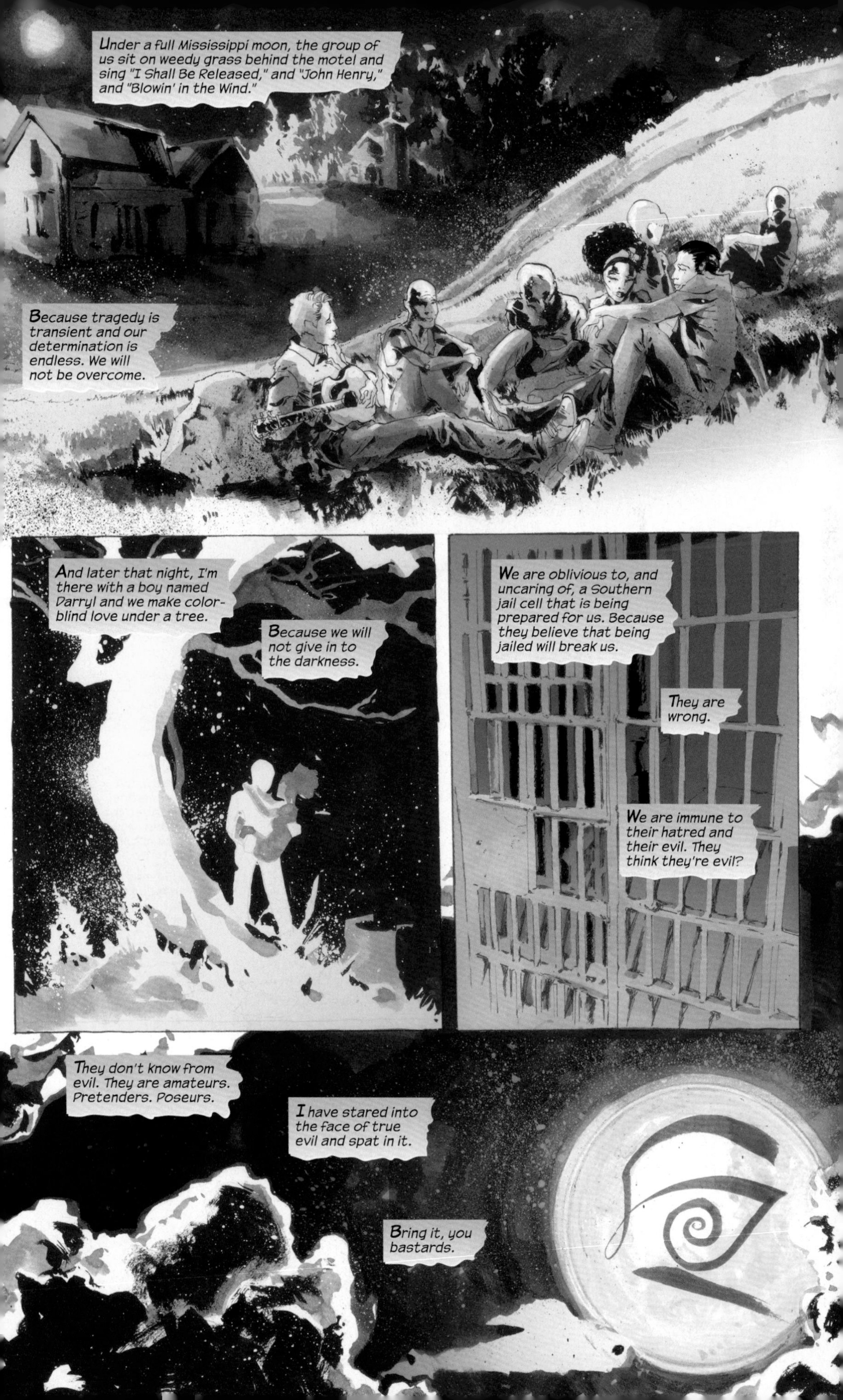
Under a full Mississippi moon, the group of us sit on weedy grass behind the motel and sing "I Shall Be Released," and "John Henry," and "Blowin' in the Wind."
Because tragedy is transient and our determination is endless. We will not be overcome.
And later that night, I'm there with a boy named Darryl and we make color-blind love under a tree.
Because we will not give in to the darkness.
We are oblivious to, and uncaring of, a Southern jail cell that is being prepared for us. Because they believe that being jailed will break us.
They are wrong.
We are immune to their hatred and their evil. They think they're evil?
They don't know from evil. They are amateurs. Pretenders. Poseurs.
I have stared into the face of true evil and spat in it.
Bring it, you bastards.

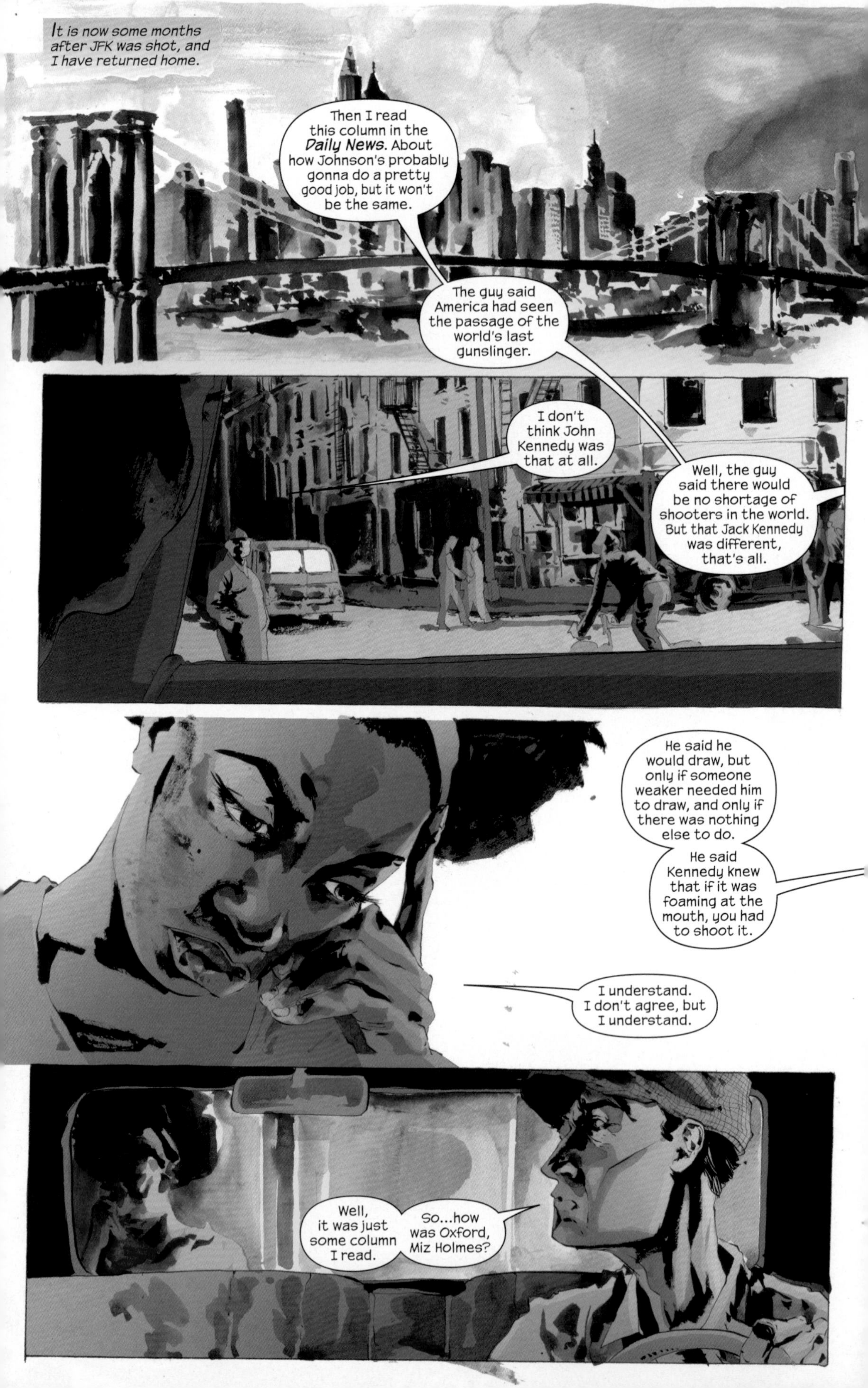
It is now some months after JFK was shot, and I have returned home.
Then I read this column in the Daily News. About how Johnson's probably gonna do a pretty good job, but it won't be the same.
The guy said America had seen the passage of the world's last gunslinger.
I don't think John Kennedy was that at all.
Well, the guy said there would be no shortage of shooters in the world. But that Jack Kennedy was different, that's all.
He said he would draw, but only if someone weaker needed him to draw, and only if there was nothing else to do.
He said Kennedy knew that if it was foaming at the mouth, you had to shoot it.
I understand. I don't agree, but I understand.
Well, it was just some column I read.
So...how was Oxford, Miz Holmes?

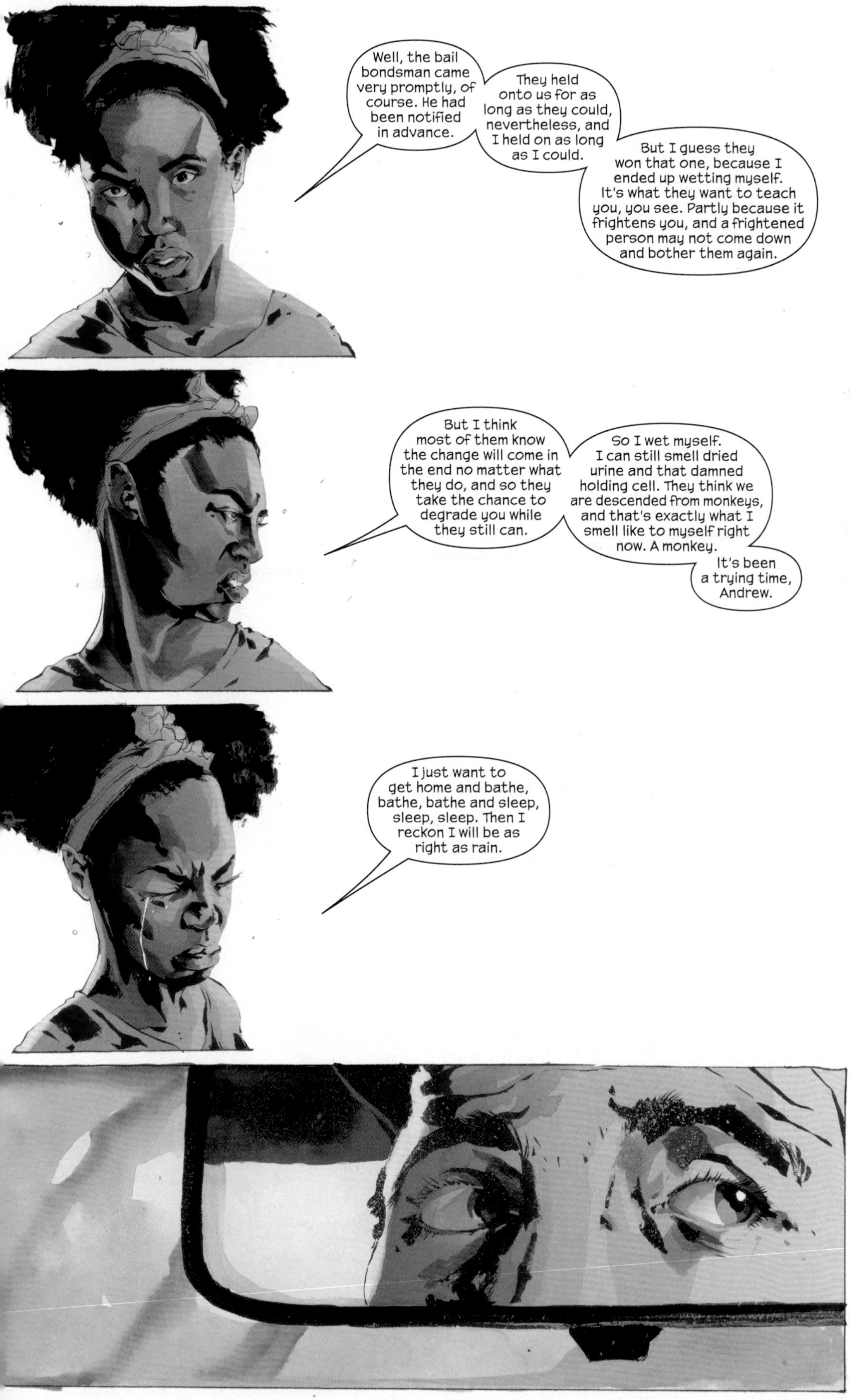
Well, the bail bondsman came very promptly, of course. He had been notified in advance.
They held onto us for as long as they could, nevertheless, and I held on as long as I could.
But I guess they won that one, because I ended up wetting myself. It's what they want to teach you, you see. Partly because it frightens you, and a frightened person may not come down and bother them again.
But I think most of them know the change will come in the end no matter what they do, and so they take the chance to degrade you while they still can.
So I wet myself. I can still smell dried urine and that damned holding cell. They think we are descended from monkeys, and that's exactly what I smell like to myself right now. A monkey.
It's been a trying time, Andrew.
I just want to get home and bathe, bathe, bathe and sleep, sleep, sleep. Then I reckon I will be as right as rain.

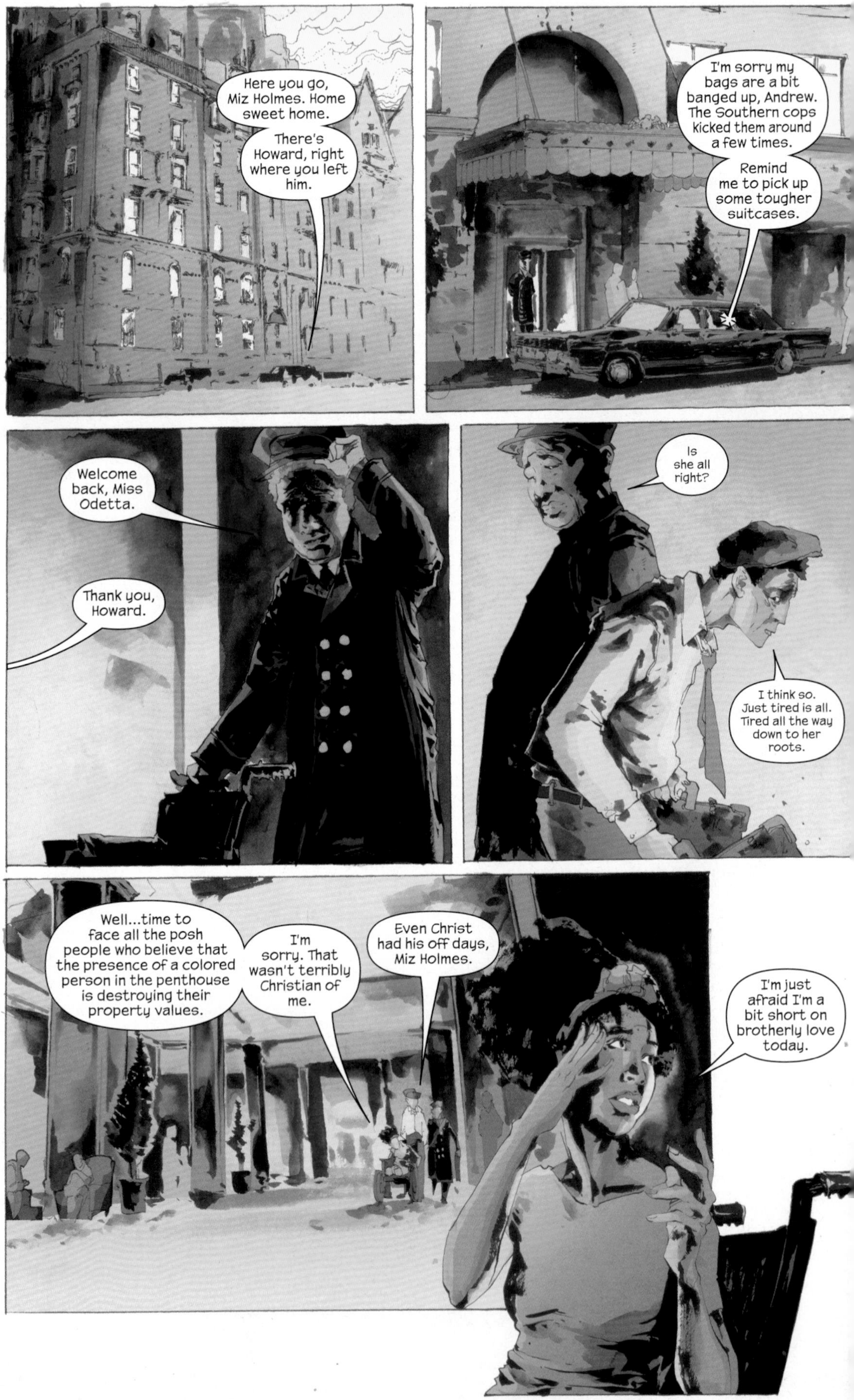
Here you go, Miz Holmes. Home sweet home.
There's Howard, right where you left him.
I'm sorry my bags are a bit banged up, Andrew. The Southern cops kicked them around a few times.
Remind me to pick up some tougher suitcases.
Welcome back, Miss Odetta.
Thank you, Howard.
Is she all right?
I think so. Just tired is all. Tired all the way down to her roots.
Well...time to face all the posh people who believe that the presence of a colored person in the penthouse is destroying their property values.
I'm sorry. That wasn't terribly Christian of me.
Even Christ had his off days, Miz Holmes.
I'm just afraid I'm a bit short on brotherly love today.

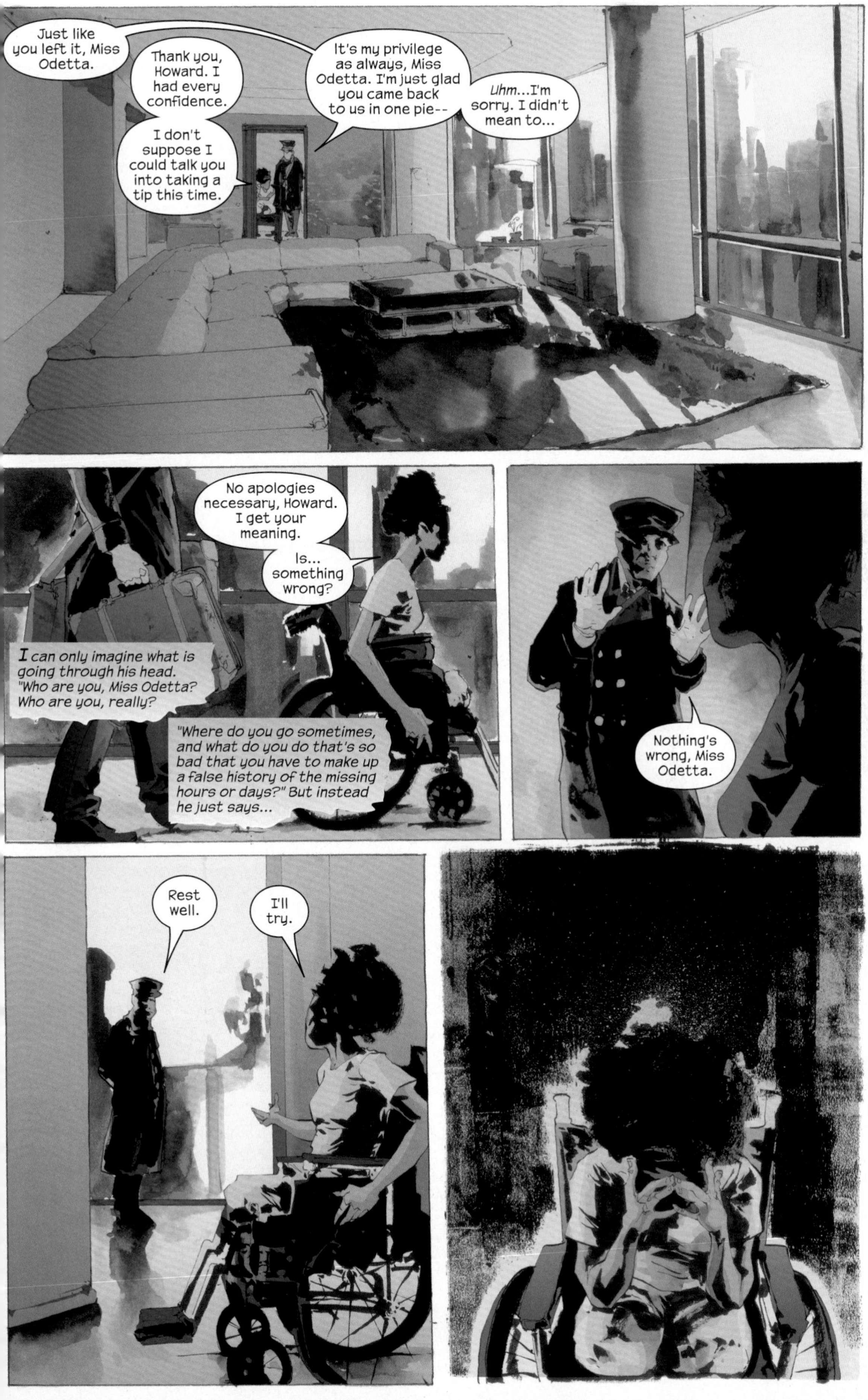
Just like you left it, Miss Odetta.
Thank you, Howard. I had every confidence.
I don't suppose I could talk you into taking a tip this time.
It's my privilege as always, Miss Odetta. I'm just glad you came back to us in one pie--
Uhm...I'm sorry. I didn't mean to...
No apologies necessary, Howard. I get your meaning.
Is... something wrong?
I can only imagine what is going through his head. "Who are you, Miss Odetta? Who are you, really?
"Where do you go sometimes, and what do you do that's so bad that you have to make up a false history of the missing hours or days?" But instead he just says...
Nothing's wrong, Miss Odetta.
Rest well.
I'll try.

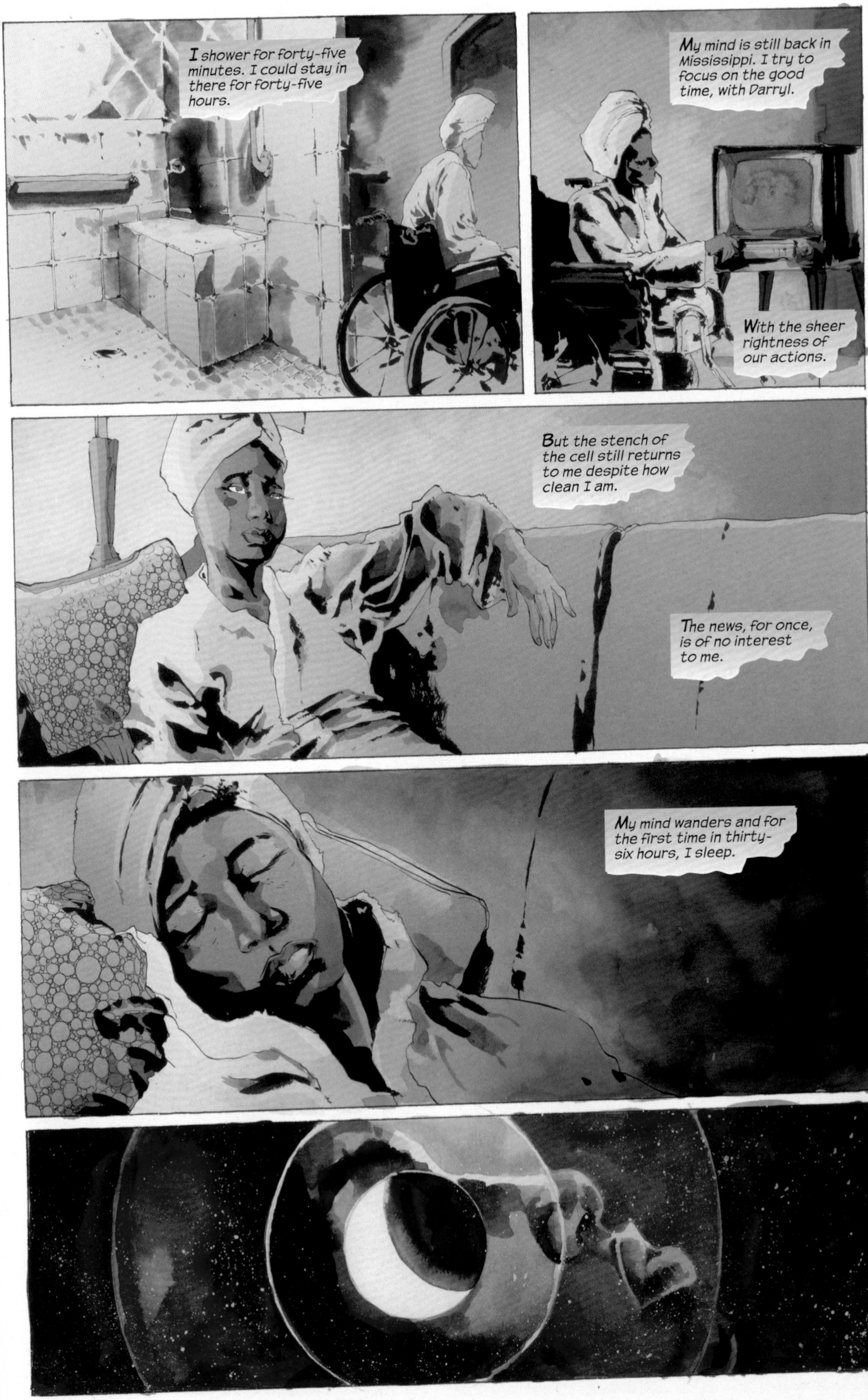
I shower for forty-five minutes. I could stay in there for forty-five hours.
My mind is still back in Mississippi. I try to focus on the good time, with Darryl.
With the sheer rightness of our actions.
But the stench of the cell still returns to me despite how clean I am.
The news, for once, is of no interest to me.
My mind wanders and for the first time in thirty-six hours, I sleep.

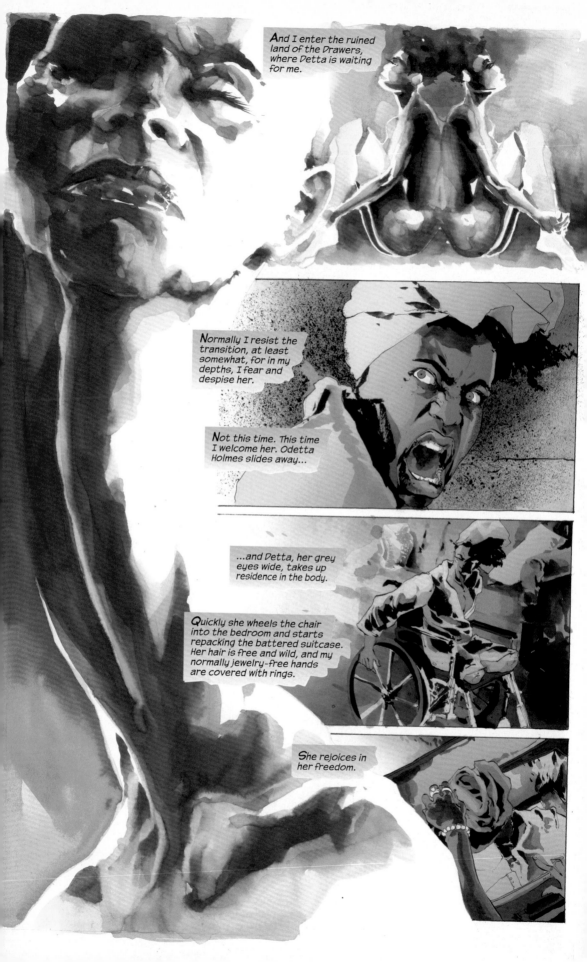

And I enter the ruined land of the Drawers, where Detta is waiting for me.

Normally I resist the transition, at least somewhat, for in my depths, I fear and despise her.

Not this time. This time I welcome her. Odetta Holmes slides away...

...and Detta, her grey eyes wide, takes up residence in the body.

Quickly she wheels the chair into the bedroom and starts repacking the battered suitcase. Her hair is free and wild, and my normally jewelry-free hands are covered with rings.

She rejoices in her freedom.

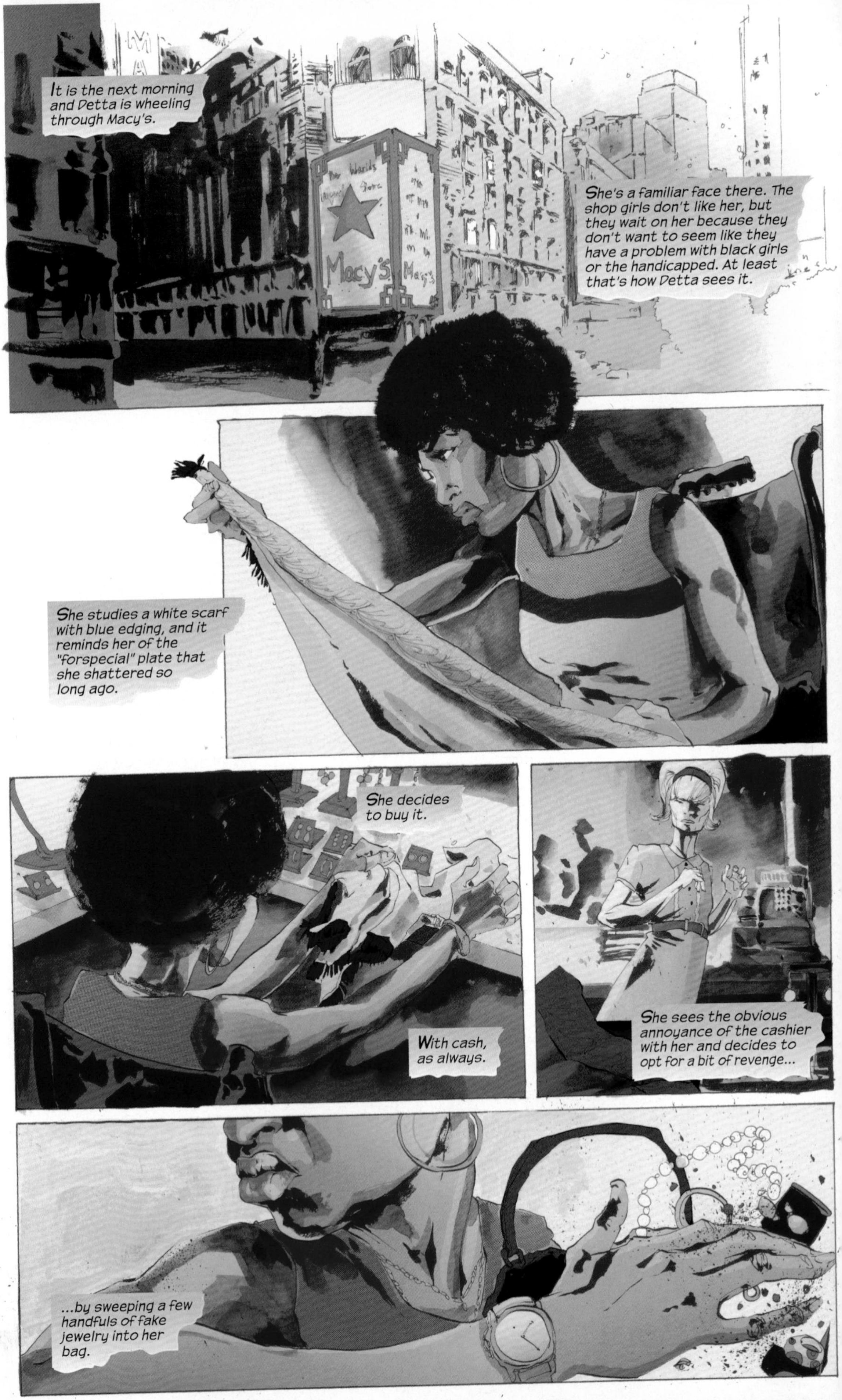
It is the next morning and Detta is wheeling through Macy's.
Macy's
She's a familiar face there. The shop girls don't like her, but they wait on her because they don't want to seem like they have a problem with black girls or the handicapped. At least that's how Detta sees it.
She studies a white scarf with blue edging, and it reminds her of the "forspecial" plate that she shattered so long ago.
She decides to buy it.
With cash, as always.
She sees the obvious annoyance of the cashier with her and decides to opt for a bit of revenge...
...by sweeping a few handfuls of fake jewelry into her bag.

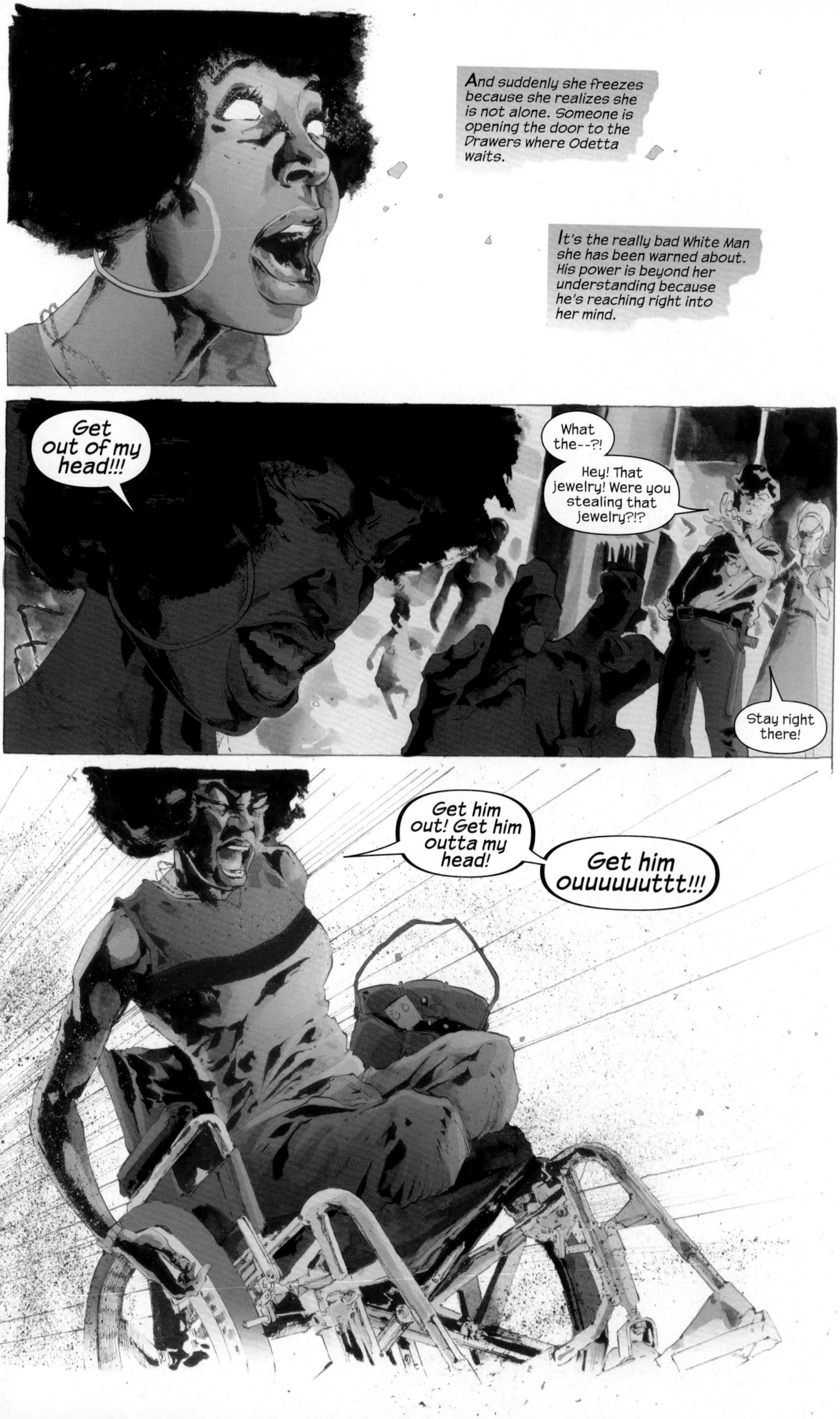
And suddenly she freezes because she realizes she is not alone. Someone is opening the door to the Drawers where Odetta waits.
It's the really bad White Man she has been warned about. His power is beyond her understanding because he's reaching right into her mind.
Get out of my head!!!
What the--?!
Hey! That jewelry! Were you stealing that jewelry?!?
Stay right there!
Get him out! Get him outta my head!
Get him ouuuuuuttt!!!

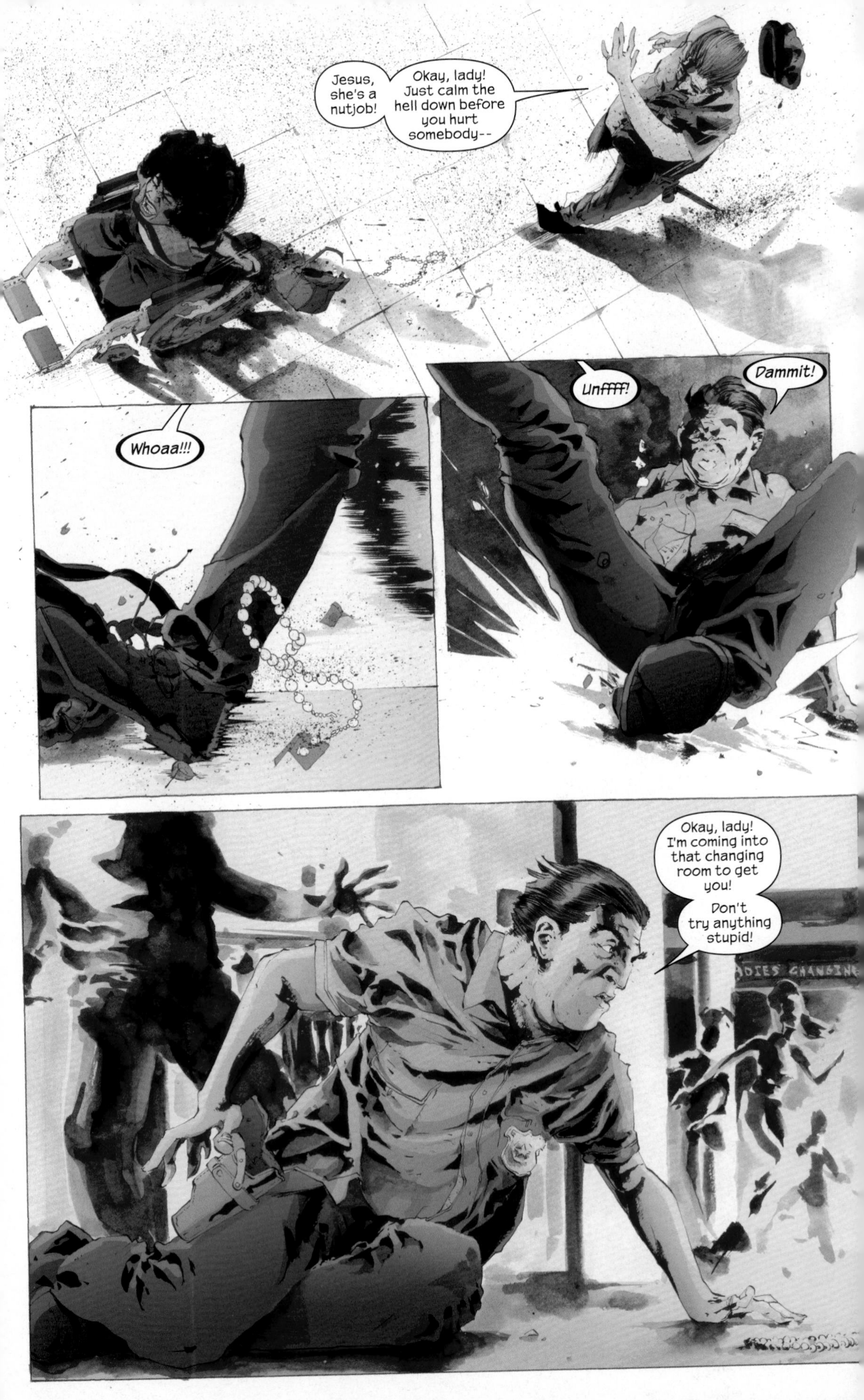
Jesus, she's a nutjob!
Okay, lady! Just calm the hell down before you hurt somebody--
Whoaa!!!
Unffff!
Dammit!
Okay, lady! I'm coming into that changing room to get you!
Don't try anything stupid!

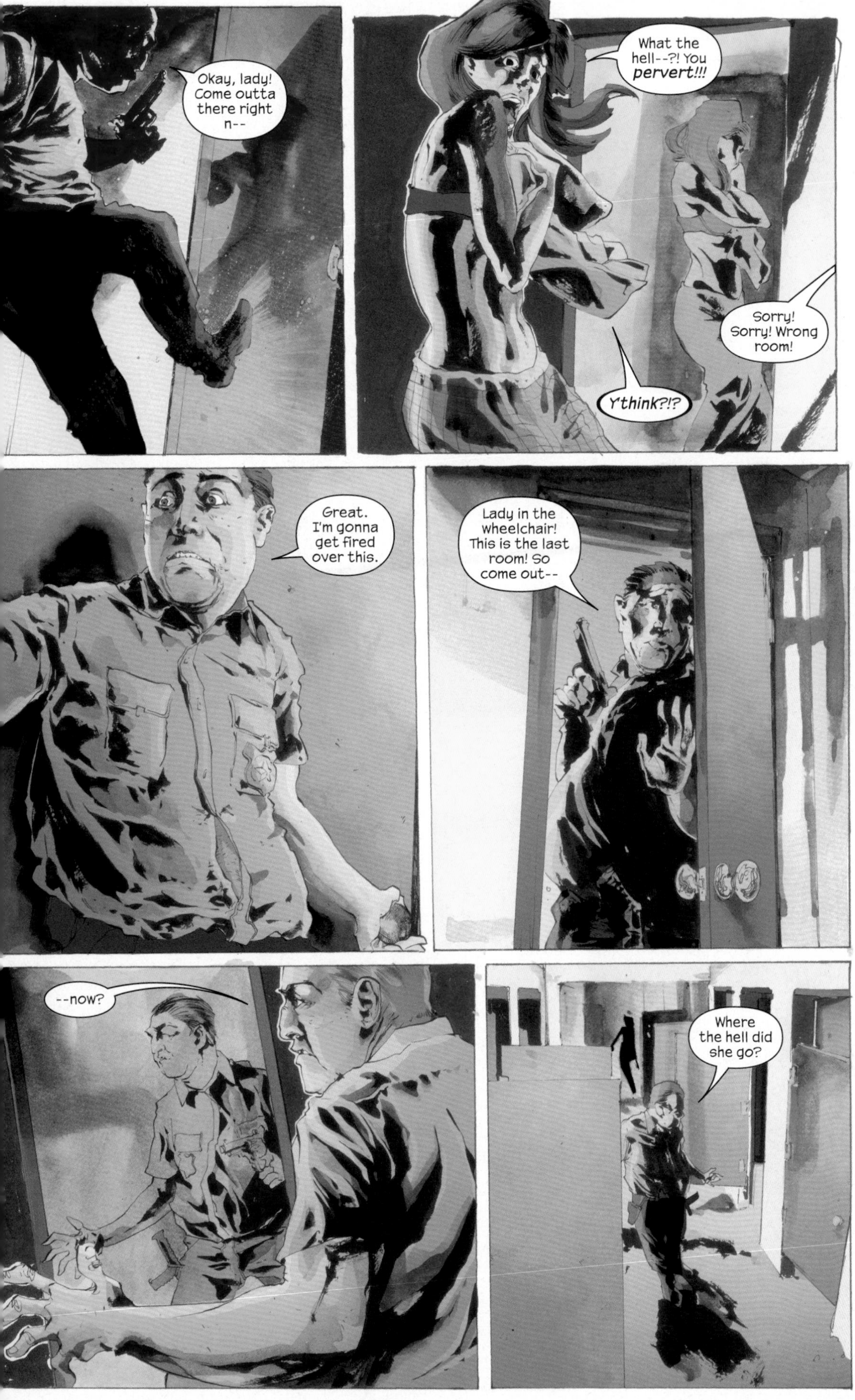
Okay, lady! Come outta there right n--
What the hell--?! You *pervert!!!*
Sorry! Sorry! Wrong room!
Y'think?!?
Great. I'm gonna get fired over this.
Lady in the wheelchair! This is the last room! So come out--
--now?
Where the hell did she go?

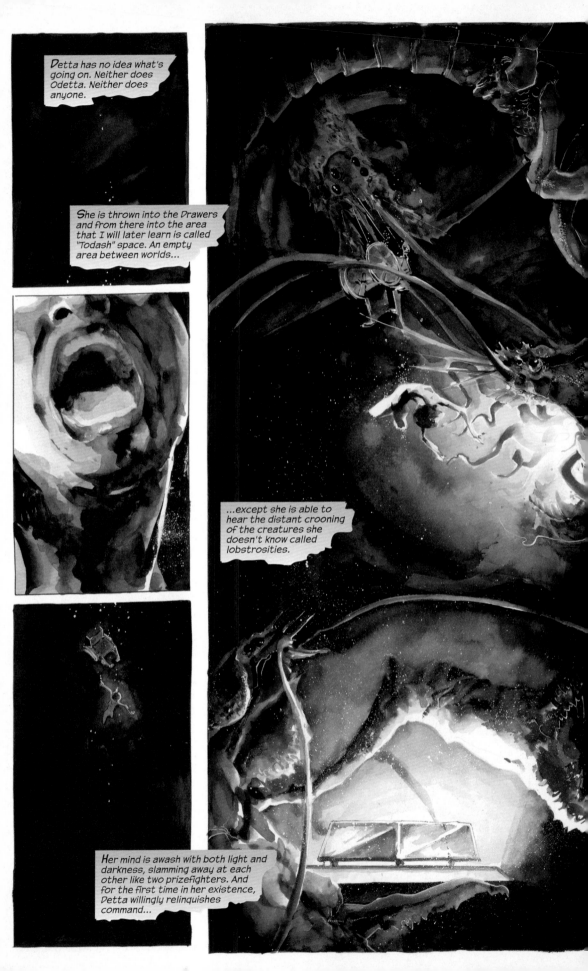

Detta has no idea what's going on. Neither does Odetta. Neither does anyone.

She is thrown into the Drawers and from there into the area that I will later learn is called "Todash" space. An empty area between worlds...

...except she is able to hear the distant crooning of the creatures she doesn't know called lobstrosities.

Her mind is awash with both light and darkness, slamming away at each other like two prizefighters. And for the first time in her existence, Detta willingly relinquishes command...

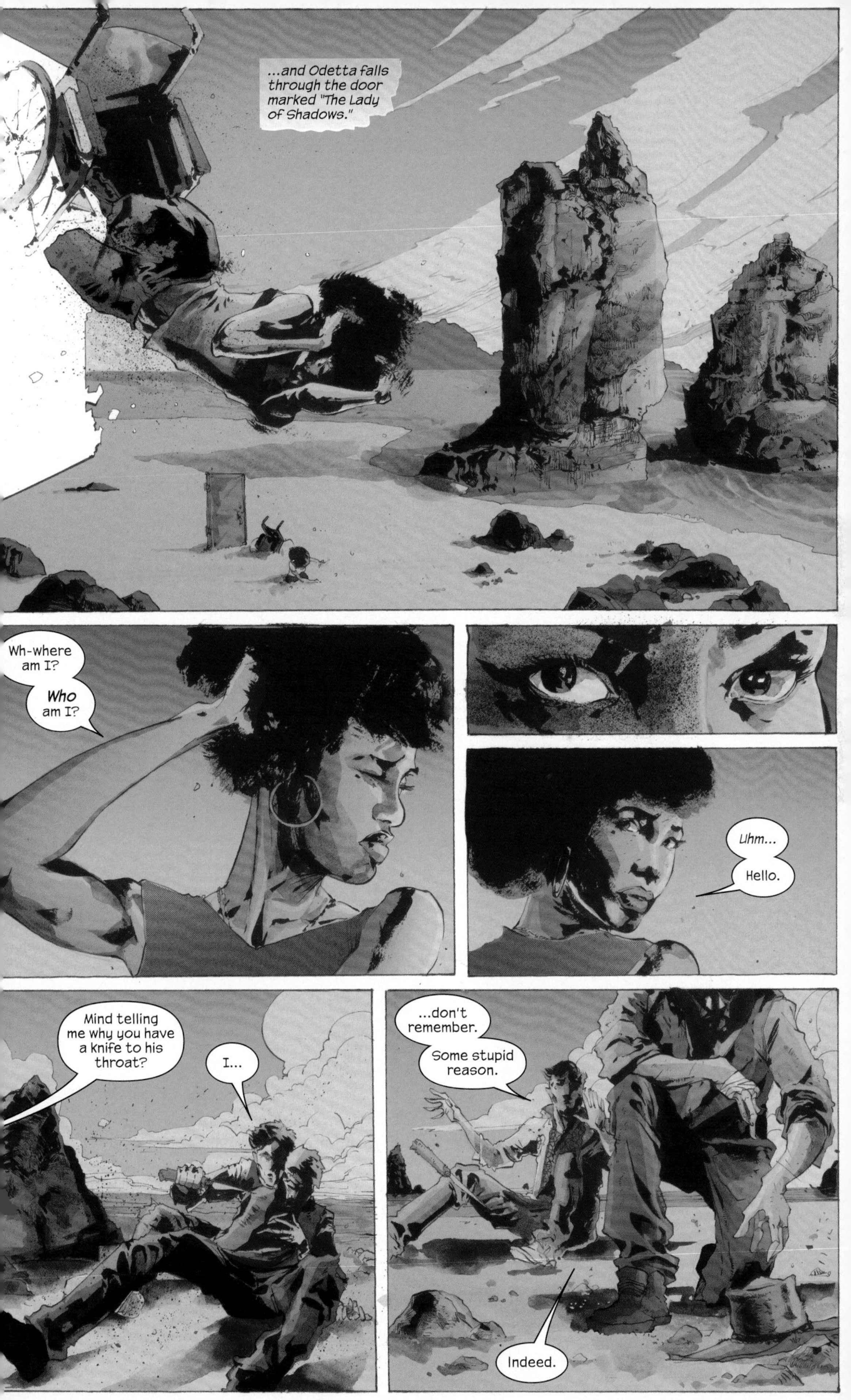
...and Odetta falls through the door marked "The Lady of Shadows."
Wh-where am I?
Who am I?
Uhm...
Hello.
Mind telling me why you have a knife to his throat?
I...
...don't remember.
Some stupid reason.
Indeed.

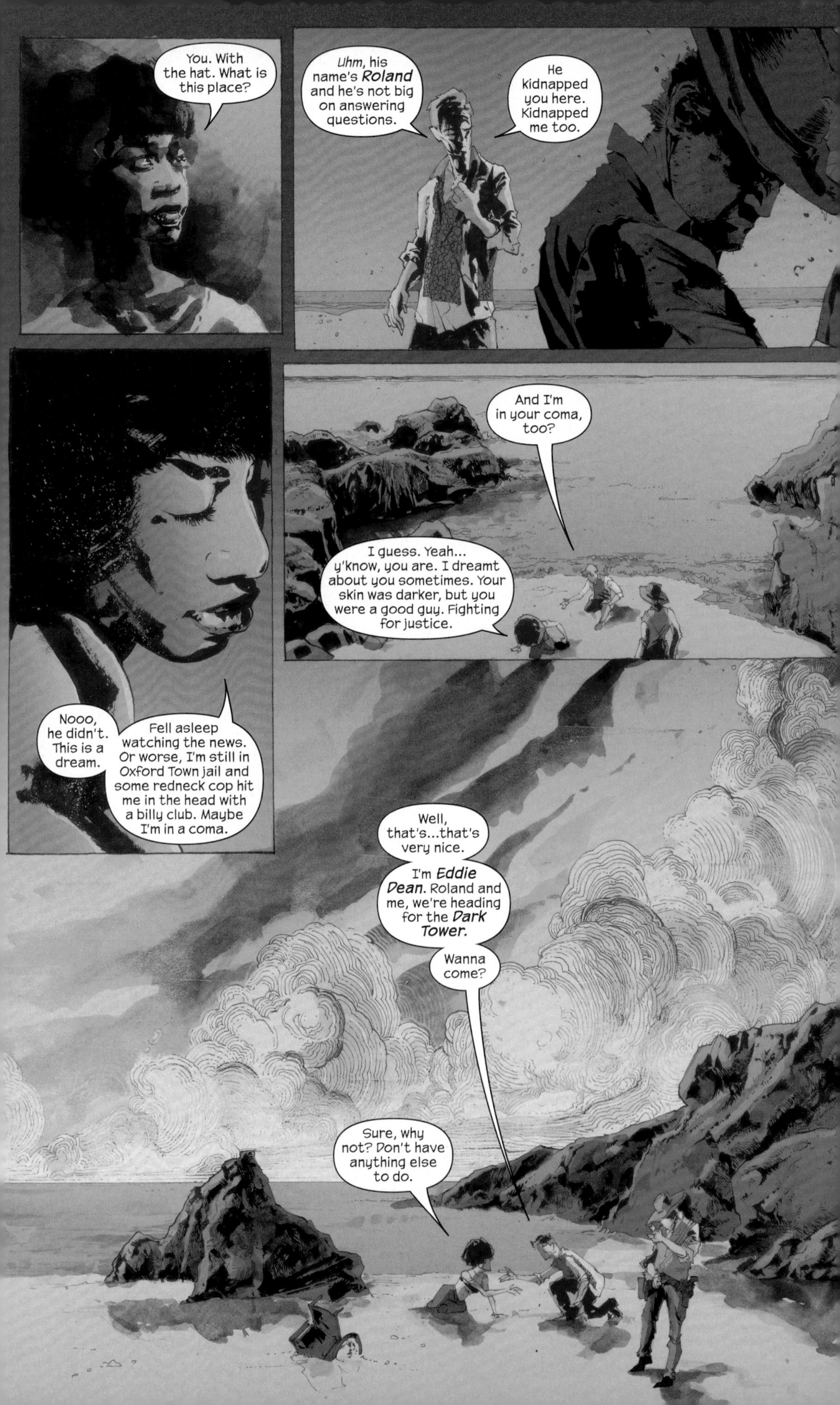
You. With the hat. What is this place?
Uhm, his name's Roland and he's not big on answering questions.
He kidnapped you here. Kidnapped me too.
Nooo, he didn't. This is a dream.
Fell asleep watching the news. Or worse, I'm still in Oxford Town jail and some redneck cop hit me in the head with a billy club. Maybe I'm in a coma.
And I'm in your coma, too?
I guess. Yeah... y'know, you are. I dreamt about you sometimes. Your skin was darker, but you were a good guy. Fighting for justice.
Well, that's...that's very nice.
I'm Eddie Dean. Roland and me, we're heading for the Dark Tower.
Wanna come?
Sure, why not? Don't have anything else to do.

The story continues in *The Dark Tower: The Drawing of the Three — Bitter Medicine*

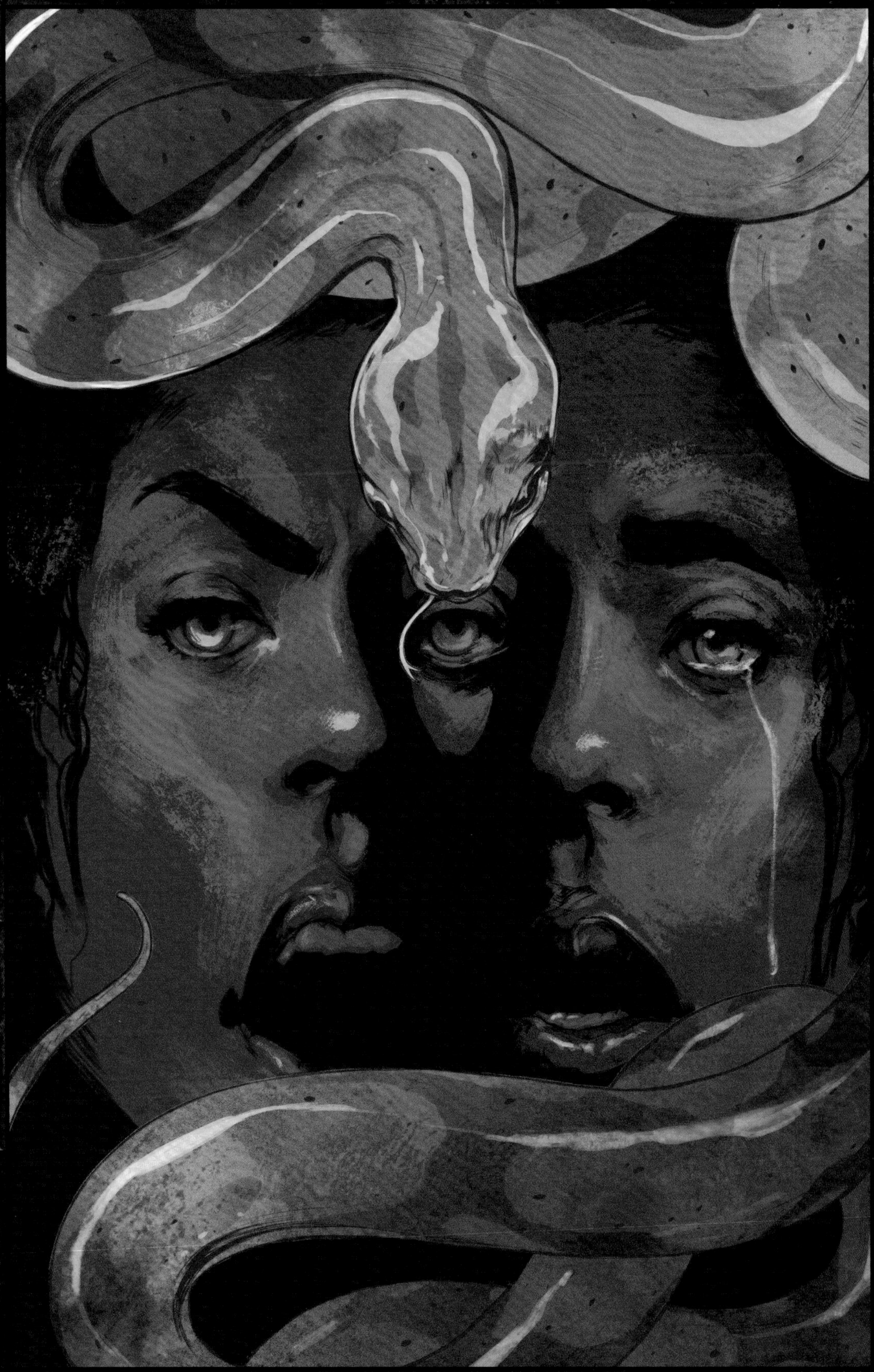

The Dark Tower: The Drawing of the Three — The Lady of Shadows #1 **Cover by Nimit Malavia**

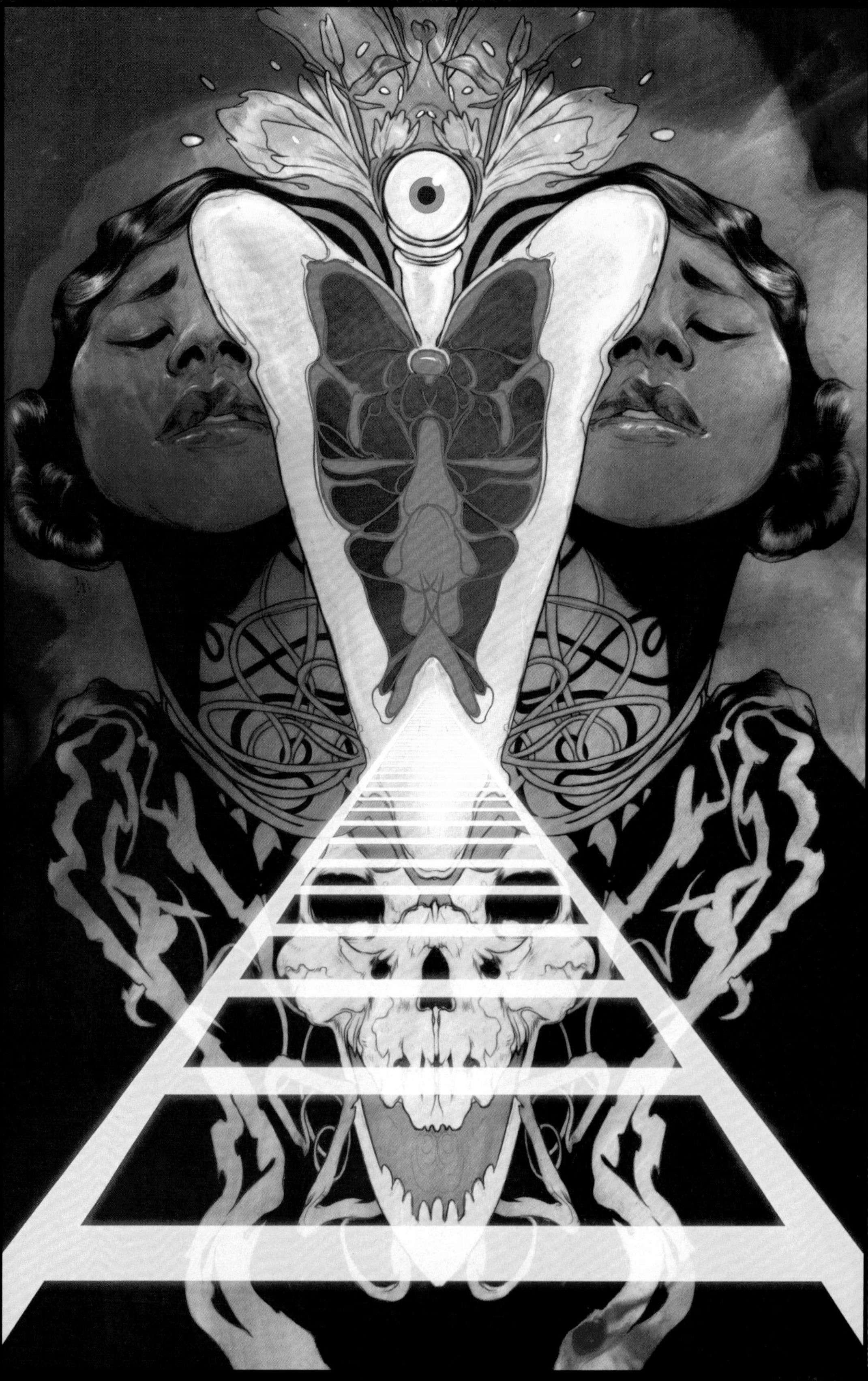

The Dark Tower: The Drawing of the Three — The Lady of Shadows #2 **Cover by Nimit Malavia**

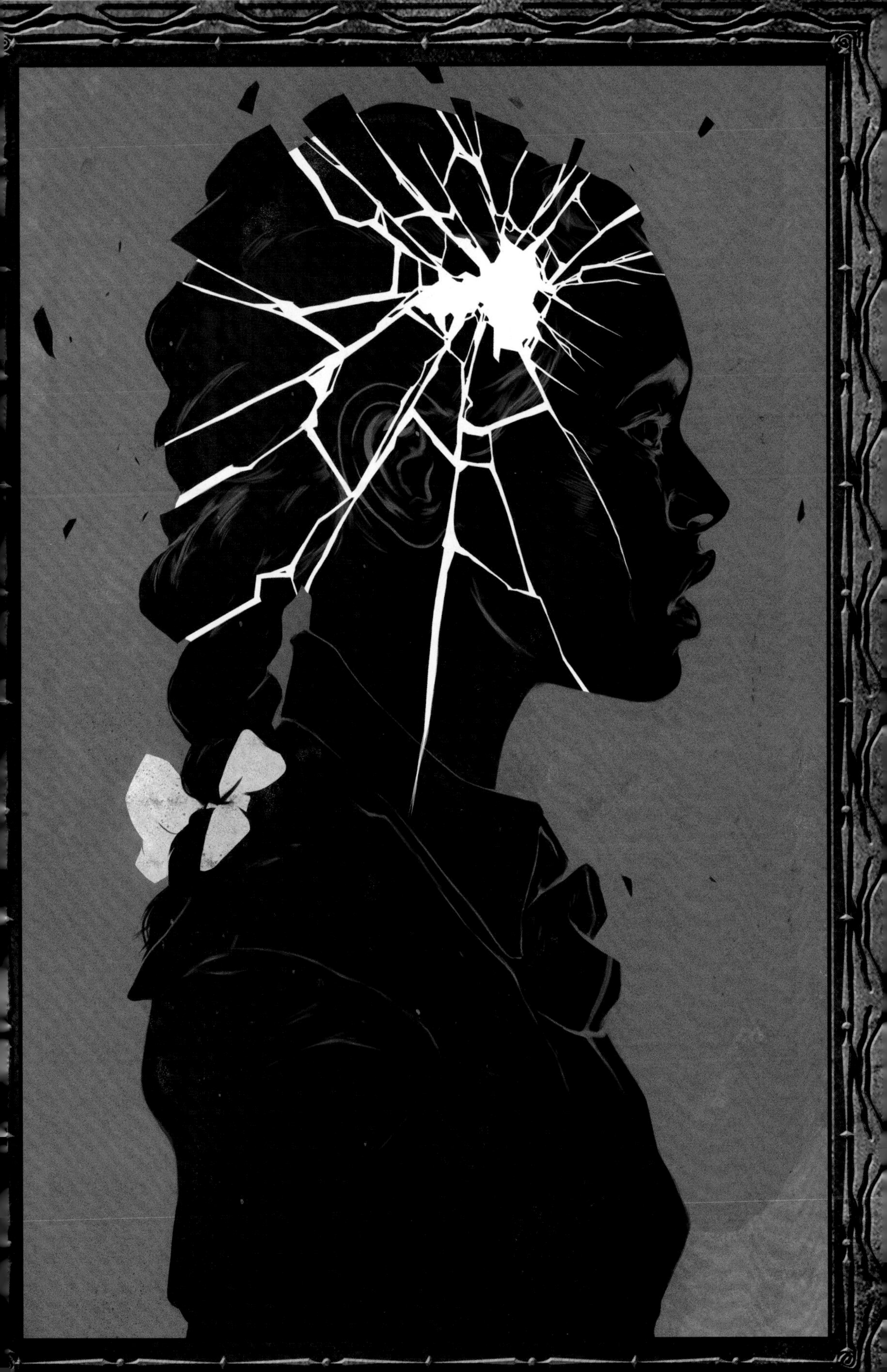

The Dark Tower: The Drawing of the Three — The Lady of Shadows #3 **Cover by Nimit Malavia**

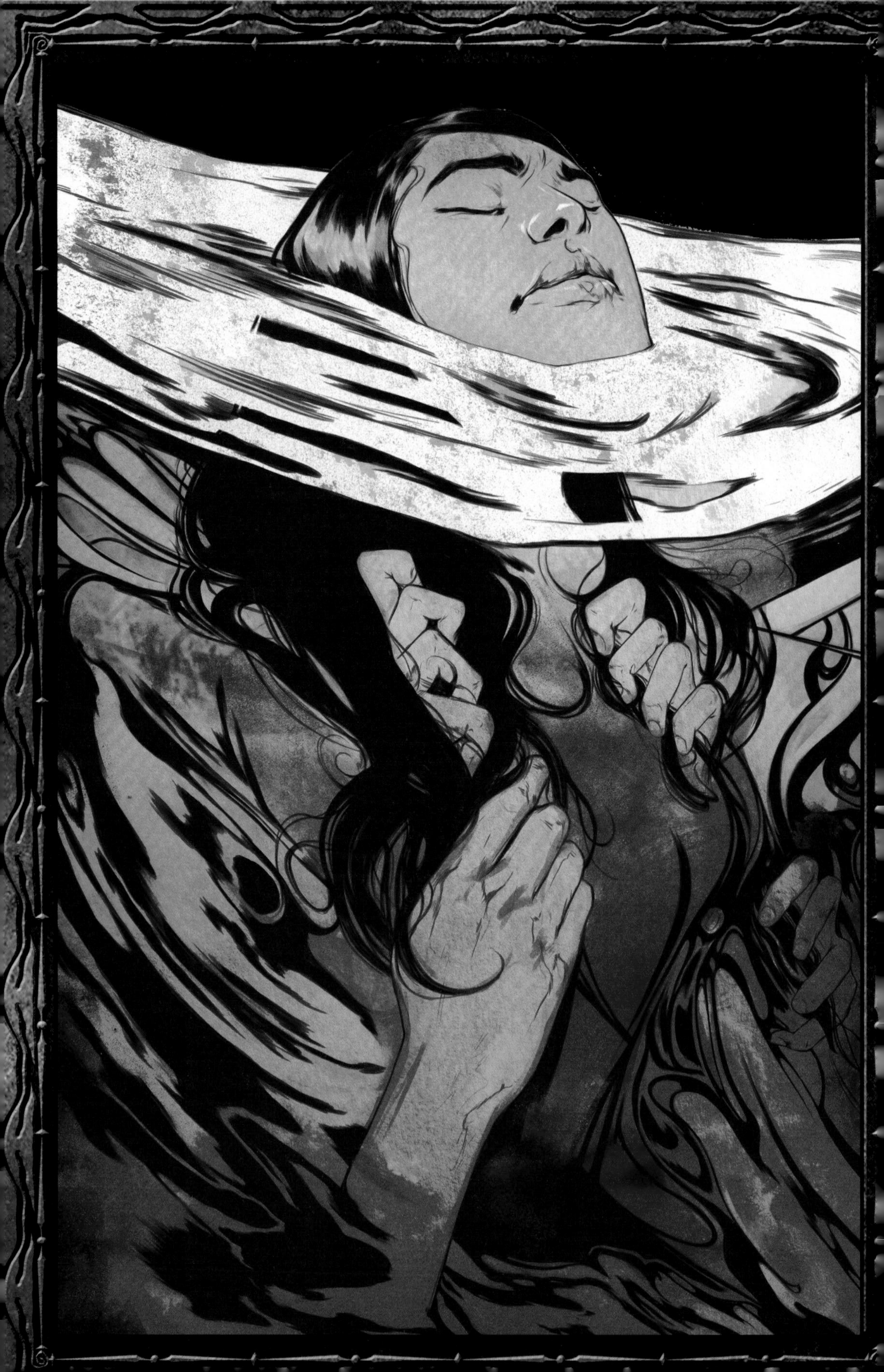

The Dark Tower: The Drawing of the Three — The Lady of Shadows #4 **Cover by Nimit Malavia**

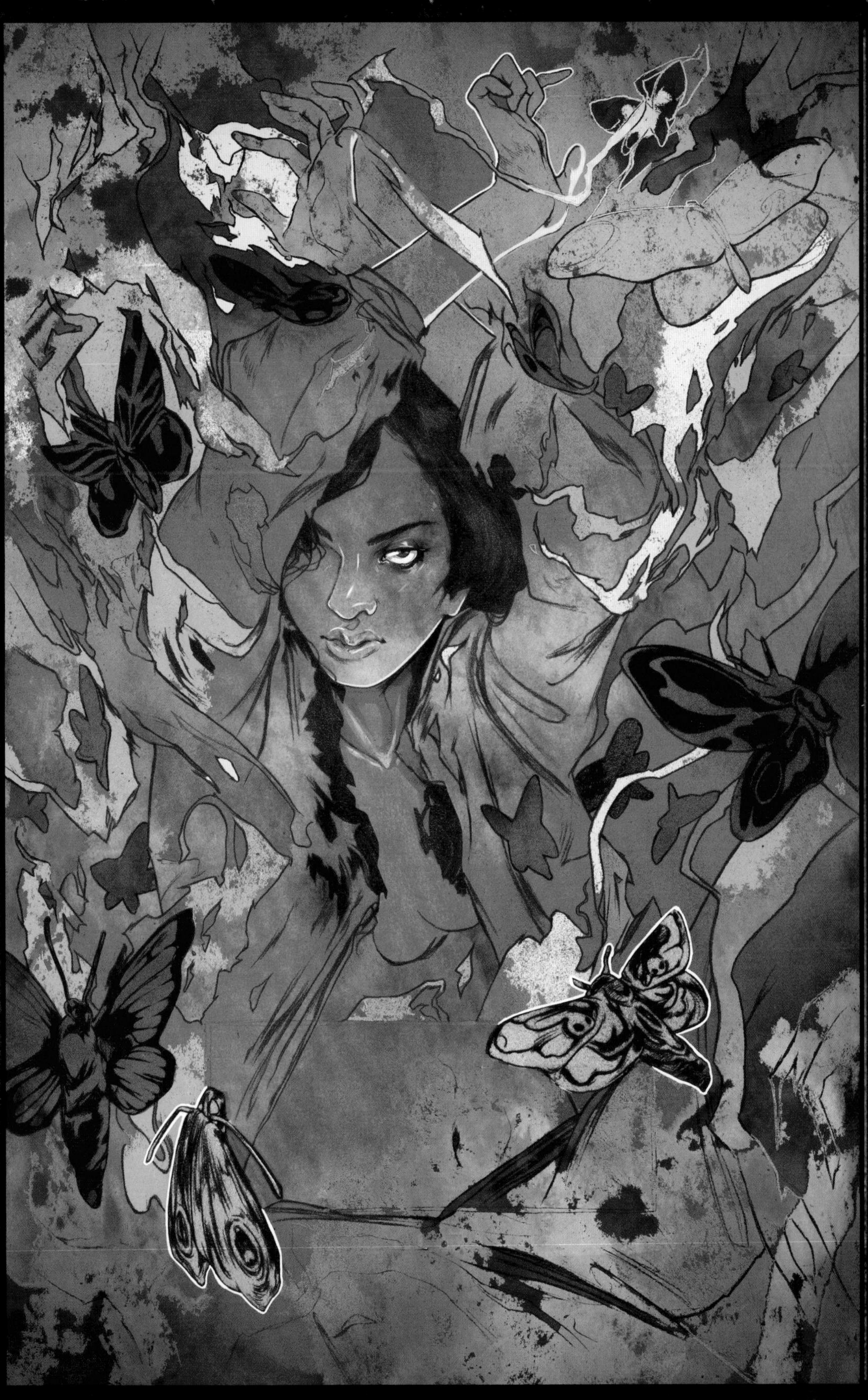

The Dark Tower: The Drawing of the Three — The Lady of Shadows #5 **Cover by Nimit Malavia**

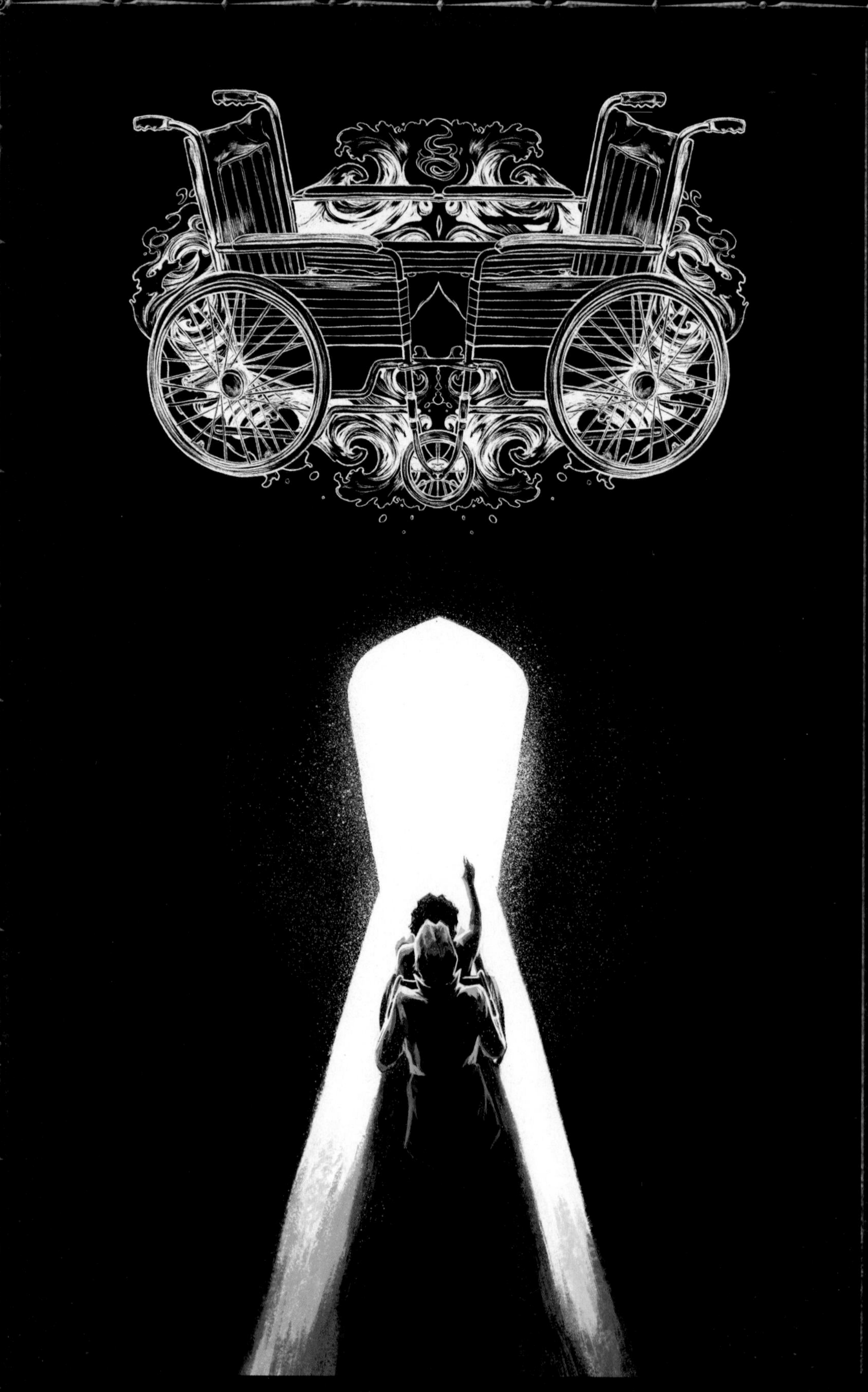

The Lady of Shadows #1, page 5 **alternate versions of panel 1 by Jonathan Marks**

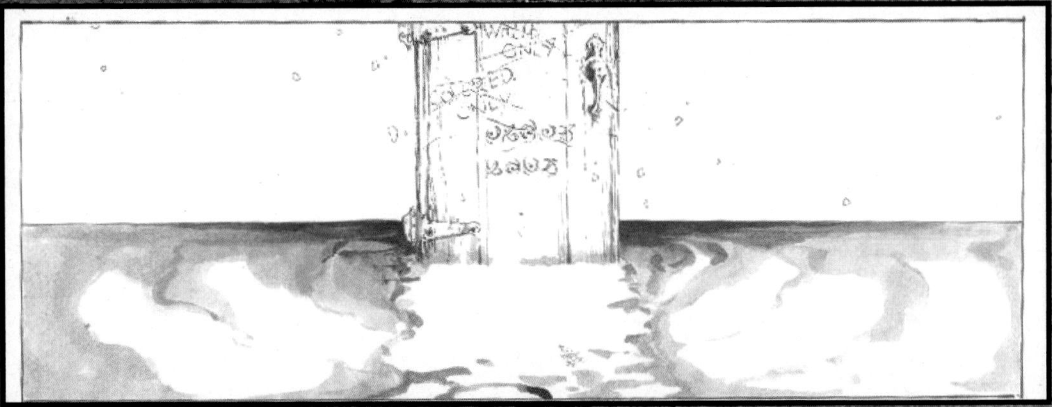
WHITE ONLY
COLORED ONLY

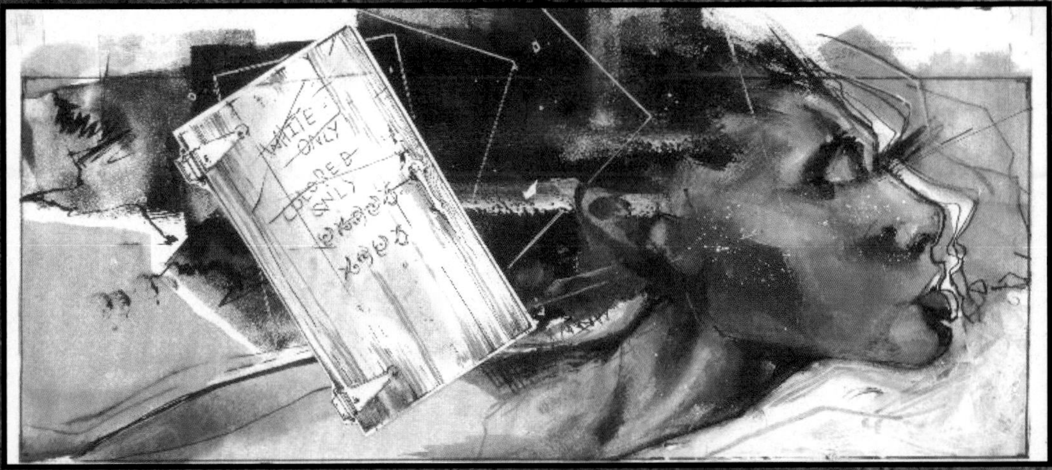
WHITE ONLY
COLORED ONLY

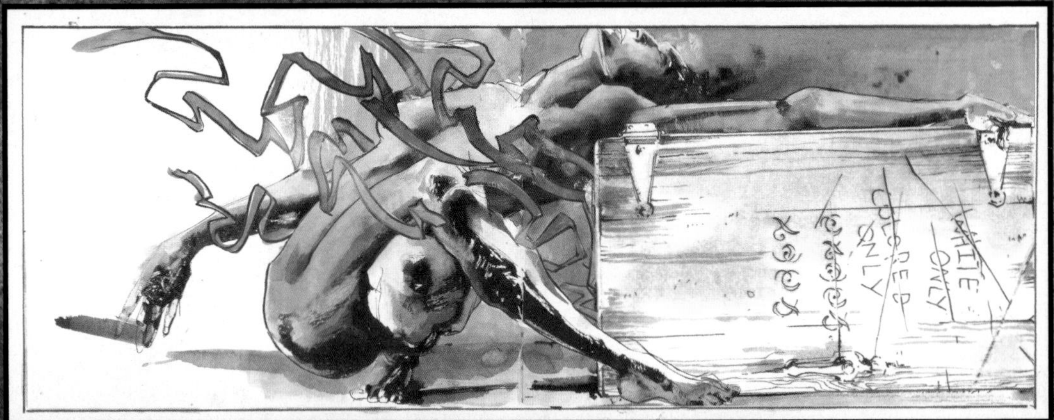
WHITE ONLY
COLORED ONLY

Page 12

1. It is almost midnight. Wearily Odetta rolls out of the shower. She wears a bathrobe and a towel around her head.

2. Odetta flips on the news.

3. Odetta has transferred to the sofa to watch the news.

4. She nods off.

5. We have a shot of the moon. It is waning.

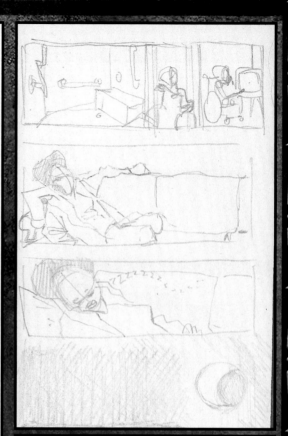

JM 15

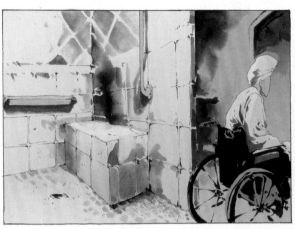

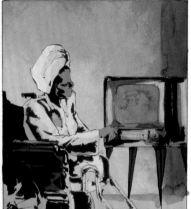

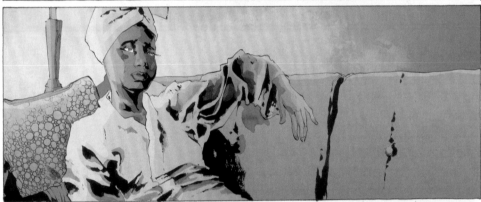

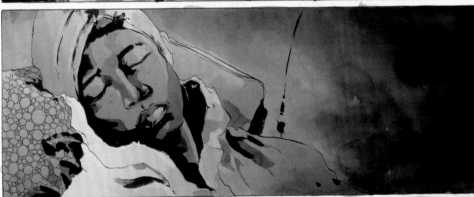

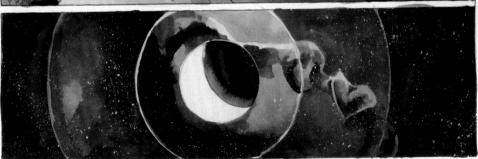

Page 13

1. In her dream, Odetta is entering the ruined land of the Drawers, where the ring of fire is located. (Once again, she is back-to-back with Detta in that ring of fire.)

2. She switches places with Detta.

3. Detta wakes up. Her grey eyes are wide.

4. Quickly, Detta rolls her wheelchair to the bedroom.

5. She is repacking her suitcase, which still sits on the bed. Her hands, which are usually ringless, are now covered in gaudy rings. Her hair is free and wild.

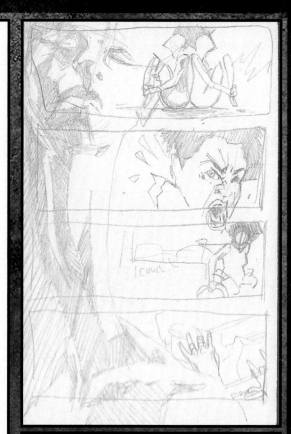

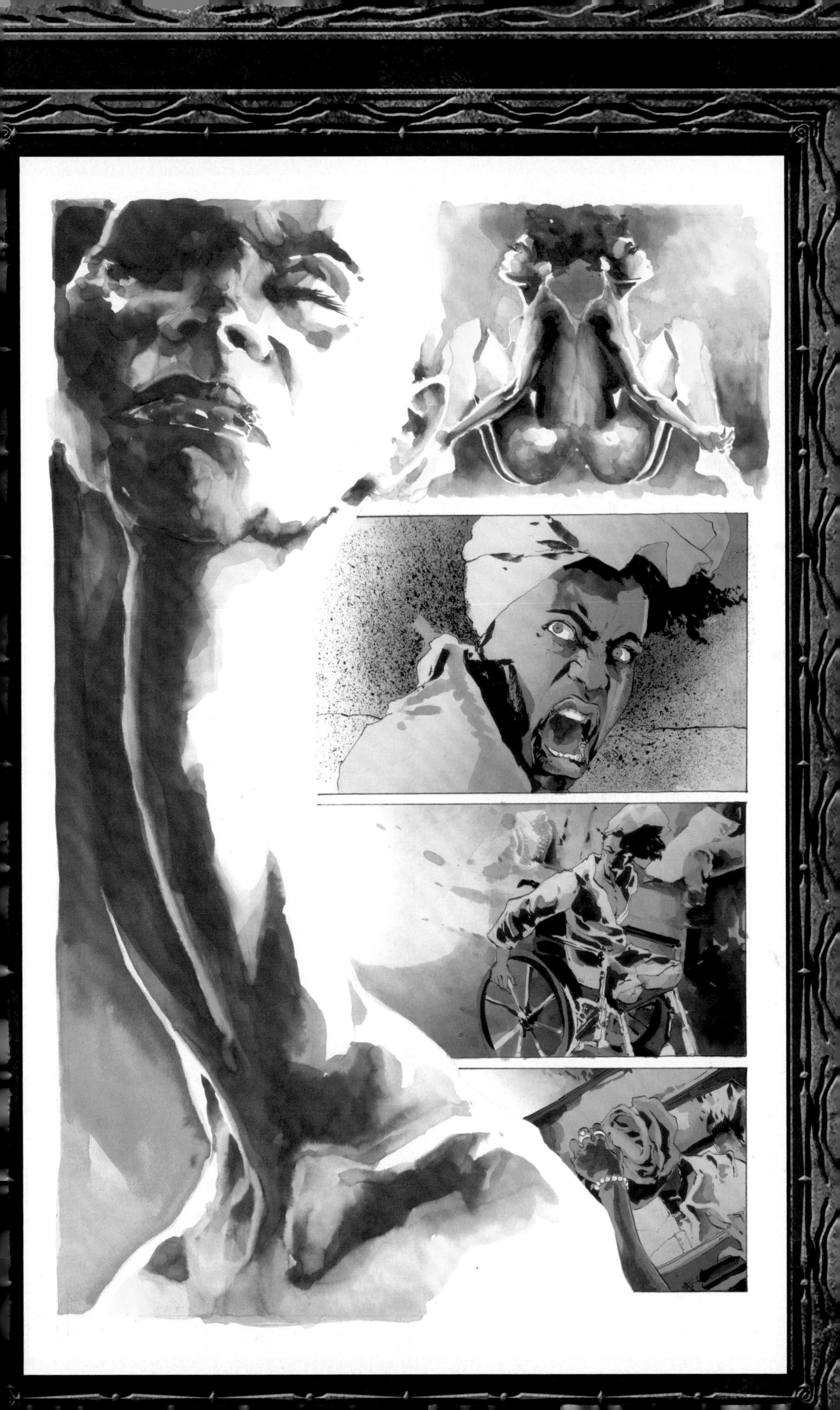

Page 14

1. It is now the next morning. Detta is rolling through Macy's.

2. She is holding up a white scarf that has blue edging. It reminds her of the "forspecial plate" which her mother gave to Aunt Blue, and which she crushed. She decides to buy it.

3. Detta tells the shop girl to ring up the purchase and put it in a bag. She's paying cash, as always. It's obvious that the shop girl doesn't like Detta.

4. As the snotty shopgirl is ringing up Detta's purchase, Detta starts to sweep fake jewelry into her bag. It is her revenge on the shop girl.

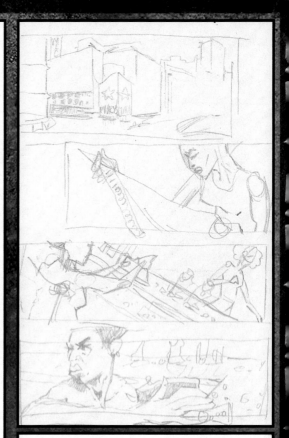

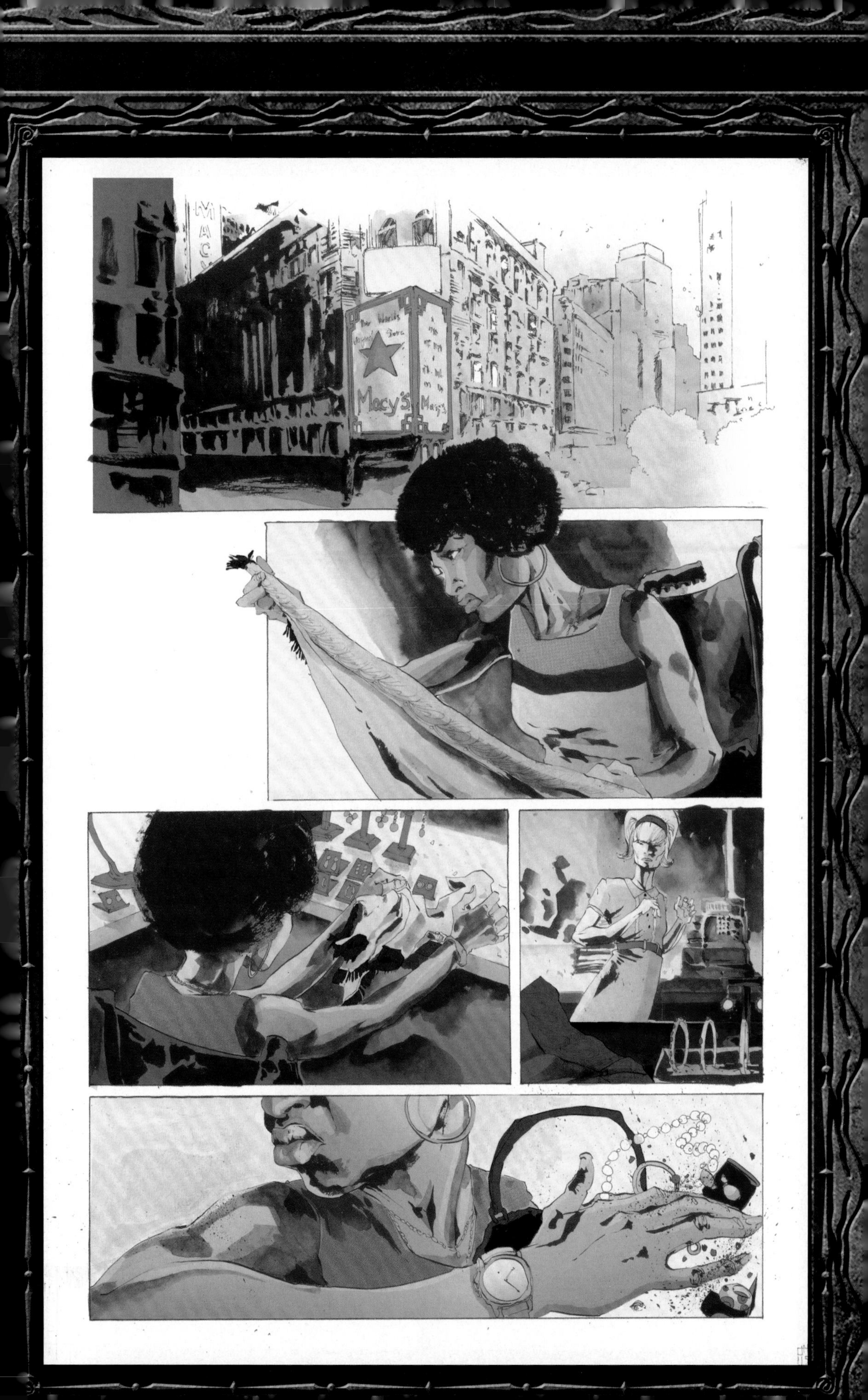
Macy's

Page 15

1. At this moment, Detta freezes, her hands mid-scoop. She feels SOMEONE entering her mind and opening the door to the "Drawers" where Odetta waits. Worse still, she knows it's a WHITE MAN opening the portal! In fact, it's the REALLY BAD MAN from her nightmares!

2. Detta screams, "Get out of my head!" But the shop girl and a cop have turned to stare at her. A security guard with a big gut sees that Detta is in the process of stealing jewelry and shouts "Stop! Stop right there!"

3. Detta is rolling her wheelchair towards the changing room, but she's shouting at herself to stop. She is not in control of this movement, though her own hands are wheeling the wheelchair. The REALLY BAD MAN has finally come for her!

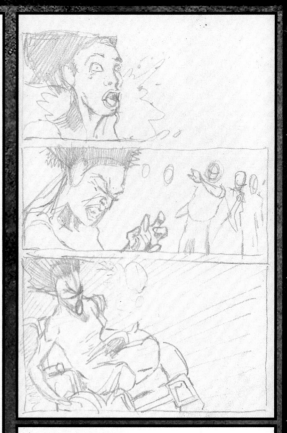

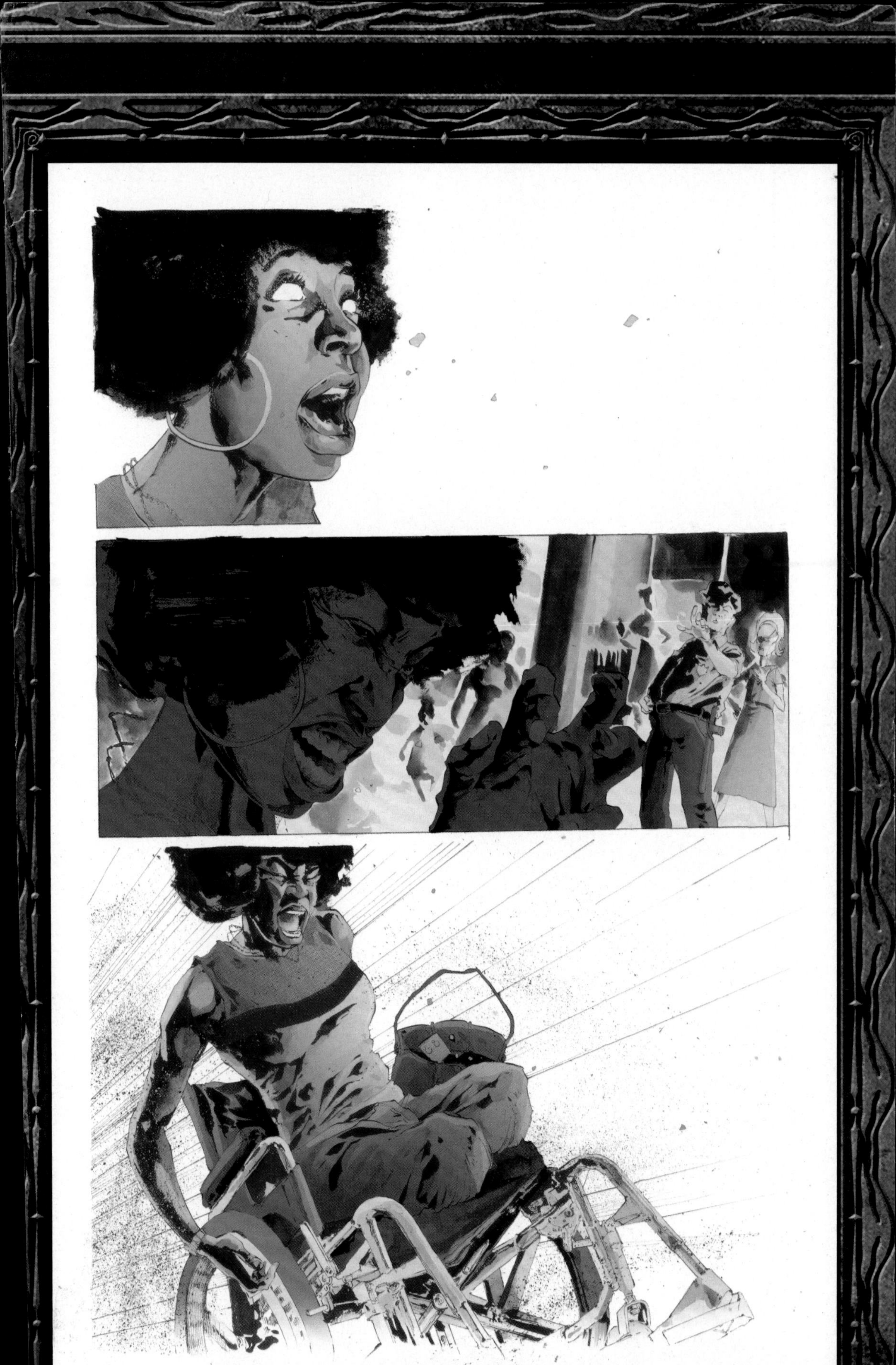